Decolonial Imaginings

T0347012

This book is a transdisciplinary study of the ways in which mobilities take social forms and result in multiple belongings. Situated within the confluence of decolonial feminist theory, border theory, and diaspora studies, it explores borders and boundaries and how politics of connectivity are produced in and through struggles over 'difference'. It examines multiple formations of power embedded in the intersections between gender, race, class, ethnicity, and sexuality. Inter alia, the text analyses this intersectionality in relation to diaspora; theorises the relationship between diaspora, law, and literature; and between affect, memory, and cultural politics.

In detailing crossings of impervious borders, the book foregrounds the economies of abandonment such as the plight of people in boats in the Mediterranean when a number perished because of a catalogue of failures by NATO warships and European coastguards. Such examples of violent histories leave deep scars and traumas, yet there can be a creative reckoning and resistance in biographies marked by them, as exemplified here by the lives and mobilities of young Black women at the turn of the twentieth-century USA mapped by Saidiya Hartman who describes the women as making a sexual revolution. The book revisits the Gilles Deleuze and Felix Guattari's notion of 'nomad thought' and seeks to assess this framework's value today. It analyses the politics of 'Black' in Britain with a focus on feminism constituted by women of African-Caribbean and South Asian background. The book also explores stereotypic representation of Muslim women in the context of Islamophobia and anti-Muslim racism, and the complexities of the #MeToo movement and how whiteness is configured in these contestations.

Decolonial Imaginings

Intersectional Conversations and Contestations

Avtar Brah

Goldsmiths
Press

Copyright © 2022 Goldsmiths Press
First published in 2022 by Goldsmiths Press
Goldsmiths, University of London, New Cross
London SE14 6NW

Printed and bound by Versa Press, USA
Distribution by the MIT Press
Cambridge, Massachusetts, USA, and London, England

Copyright © 2022 Avtar Brah

A CIP record for this book is available from the British Library

ISBN 978-1-913380-08-3 (pbk)
ISBN 978-1-913380-07-6 (ebk)

www.gold.ac.uk/goldsmiths-press

Goldsmiths
UNIVERSITY OF LONDON

In memory of my brother Tar
Much loved, much missed

Contents

Acknowledgements

One of the pleasant tasks of writing this book is the opportunity it gives me to thank all those who have encouraged and supported me while it was being written. The idea for the book came from Yasmin Gunaratnam, who nudged me into action through continuing encouragement. I am deeply grateful to her for that. Sreya Banerjea's assistance in preparing the manuscript has been indispensable. Thanks to Susan Kelly and Ellen Parnavelas at Goldsmiths Press for their enthusiasm for the project.

I am incredibly lucky to have very supportive friends. They have provided encouragement throughout this project. Special thanks go to: Floya Anthias; Les Back; Filomena Fernandes; Irene Gedalof; Catherine Hall; Sushila Khoot; Gail Lewis; Lata Mani; Sulekha Nath; Ann Phoenix; Nirmal Puwar; and Nira Yuval-Davis. Irene Gedalof, Catherine Hall, and Sarah Kember read the manuscript in its entirety. I am grateful to them for their valuable comments.

Until recently, I have been a long-term member of the Editorial Collective of the journal *Feminist Review*. I am grateful to the members of the Collective for making this an important political and intellectual experience. I have also been a trustee of the Feminist Review Trust, which has been providing grants to projects in the UK and internationally that support women. I would like to acknowledge the support of my fellow trustees of the Feminist Review Trust.

I wish to thank Klaus Stierstorfer for convening the stimulating colloquia at Villa Vigoni, German-Italian Centre for the European Dialogue, on Lake Como, Italy, where some of the work in the book was first presented. Thanks also to Nilufer Bharucha and Sridhar Rajeswaran whom I met at Villa Vigoni, and who have since become friends. I appreciate their support.

I wish to remember the late Stuart Hall for his friendship and inspiring work.

I am grateful to my family for their support over the years. No words can fully express my debt to my late parents, Dhan Kaur and Bachan Singh. Very special thanks to Bhupinder, Sareeta, Balraj, and Amerjit for their ongoing encouragement and support. Much love to the youngest members of the family, Amara and Yash, children still, with the future yet to unfold. They never fail to bring a smile to my face.

I am immensely thankful to Pervaiz Nazir for constant help, support, and encouragement.

This book is dedicated to the memory of my brother, my namesake, Avtar Singh Brah, whom we lovingly called Tar and who left us while I was working on the book. We spent a carefree childhood together in Jinja on the banks of Lake Victoria and at the source of the River Nile. In London, he was a means of great support. I always knew I could rely on him. I will always miss him.

Acknowledgement of Sources

Some of the chapters that follow are revisions of material published previously. For permission to reprint I would like to thank the following: For Chapter 3 'Borders, Boundaries, and the Question of Commonality and Connectivity', in N. E. Bharucha, S. Rajeswaran and K. Stierstorfer (eds) (2018) *Beyond Borders and Boundaries: Diasporic Images and Re-Presentations in Literature and Cinema*, CoHab IDC, University of Mumbai; for Chapter 4, interview by Katy P. Sian, in, *Conversations in Postcolonial Thought* (2014), Palgrave Macmillan; for Chapter 5 'Diaspora in and Through Feminist Inflections', R. Goodman (ed.) (2019) *The Bloomsbury Handbook of 21st Century Feminist Theory* Bloomsbury Academic, published as Chapter 31 titled 'Diaspora'; for Chapter 6, A. Brah and C. Clini (2017) 'Contemporary Feminist Discourses and Practices within and across Boundaries: An Interview with Avtar Brah', *Feminist Review* 117, 163–170; for

Chapter 7, 'Multiple Axes of Power: Articulation of Diaspora and Intersectionality', in K. Stierstorfer and J. Wilson (eds) (2018) *Routledge Diaspora Studies Reader*, Taylor and Francis; for Chapter 8, 'Articulations Across Diaspora, Law and Literature' in D. Carpi and K. Stierstorfer (eds) (2017) *Diaspora Law and Literature*, De Gruyter; for Chapter 9, Interview with Avtar Brah by Brenna Bhandar and Rafeef Ziadah (2020) *Revolutionary Feminisms*, Verso.

Chapter 1

Introduction: Multiple Configurations of Power: Framing the Decolonial

In December 2019 the world began to change under the seismic impact of the Covid-19 pandemic. By the middle of May 2021, over three and a half million people had died of the virus worldwide. Populations have been devastated as have the economies. Global lockdowns have been introduced in which households, friends, lovers, colleagues, indeed whole populations, have had to go into self-isolation. Media reports for England and Wales reveal that people in deprived areas have experienced a death rate that is twice that of those living in more affluent areas. There have also been disproportionate deaths among men, older people, frontline workers, and Black and minority ethnic groups. The reasons for these disparities are complex and there is ongoing debate. In the case of Black and minority ethnic groups, socio-economic disadvantage for which sustained evidence has accumulated over the decades, and the effects of racism would seem to be among the key factors at work. Black and minority ethnic groups in Britain are more likely to work in high-risk 'frontline jobs' in health care, public transport, caring professions, and retail, especially in essential 'corner' shop work. They tend to live in deprived, crowded areas, and some reside in multigenerational households with limited space. Black and minority ethnic patients with Covid-19 have been found to be more likely to have pre-existing medical conditions such as high blood pressure and diabetes compared to white patients but this differential too has been found to be related to socio-economic disadvantage. There is much that is still unknown but Nish Chaturvedi, professor of clinical epidemiology at University College London, insists against one misconception: "Some suggest that genes can account for the excess risk of

Covid-19 in BAME (Black and Minority Ethnic) groups, and I just want to say that it's not the case. Genetic heterogeneity is far greater within than between populations. This is a story about social inequality, not biology" (Chaturvedi qtd in Hattenstone, 2020: 28). In other words, the pandemic has highlighted political cleavages when multiple social dimensions such as gender, class, age, sexuality, disability/debility and racialised difference intersect and define everyday individual and group realities at the heart of the major crisis we face today.

In this book I combine substantive analysis of themes central to the concerns of the text with material drawn from chapters that consist of interviews with me carried out by other scholars. These interviews introduce personal reflections on theoretical as well as political dimensions of the material under investigation. Hence, they highlight the imbrication of the personal with the political, thereby underlining the importance of the longstanding feminist slogan 'the personal is political'. The interviews or conversations foreground, concretise, and provide both conceptual clarification and express my position on particular political issues. Concepts discussed and elaborated include coloniality/decoloniality, diaspora, intersectionality, Gramscian common sense, and critical multiculturalism. Substantive issues tackled in the conversations cover such topics as transnational feminism, sexual assaults on New Year's Eve in Germany (2015–2016), politicised religious identities, and questions of belonging.

A Decade of Shifting Political Landscape

The past decade has witnessed dramatic changes ranging from the Arab Spring uprisings (2010–2012), through the ongoing war in Syria, to the worsening climate global emergency. In 2017, Donald Trump was catapulted from being a reality TV star to president of the United States, and Boris Johnson assumed office as prime minister of Britain in 2019, from being mayor of London. As David Olusoga notes, while people in 2010 were debating whether Barack Obama's presidency might usher a post-racial society, Trump spoke of white supremacists as "very fine people" (*Observer*, 22 December 2019: 23). Along a similar vein, Boris Johnson called gay men "bumboys" and women as "hot totty" and compared Muslim women to "letterboxes". He has also described African heritage Black people as "piccaninnies" with "watermelon smiles" (Johnson quotes cited in Bienkov, 2020). It is noteworthy that such racialised, sexist, and homophobic discourses have emanated from high citadels of the political elite. In Hungary, Viktor Orbán, the president, rides high on an anti-immigration platform. In Brazil a far-right president, Jair Bolsonaro, is in power. In India, the country has Narendra Modi as its prime minister who is a member of the Bharatiya Janata Party, a Hindu right nationalist organisation with Rashtariya Swayamsevak Sangh (RSS) as its military wing. One can cite many more examples. The point is that the political right has experienced a considerable resurgence over the course of the last decade and it now features as a distinctive element in global politics. In Britain, the UK Independence Party (UKIP), and the Brexit Party (renamed Reform UK in January 2021) have exercised visible influence on political direction to the right, especially that of the Conservative Party. This turn to the right as a global phenomenon is associated with the normalisation and legitimisation of racism and far right ideologies, ideas, and perspectives (Farris, 2017; Kaufmann, 2019; Mondon and Winter, 2020).

By contrast the beginning of the 'noughties' had begun with an optimistic outlook, especially when Barack Obama was elected as the first Black president of the United States in 2008 to the loud refrain of "Yes We Can (change the world)!". There was an expectation that this would install a new dawn for a better world. Although this optimism might have been exaggerated and somewhat misplaced, nevertheless the election was a momentous event on a world scale that marked major shifts in political sensibility. The 2012 London Olympics held in London injected considerable feelings of solidarity, positivity, and connectivity among British people. The election of the left-wing candidate Jeremy Corbyn in 2015 as leader of the British Labour Party promised to introduce a future in which egalitarian politics would stand a good chance. As Andy Beckett notes in the British newspaper

The Guardian (17 December 2019), space opened up for the emergence of political movements, not witnessed since the 1960s:

> Some of these movements, such as #MeToo and Black Lives Matter, are revolts against age-old injustices, largely made possible, and then accelerated and amplified, by the new digital networks. Others, such as Extinction Rebellion and Corbynism, have been reactions to glaring inadequacies in modern mainstream politics: its inability, or unwillingness, to address the problems; or to create an economy and society that works for the majority.
>
> (Beckett, 2019: 9)

More right-wing developments such as the Brexit campaign, he adds, have been nostalgic in tone but remain modern with a commitment to a "more footloose, disruptive capitalism" (Beckett, 2019: 9).

The recent inauguration in January 2021 of Joe Biden as president of the US and Kamala Harris as vice-president once again portends to usher a comparatively more hopeful political climate in the US. Importantly, Kamala Harris is the first woman vice-president with an African-Caribbean and South Asian background. It is, of course, too early to predict the global impact of this election but a degree of optimism is perhaps not totally misplaced.

In Britain there have been four elections during the previous decade (2010, 2015, 2017, 2019) and the last one quite definitively marks the beginning of a new phase in politics with Boris Johnson at the helm of the government. The Brexit referendum in 2016, and the process of withdrawal from the European Union on 23 January 2020, is likely to transform the socio-economic, political, and cultural terrain on which the present decade will manifest itself. The processes unleashed by the economic crash of 2008 will continue to have an impact on the life chances of people. Events such as the economic crash take a long time to work through, and their consequences are differentially distributed among the population. The austerity policies of the Conservative government have left an indelible mark on the experiences of significant levels of the population (Cooper and Whyte, 2017; Gedalof, 2018). Downturns tend to hurt the poorest most, not least because those on lower incomes are more likely to lose their jobs. Over the years, there has been a cas-ualisation of the labour market as zero-hours contracts, low wages, and insecure employment have increasingly created precarious work and we now speak of a new category, that of the 'precariat'. Certain areas of Britain witnessed not only austerity but also the unequal impact of the recession along with underinvestment so that these localities tend now to be referred to as the 'left behind'.

Hostile Environment

One key figure demonised in political and popular discourse as a major problem throughout the previous decade, and of course before, has been that of the 'migrant'. David Cameron's promise on the Andrew Marr Show on 10 January 2010 of bringing down immigration numbers in the UK to "tens of thousands" set the tone for highly toxic debates about immigration. The announcement was followed by harsh policies to meet this target such as the singularly punitive minimum income threshold for people with spouses from overseas; severe measures to clamp down on supposed 'bogus colleges' or 'bogus migrants'; and, the setting in motion of the notorious 'hostile environment' policy designed to either deport migrants or put pressure on them to leave voluntarily (see below). There is a long history in Britain of hostility towards migrants from non-European Union countries, even when their contribution was necessary for economic reasons. In other words, for racialised groups, this expression of antagonism was nothing new. But during the decade of the 2010s, even European migrants (albeit mostly East European ones) came to be viewed as threatening. Indeed, during the general election of 2015, both Labour and Conservatives tried to out-perform each other by being, in government parlance, 'tough on immigration'. The political climate created by the noxious discourse and policy of 'hostile environment' deeply impacted the lives of a variety of people including migrants, refugees, asylum seekers, and diasporic groups whose life chances are discussed in the book.

In 2012, Theresa May, the then Conservative home secretary, put forward the Hostile Environment Policy. She introduced it with the view that the aim was to create, "a really hostile environment for illegal immigrants" (Goodfellow, 2019: 2). This policy consisted of a raft of administrative and legislative measures that were intended to make life intolerable for people without leave to remain in the United Kingdom so that they would 'voluntarily leave'. In May 2007, Liam Byrne, the then Labour immigration minister, had already used similar language while announcing a consultation document on immigration (Travis, 2007, 2013). The policy by Theresa May included the removal of homeless citizens of other European Union countries. It implemented the Immigration Act 2014 and Immigration Act 2016, thereby instituting practices such as the requirement for landlords, the NHS, charities, community interest companies, and banks to carry out identity checks. The application process for 'leave to remain' came to rely on the principle of 'deport first appeal later'. Voluntary deportation was enforced through the deployment of strategies such as the infamous 'Go Home Vans' as part of 'Operation Vaken', an advertising campaign by the British Home Office, which was piloted for a month between 22 July and 22 August 2013 in six London boroughs. These vans travelled the streets carrying huge government billboards with the words "In the UK illegally? GO HOME OR FACE ARREST". A group of researchers conducted an investigation into this issue. They worked collaboratively with civil society organisations to map the impact this policy had on individuals and groups such as refugees and asylum seekers and others considered as 'migrants'. Inter alia, the research project analysed Vaken-related policy, media narratives, the social and political context of immigration regimes and debates in Britain, and how Vaken was experienced in local communities (Jones et al., 2017). It draws attention to the similarity between the language of the billboards and the rhetoric on immigration of the far-right racists. Some of the interviewees in the project found the vans "extremely scary", others were concerned it would fuel "racial tension", and all felt stigmatised and 'othered', even when they had full legal rights to remain in the country. The vans generated such heated controversy that their deployment was cancelled on 21 October 2013. However, they signified a turning point in the political climate of immigration policy.

As noted above, the UK referendum to join the European Union took place in June 2016 in the midst of polarised debate on the supposed problem of immigration control and resulted in a vote to leave the European Union. There were reports of racial abuse directed at migrants as well as settled racially minoritised groups who were exhorted to 'go home!' This was the height of the activities of the UK Independence Party (UKIP), a right wing, anti-immigration, populist party, which exerted pressure on the government that led to the 2016 referendum. They launched a poster that had the words "Breaking Point: The EU has failed us all. We must break free of the EU and take control of our borders" inscribed above an image of a crowded queue of Syrian refugees at the Slovenian border. As Jones et al. (2017) remind us, the anti-immigration rhetoric seamlessly blurs into racism and Islamophobia. This period also witnessed raids at places of work and in homes to locate individuals. Such government and media attention to immigration created a great deal of fear and distress in local communities and violated their sense of belonging:

Several participants wept as they considered the implication of this hostile environment for themselves and people they know. From witnessing night-time raids in shared houses to seeing people on the street being carted off, they talked about the visceral impact of immigration policy on their lives and their new or increasing sense of precariousness.

(Jones et al., 2017: 101)

Another casualty of the policy of 'hostile environment' were the thousands of law-abiding, pension-age people who had been born in Commonwealth countries but had lived for much of their childhood and adult lives in Britain. They were wrongly classified by the Home Office as 'illegal immigrants'. By 2017, when Amelia Gentleman started to investigate what came to be known as the 'Windrush Scandal' some of these individuals were detained and threatened with deportation or actually deported, others were not permitted to return after visiting the country of their birth, yet others lost their jobs, homes, and were denied NHS treatment. Initially, their experience was highlighted in *The Guardian* newspaper. Gradually, as the evidence mounted, the government was forced to acknowledge what a catastrophic mistake they had made. Although exact figures were not easily available, it was estimated that as many as thirty thousand individuals may have been affected by this policy. Although referred to in common usage as the 'Windrush Generation', this description of the group was somewhat inaccurate. This terminology is normally applied to the 492 passengers, the vast majority from Jamaica, who arrived on the ship *Empire Windrush* at Tilbury Docks in Essex on 22 June 1948. Their arrival has become a central signifier of the history that marks the beginning of the Black Caribbean post-World War II immigration to the UK. But those who were impacted by the Windrush Scandal came to Britain in the 1950s and 1960s to take up low-paid jobs in the NHS, on the London underground, as construction workers, on the railways, as healthcare assistants, and so on. These jobs were vital to the economy but concentrated at its lower rungs. They worked hard, experiencing all the hardships associated with not just low pay and injuries of working-class subordination but also racism arising from colonial and imperial histories and the current context. In time, they made well-settled lives for themselves and their families and were edging retirement when they started receiving letters from the Home Office to produce documentary proof to show they were here legally. This infamous criminalisation of Black British residents emerged in the context of a heightened frenzy about immigration fuelled by media scare stories about refugees and migrants coming in 'swarms' as David Cameron announced in July 2015. As Gentleman (2019) demonstrates, both David Cameron and Theresa May pushed the 'hostile environment' policies with equal enthusiasm. Not that opposition within the government was totally absent. Bob Kerslake, the then head of the UK civil service, told the BBC that these policies were regarded by some ministers as "almost reminiscent of Nazi Germany".

Moreover, the popularity of UKIP also influenced the Labour Party. Like the Conservatives, Labour too responded by adopting a hardened position on immigration symbolised by a mug that was offered for sale during the 2015 election that read: "Controls on immigration. I'm voting Labour". The middle years of the decade witnessed acutely distressing scenes of people fleeing conflict, war, and poverty in Africa and the Middle East to seek safety in Europe. Many lives were lost on the way as a large number drowned in the Mediterranean. These desperate journeys are a key part of the discussion in Chapter 3, as are the main features of immigration control. These scenes have kept the debate on immigration high on the political agenda. People born and brought up in Britain have experienced being referred to as 'immigrants' or 'migrants' and seen through the lens of 'them' and 'us' (Anderson, 2013). In public debate, the word migrant and immigrant are often used interchangeably. These labels come to mean different things in different discourses: sometimes they serve to stand for racialised and ethnicised groups; at other times they refer to refugees and asylum seekers, and, on yet other occasions they have been used to refer to Roma people or Eastern Europeans. On the whole, this terminology is likely to be used as a term of exclusion and disapproval within debate on immigration control. The UK's first major piece of legislation to deal with immigration – the Alien's Act 1905 – was designed to limit the number of Jewish people entering the country. Since then, several Acts have been implemented to exclude particular categories of people. For instance, the Commonwealth Immigration Act 1968, instituted by Harold Wilson's Labour government to deter Asians from Kenya from migrating to Britain, made every citizen of the United Kingdom or the colonies subject to immigration control unless they had one parent or grandparent born, adopted, naturalised, or registered in Britain as a citizen of Britain or its colonies. In other words, entry came to be restricted primarily to white groups. Three years later this Act was replaced by the Immigration Act 1971 but the 'patriality' clauses were retained. This legislation was widely regarded as blatantly discriminatory. Both the Conservative and Labour parties have been implicated over the decades since World War II in the introduction of increasingly restrictive immigration law. This has served to construct and represent certain groups as outsiders, 'a foreign element.'

As Virdee (2014) has pointed out, working-class resistance has often been accompanied by intense racism and anti-Semitism in all social classes. Britain has had a dual policy with introduction of immigration control on the one hand, and race equality on the other. In response to widespread discrimination in society and political pressure to eliminate its effects, the government passed Race Relations Acts, with the intention to outlaw discrimination. The 1965 Race Relations Act, for instance, made it illegal to discriminate along lines of race, ethnicity, or nationality. These provisions were extended to cover housing, employment, and public services by the 1968 Race Relations Act, which also created the Community Relations Commission to promote good community relations. These Acts were followed by the Race Relations Act 1976, which covers employment, education, training, housing, and the provision of goods and services; the Race Relations Amendment Act 2000, and the Equality Act 2010. The last supersedes and consolidates previous discrimination legislation. Of course, legislation is only one measure that can be taken to engender positive or negative social relations. The civil society actions are perhaps immeasurably more important. Yet the social climate created by the discourse and practice surrounding the introduction and implementation of law, especially the immigration Acts – jingoistic nationalism, for instance – foreground alterity, raising questions as to who can or cannot stake a claim to a place as home. Hence, home remains a contested idea even as generations have made their home in the UK in the post-world war period.

Decolonial Framings

How do we think about decoloniality? How do we address the present-day consequences of processes of colonisation and decolonisation? In its commonly accepted meaning, decolonisation refers to processes, events, and histories of political challenge and resistance that resulted in the formal 'independence' of former colonies from the colonisers so as to establish self-governing new 'sovereign' states. However, achievement of political independence did not always lead to socio-economic, cultural, or psychological 'independence'. There has been a long-standing debate on this subject. For instance, the collection of essays by Ngũgĩ wa Thiong'o, the Kenyan novelist and theorist, titled 'Decolonising the Mind: The Politics of Language in African Literature' was published over 30 years ago in 1986. And, ten years later, Linda Tuhiwai Smith argued that decolonisation was not simply a formal process of handing over the instruments of government, but rather it was a long-term process that involved cultural, linguistic, and psychological divesting of colonial power (Smith, 1999). More recently, scholars such as Walter Mignolo draw attention to the importance of coloniality/decoloniality in the modern world, especially in relation to its epistemic genealogies (Mignolo, 2011; Mignolo and Walsh, 2018). Why is it important to think decolonially, Mignolo asks. Mainly because coloniality is understood as constitutive of modernity and that *"knowledge itself is an integral part of imperial processes of appropriation"* (Mignolo, 2011: 205, original emphasis). Hence the importance of a focus on knowledge regimes alongside analysis of economic and political dimensions of coloniality/decoloniality.

The term 'decolonisation' was transformed into 'decoloniality' towards the end of the Cold War with a view, in part, to foreground decolonisation of knowledge. This emphasis on 'epistemic reconstitution' is essential so as to critique, challenge, and dismantle colonial epistemic hierarchies. The aim is to install instead knowledge regimes that

open up to the richness of knowledges and praxis of living that the rhetoric of modernity demonised and reduced to tradition, barbarism, folklore, underdevelopment, denied spirituality in the name of reason, and built knowledges to control sexuality and all kinds of barbarians.

(Mignolo and Walsh, 2018: 228)

There is a tendency in decolonial thought to claim that analysis of colonialism was likely to overemphasise the study of economic and political consequences of colonialism rather than that of knowledge practices. The veracity of this claim in my view is debatable since a number of theorists long ago addressed questions of knowledge production and the colonial context (cf. Asad, 1973, 2003; Said, 1978; Hall, 1992; Wynter, 2003). But, in any case, I would suggest that an effective political strategy would always include analysis of epistemic as well as socio-economic, cultural, and political differentiations and/or cleavages.

It is important to bear in mind that decoloniality has developed in parallel with the discourse of postcoloniality. The two have comparable, though distinct, developments. How do we distinguish between these analogous formations? The two represent separate genealogies of discourse and distinct points of origination, with the concept of postcoloniality connected primarily with the experience of British colonisation, whereas the notion of decoloniality is largely associated with the experience of South America, the Caribbean, and Latino/as in the United States of America. They are, in my view, complementary projects with similar goals of transformation. The discourse of the 'postcolonial' refers to the ways in which decolonisation processes underpinned both colonising and colonised societies, albeit differently. According to Stuart Hall, the postcolonial signifies transnational and transcultural 'global' processes that he described as a decentred, global, diasporic rendering of earlier imperial grand narratives that focused on the nation. In the publication titled 'When Was the "Postcolonial"? Thinking at the Limit' Hall argues that the postcolonial has poststructuralist underpinnings, and it restages colonisation as a major, world historical event:

By 'colonisation' the 'post-colonial' references something more than the direct rule over certain areas of the world by the imperial powers. I think it is signifying the whole process of expansion, exploration, conquest, colonisation and imperial hegemonisation which constituted the 'outer face', the constitutive outside, of European and then Western capitalist modernity after 1492.

(Hall, 1996d: 249)

Comparing the two analytical and political formations, Mignolo suggests that postcoloniality emerged as an option to poststructuralism and postmodernity, but decoloniality emerged as an option to the rhetoric of modernity and to the combined rhetoric of "development and modernization".... Decoloniality came to light also as an option to the discourse of decolonization during the Cold War and as a critical option in relation to Marxist-dialectical materialism.

(Mignolo, 2011: xxviii)

Though common to both projects, the legacies of colonialism, then, are addressed somewhat differently.

In terms of praxis, decoloniality stakes a claim to contributing to scholarly activism, to political work of building new futures whereby multiple worlds can coexist and sustain life-affirming practices. Decoloniality embraces pluriversality, and dialogue between different epistemic traditions such as postcolonialism and decoloniality. Such 'theoretical synergy', to use Ali Meghji's (2021) phrase, and my notion of 'creolised theory' (Brah, 1996), are useful pointers that studying the complexity of social reality demands the deployment of multiple theoretical and conceptual tools.

Thus, there would seem to be considerable overlap between decolonial and postcolonial discourses and practices, especially as evidenced in Hall's formulation above. Hall shows that the key concepts in the postcolonial conceptual armoury may be read under Derridean erasure so that they are repositioned rather than overcome. This would be similar to reading decoloniality 'under erasure' whereby the regimes of coloniality continue to be refracted in and through a decolonial lens.

I have explored the concepts of decoloniality and postcoloniality in some detail because they inform my analysis in the book, especially in terms of feminist decoloniality, which proposes a gendered reading of capitalist modernity. As Maria Lugones argues, such a project demands dismantling the logic of colonial modernity:

I propose the modern, colonial gendering system as a lens through which to theorise further the oppressive logic of colonial modernity, its use of hierarchical dichotomies and categorical logic. I want to emphasize categorical dichotomous, hierarchical logic as central to modern, colonial, capitalist thinking about race, gender and sexuality.

(Lugones, 2010: 742)

She draws upon Anibal Quijano's notion of 'coloniality of power' as it developed from his analysis of the 'capitalist world system' in which there is an inseparability of racialisation and capitalist exploitation. In parallel to 'coloniality of power', Lugones uses the term 'coloniality of gender', which references gender-specific processes that have lasted beyond colonisation into the present. Methodologically, she shifts from women of colour feminism to decolonial feminism with a focus on grassroots politics and the 'colonial difference' where the idea of colonial difference is understood as the site where coloniality of power is enacted. As she points out: "I call the analysis of racialised, capitalist, gender oppression 'the coloniality of gender'. I call the possibility of overcoming the coloniality of gender 'decolonial feminism'" (Lugones, 2010: 747).

Another important deployment of the concept of decolonial in feminist work is that by Françoise Verges (2021). She seeks to anchor decolonial feminism in a struggle against exploitation and all forms of domination, that is to say "in the desire to smash sexism, racism, capitalism and imperialism" (Verges, 2021: vii). Among the possible agents of oppression she includes "feminist racism", a term coined by Sabine Hark and Paula Irene Villa (2020). She analyses the role of what she calls *"civilizational feminism"*, which borrows the language and aims of the colonial civilising mission, and mounts a counter-strategy to the revolutionary changes introduced by the combined struggles of the subaltern. While this putative feminism puts women's rights at the forefront of the politics of equality, it does so in ways that bolster neoliberal and imperialist agendas. In France, Verge argues, this feminism came to be theorised by feminists on the Left in the 1980s, and, inter alia, it succeeded in criminalising the veil. The arguments they used to support their political position are now at the heart of those particular feminist formations that have set up essentialist binaries between

Western cultures which are seen as open to gender equality and those others, especially Islamic ones, which are construed as impervious to such politics. Decolonial feminism, then, is a counter-narrative to this neoliberal and imperialist feminist project and as such it offers a vision of a world that is "post-racist, post-capitalist, post-imperialist, thus post-hetero-patriarchal" (Verges, 2021: ix). These are global phenomena that warrant planetary solutions through analysis and political activism. Such praxis combines a recognition of difference with a grounded politics of solidarity. Such decolonial solidarity agendas are intersectional and multidimensional. They are designed to address simultaneously the impact of the state and civil society.

Decoloniality enables us to prioritise and foreground regimes of knowledge that have been sidelined, ignored, forgotten, repressed, even discredited by the forces of modernity, colonialism, imperialism, and racial capitalism. It is a method to restore and resituate the marginalised to the centre and thereby validate the lived experiences, cultures, and multiplicity of forms of knowledge of subordinate groups such as Indigenous people, racialised groups, and those suffering all manner of exploitation and discrimination. The project of decoloniality is designed to interrogate and decentre the hegemonic moves of hetero/cis normativity. It challenges intersectional hierarchies of 'race', class, gender, and de/disability. While an interrogation of the histories of colonialism and imperialism is central to decolonial projects, their primary concern is with the present, especially with the ways in which systems of knowledge production are structured. Decoloniality is associated with recovery and development of subaltern epistemologies and it aims to enact a radical break with regimes of knowledge that underpin Eurocentric episteme. In other words, decoloniality embodies a ground-breaking, innovative critique that poses a serious challenge to the hegemony of claims surrounding the perceived superiority and universality of Western culture. It embraces analytical approaches and socio-economic and political practices that delink from the oppressive imperatives of coloniality, racial capitalism, and the contradictory effects of modernity.

As part of decolonizing epistemology, there is a growing move to critique and revise academic subject disciplines from the inside (Bhambra and Holmwood, 2021; Meghji, 2021). These three authors address colonial moves in the development of sociology and social theory. The academic discipline of sociology, for instance, emerged in the nineteenth century during the high noon of colonialism. It internalised the logic of colonialism and in some ways reproduced and propagated this logic even when the individual practitioners of the discipline were avowedly anticolonial. This is not surprising, given that colonial epistemic formations have impact at both the conscious and unconscious level. That is, they influence how we think, perceive, and feel the world. It is important to recognise the effects of the unruly unconscious as it circumscribes the workings of conscious mental activity marked by the articulations between power, ontology, and epistemology. One of the major outcomes of these processes was that the colonised came to be socially constructed as inferior to the coloniser. The emergence of the idea of race in the sixteenth century, and its growing hegemony over the following centuries, has helped consolidate racialised hierarchies of difference between different categories of people. As is commonly known, W. E. B. Du Bois was one of the first sociologists to analyse the construction of global hierarchies of racialised peoples. In Britain, the work of sociologists such Sheila Allen at Bradford University, Michael Banton at Bristol University and Stuart Hall at the University of Birmingham, and John Rex at Warwick University analysed questions of racism from the 1960s and 1970s onwards. Anibal Quijano's concept of the 'colonial matrix of power' has been important in helping theorise social, cultural, and political divisions that permeate the developments of academic disciplines.

We noticed above that colonial epistemic practices inferiorised the colonised peoples. Simultaneously, of course, they came to represent the coloniser as the 'superior race' with a more advanced civilisation. Hence the emergence of the myth of the 'civilising mission' of the West whereby the West was assumed as being charged with a moral duty to transport their civilisation to the rest of the world. This gave rise to the highly problematic and contradictory notion of democratic imperialism when, in fact, democracy was as yet far off the agenda. Some eminent sociologists of the time such as Robert Park in the 1930s and 1940s as well as politically radical theorists such as Karl Marx in the nineteenth century tended to regard imperialism as beneficial to the dominated countries in so far as it was thought to help economic prosperity though how far this supposed prosperity was realised in practice has been debatable. While not all classical sociologists were active agents of empires, some such as Patrick Geddes in Britain were critical of colonialism but at the same time Geddes was working as a colonial town planner (Meghji, 2021). A critical point to register here is that imperial legacies played their part in the development of sociology as an academic field of inquiry; that is to say, in the constitution of epistemic regimes. Formal colonialism may be over but the power relations derived from colonialism still retain their resonance. In other words, the relationships produced during colonialism may outlive the collapse of colonial administrations and this reality is signified today by the concept of coloniality, which receives its sustenance through the colonial matrix of power.

Decolonial feminist politics then entail interrogating, challenging, and, finally, erasing the colonial difference and, in the process, decolonising gender which is a critique and praxis of resistance. It involves valuing and affirming life over profit, and enacting coalitions and non-hierarchical relationality. In Britain, such practices were the life force underlining the 'politically Black feminism' that emerged as a feminist coalition among women of African, Caribbean, and South Asian heritage during the 1970s, with the first Black women's conference taking place in 1979. Currently, this category includes feminists with ancestry in Africa, Asia, the Middle East, and Latin America, as well as Indigenous women. Chapter 2 details aspects of the history of British Black feminism in the broader context of its colonial and imperial genealogies and of global as well as local mobilities. British Black feminism contested racialised imperatives of white feminism. Drawing on Gail Lewis, I address the figure of the Black woman, "not as an abject figure of absolute alterity, but as separate from, equal to and essential to the self" (Lewis, 2017: 15). Chapter 2 also discusses the theme of 'mobilities' ranging from physical migrations, especially of people trying to cross the Mediterranean from Africa or Asia into Europe, through conceptual border crossings, to theoretical mobilisation of the figure of the nomad. Nomad thought, though not as central to contemporary debate as it once was, still retains purchase, especially in terms of feminist critique and contestation surrounding its use. I present some features of this debate through Irene Gedalof's engagement with Rosi Braidotti's feminist conceptualisation of the nomad. The chapter concludes with a discussion of the 'politics of location' as theorised, among others, by Chandra Talpade Mohanty.

The theme of movement and mobility is continued in Chapter 3 where borders, boundaries, and questions dealing with coalitions and connectivity are analysed. Using Gloria Anzaldua's classic work on borders as a point of departure, I address borders and boundaries not simply as territorial but also as social, cultural, political, psychological, psychic, and experiential. Borders facilitate crossings as much as hinder them depending on the category of person involved. People on the move may be labour migrants, highly qualified specialists, entrepreneurs, refugees, asylum seekers, students, or family dependents. Their experiences differ enormously. For instance, as we have already noted, thousands of migrants, refugees, and asylum seekers have drowned while crossing the Mediterranean during the last few years, especially since 2015. Some groups sympathetic to their plight organised search and rescue missions, but – with the political tilt towards the right in some European countries – others criminalised them. Border crossing may become highly politicised events and international politics is thoroughly enmeshed in the governance of border crossings. Overall, following Etienne Balibar (2002, 2004), my focus is upon *what borders do* at particular historical moments.

Questions of ethnicity, nationalism, national identity, and belonging are central to thinking about borders. As such, Chapter 3 explores the ways in which these concepts and the interrelation between them have been theorised. It argues for a non-essentialist conception of these categories, endorsing the view that rather than thinking of general theories of, say, nationalism, it is best to examine concrete sets of historical relations underpinning given nationalist ideologies, discourses, and practices. Inter alia, it addresses the concept of 'homonationalism' developed by Jasbir Puar and 'femonationalism' by Sara Farris. Jasbir Puar describes how nationalist discourses and practices are deployed by groups on the right of the political spectrum as they express support for LGBTQ communities while maintaining their racist, xenophobic, and anti-Muslim positions. In a similar vein, femonationalism refers to the ways in which the European right-wing parties and neoliberals promulgate gender equality while touting xenophobic and racist politics. It also demonstrates how well-known feminists and femocrats are involved in the current framing of Islam as a quintessentially misogynistic religion and culture from which Muslim women, often portrayed as passive, need to be 'rescued'. Accordingly, they are likely to endorse legal proposals such as veil bans.

In Britain, the history of immigration law is instructive in helping us think through borders and boundaries of 'them' and 'us' and Chapter 3 analyses key features of immigration control, and how the anti-migrant discourse is exploited by the political right. On a somewhat different though related note, it also explores questions of commonality, connectivity and conviviality beyond social divisions marked by borders. I discuss a modality of the non-essentialist notion of 'universalism' or 'pluriversalism' (Mignolo and Walsh, 2018). The chapter concludes on the problematic of connectivity and cosmopolitanism with a brief reflection on perspectives drawn from David Harvey, Seyla Benhabib, and Antony Appiah.

Chapter 4 is based on an interview with me conducted by Katy P. Sian and it is part of a discussion with British thinkers writing on coloniality/postcoloniality. It begins with a consideration of early influences on the development of my political consciousness. We explore the bearing Panjabi literature had on my emerging political orientation, especially the impact of that particular branch of Panjabi literature that had a focus on class, caste, and gender relations. It charts my childhood experiences of growing up in colonial Uganda, with its racialised social and cultural hierarchies and relations, with whites at the top, Asians in the middle, and Black Africans at the lowest end. We reflect upon my sojourn as a university student in the USA during the period of radical student politics, Black Power movement, and emerging feminist organising at the end of the 1960s/early 1970s. We look at my experiences of postgraduate study and work in the UK and discuss my writing on culture and politics and on developing a theoretical framework to study diaspora, and the influence of poststructuralist and postcolonial thought on my work. The chapter describes the epistemic struggles, contestations, and change within the academy in relation to the study of racism, ethnicity, and postcoloniality.

My concept of 'diaspora space' has become established as a key construct in feminist and diaspora studies and has been widely used in analysing diasporic formations. Yet, while there is by now a substantial body of literature on diasporas, there is limited material that addresses the field of diaspora studies and feminism together. This intersection forms the basis of discussion in Chapter 5. My attempt to tackle the subject is one of the first to foreground the articulation of gender and diaspora. I argue that diasporas are inherently intersectional formations and foreground the important insight of the Combahee River Collective that speaks of "integrated analysis and practice based upon the fact that the major systems of oppression are interlocking" (The Combahee River Collective Statement, 1977). I revisit my theorisation of diaspora as historically contingent 'genealogy' in the Foucauldian sense, and diaspora space as an articulation of diaspora, border, and the feminist concept of 'politics of location'. The chapter explores the concept of intersectionality and engages the emerging field of 'queering diasporas', using in particular the work of Fatima El-Tayeb and Gayatri Gopinath. Such work interrogates the demands placed by racialised heteronormativity on bodies, desires, subjectivities, and identities. This scholarship challenges nationalist ideologies by highlighting diaspora as the space of the impure, inauthentic, and non-essentialist.

An interview with myself by Clelia Clini forms the basis of Chapter 6. It highlights my involvement in anti-Vietnam War mobilisation. We discuss the ambivalence and contradiction entailed in my simultaneous attraction to the peace movement alongside support for more militant strategies of, say, the Black Power movement. This raises the predicament of engaging militant as compared with pacifist strategies of political organising. We address my engagement with socialist feminist politics and transnational feminism. A critical focus of our conversation here is the 'refugee crises', which we think through and address in terms of a crisis in global governance, set against the backdrop of deepening global inequities and inequalities. At the local level, we discuss the toxic nature of racism, and its exclusionary imperatives as when individuals born and brought up in Britain are told to 'go home' by their fellow citizens. We discuss the need for having political clarity in dealing with complex situations when, for instance, there might be allegations of the involvement of racialised men in sexist incidents. This was the case in Germany on New Year's Eve 2015/2016 when there were claims of 'sexual assaults' by men of African, Muslim, or "otherwise somehow 'not German'" origin (Hark and Villa, 2020). Such events call for a principled response, if and when there is clear evidence of culpability.

While there is a very significant body of literature that treats the subject of diaspora and intersectionality separately, there is comparatively limited material that analyses these two fields together. Chapter 7 represents an attempt to fill this gap. This chapter further develops my argument, introduced in Chapter 5, that diasporas are inherently intersectional, and that the study of diaspora and intersectionality is closely connected. For instance, a specific diaspora is differentiated according to diverse dimensions of power and differentiation such as gender, class, caste, sexuality, and ethnicity. As a concept too, diaspora is an articulation of diverse narratives enunciated from different "situated" (Haraway, 1988) positions. Similarly, intersectionality addresses differentiation within and between categories: the category woman, for instance, embodies all manner of differences. I work through the relationship between diaspora and intersectionality through their

common focus on 'difference'. The chapter discusses these conceptual and embodied interconnections. It elaborates the ways in which
I have previously analysed difference in terms of four axes: difference
conceptualised as social relation; understood as experience; analysed
as identity; and marked as subjectivity. The issue of sexual harassment
underlined by the #MeToo movement is also relevant to understanding
how intersectional 'difference' is configured in these debates. Sexual
difference and its exploitation are not only about gender. They are simultaneously about race, class, ethnicity, sexuality, disability/debility,
and caste. Black men, for instance, are viewed differently from white
men in relation to the sexual threat they are presumed to pose to white
femininity. Similarly, men from high castes have more power to impose
their will upon women from all castes whereas men from lower castes
can mainly target women from their own castes. Questions of harassment and police brutality against Black women in the USA are signalled
powerfully by the document titled SAY HER NAME produced by the
'Center for Intersectionality and Social Policy Studies' in New York.

Chapter 7 also deals with some of the main critiques of
intersectionality. In thinking through a critique of standpoint theory,
I draw upon Haraway's concept of 'situated knowledge' and Chandra
Talpade Mohanty's workings of 'politics of location' to propose a
non-essentialist way of formulating the problematic. One key issue
that scholars of intersectionality have raised is whether perspectives
informed by standpoint theory and others which take inspiration from
poststructuralism are mutually exclusive. My argument elaborated
here is that this is not entirely the case, and that despite significant
differences, there is overlap and that intersectionality as a concept and
process offers the opportunity to reconcile the two.

For decades now 'law and literature' as well as 'law in literature' has
occupied an important place in academic study. But, the links between
these fields of study and diaspora studies is much less developed. How
might we theorise and analyse this set of three-way relationships? I have
attempted to do so in Chapter 8 by addressing common thematics,
concepts, and theoretical perspectives across these distinctive fields.

Some of the common elements I have identified may be described as follows: citizenship is a concept central to all three areas; law, governance, and governmentality link law to literature and diaspora studies; the position of refugee and asylum seekers has a common resonance across all three areas as does the feminist concept of intersectionality; and, questions of identity and difference feature and permeate the three areas. I address the above themes through analysis of the diasporic novel *The Reluctant Fundamentalist* by Hamid Mohsin in which many of the above issues are central. Among other things, the novel stages an encounter between corporate capital and the formation of subjectivities and identities in and through asymmetrical power relations. It addresses predicaments of diasporic identities, their complexities, and their contradictions. As a way of theorising juridical processes, this analysis is accompanied by a more substantive explication of immigration law and citizenship, in particular, feminist citizenship and intercultural citizenship. Hence, the chapter performs an interdisciplinary textual analysis together with offering an understanding of the interplay of structural dimensions of the social and the cultural lifeworld.

Chapter 9 consists of an interview with me by Brenna Bandhar and Rafeef Ziadah, which addresses 'revolutionary' feminisms that were formed out of struggles against capitalism, imperialism, and racism. Among other things, we consider the historical conjuncture in which the concept of 'diaspora' emerged as a challenge to the discourses of the 'immigrant' or 'ethnic', which were likely to marginalise and pathologise diasporic groups. The discourse of diaspora represented a critique of nation-centric debates and brought into focus questions of 'globality', and the globalisation of economy and society. We speak about my 'diasporic method' as Stuart Hall has described it, which emphasises genealogies and spatialities of performance and embodiment of 'difference' understood, as already noted, as social relation, subjectivity, identity, and as experience; and in which diaspora space is the place of immanence of diaspora, border, and politics of location. There is, thus, an entanglement of genealogies of dispersion with those of 'staying put'. We discuss diaspora as an intersectional concept, focused on both 'routes and roots' and explore my conceptualisation of intersectionality, which initially developed separately from Kimberlé Crenshaw's theorisation. Our discussion of intersectionality is not simply about its veracity as an analytic but also as political practice. Questions of home and belonging, shifting meanings of the political Black in Britain, and the resurgence of religion as a form of political identity, form the basis of thinking through racisms such as Islamophobia or anti-Muslim racism or anti-Jewish racism. We also examine the importance of secular politics in the context of the role of religion in current debate and practice.

The book culminates by thinking through the politics of alterity and alliance in Chapter 10. Inter alia, it addresses the problematic of 'the human' using the analytics of Sylvia Wynter. I also explore how the concept of cosmopolitanism with its ethos of cultural diversity, fluidity, multiplicity, and hybridity has been put to use in the service of decolonial politics. The text concludes with a discussion of feminist interculturality, Boventura de Sousa Santos' theorisation of decolonial insurgent cosmopolitanism, and it emphasises the importance of struggle for social justice.

Overall, the book is an intervention into thinking decolonially about contemporary politics. The 'de' in the decolonial is a constant reminder to challenge and seek to dismantle intersectional hierarchies of 'race', class, gender, heteronormativity, and de/disability. The aim is to help install cultural and political practices that respect 'difference' so as to ensure that not everything is reduced to the economy of the 'same'. But it is important to mobilise a resolutely non-essentialist concept of difference. The project this book endorses is designed to develop a politics of solidarity across differences.

Chapter 2

Mobilities, Political Groundings, and Feminist Decoloniality

I have had a longstanding interest in diaspora, migration, intersectional feminisms, and questions of mobilities and 'putting roots'. In this chapter, I begin with a discussion of how the concept of mobilities has been theorised and the ways in which substantive mobilities take place when different categories of people such as migrants move across the world. Issues of power are central to who travels, how, to where, and in terms of what socio-economic, political, and cultural positionality the migrating person comes to occupy at the destination. How might we think through the complexity of differing and different formations of movement and cartographies of settlement? One such cartography of 'routes and roots' consists of the ways in which formations of Black feminism have emerged and developed in Britain through the activism of African-Caribbean and South Asian heritage women from the late 1970s. In this specific formation Black was mobilised as a political colour rather than skin tone. This decolonial move is the subject of discussion in the second part of the chapter. I analyse the social and cultural history of this political development and, inter alia, consider my own feminist locationality and situatedness within it. Mobilities and 'staying put' are understood as inherently interlinked phenomena in the lives of persons whose biographies or those of their parents or grandparents are inscribed by migration. Their subjectivities and identities are constituted within the crucible of the complex relationship between globality and locality.

Mobilities

Mass population movements are one of the key factors which underpin contemporary mobilities. The beginning of the twenty-first century was characterised by a rapid increase in migrations across the world. According to the UN World Migration Report 2020 published by the International Organization for Migration (IOM), there were an estimated 272 million international migrants at the end of 2019. Of these migrants, 52 per cent were male and 48 per cent were female. Although the figure of 272 is only 3.5 per cent of the world's population, it already surpasses some projections for 2050. Indeed, the number of migrants has tripled since the 1970s. Of course, Covid-19 has interrupted all kinds of global mobilities. According to the UN Department of Economic and Social Affairs in the UN report *International Migration 2020 Highlights* (UN DESA, 2020), the pandemic may have slowed the growth in the numbers of international migrants by around two million by mid-2020. Still, the number of international migrants reached 281 million people living outside their country of origin in 2020. While most people who migrate are of working age, and leave home to work, there are equally millions who are forced to leave home due to conflict, violence, and climate change. This highlights the ways in which natural disasters and political upheavals impact upon population movements. For instance, the displacement of countless people has resulted from conflict in such countries as Syria, Yemen, Central African Republic, the Democratic Republic of the Congo, and South Sudan. There were approximately 80 million forcibly displaced people worldwide, including internally displaced people, in mid-2020. Of these, 26.3 million are refugees, and 4.2 million are asylum seekers (UNHCR, 2020). In what follows, I analyse examples of different forms that mobilities may take within varying socio-economic, cultural, and political contexts.

In the aftermath of the tragic deaths of hundreds of people when two boats sank near the Italian island of Lampedusa in 2013, the IOM started to hold statistics on the number of people dying en route. During the five years that followed, more than 30,900 people lost their lives trying to reach safety in other countries. The Mediterranean remains the deadliest route, associated with the deaths of 18,000 people in that time. Similarly, over 1,800 deaths have been recorded over the border between the United States and Mexico. A research project by Lorenzo

Pezzani and Charles Heller at Goldsmiths University, London, analyses how the Mediterranean has been turned into a military–humanitarian border zone. It examines the political anatomy of violence inflicted at and through the sea. Charles Heller and Lorenzo Pezzani produced an animation titled *Liquid Traces* for the exhibition 'Forensis' at the house of World Cultures, Berlin in March 2014. It is a reconstruction of the events associated with the 'left-to-die boat' case in which 72 passengers headed for Lampedusa from the Libyan coast on a small rubber boat on 27 March 2011. When they realised they were not going to reach their destination with limited fuel, they called out for help. But no help came. They were left to drift for 14 days in NATO's maritime surveillance area. They were ignored despite distress signals pinpointing their location, a visit by a helicopter and contact with a military ship. Left without food and water the passengers started dying. Initially, 11 survived, but one woman died on the beach just before going ashore, and one man died in prison. Eventually, nine lived to speak about their deadly ordeal. A nine-month investigation by the Council of Europe pointed to woeful neglect and documented a catalogue of failures by NATO warships and European coastguards. This case is one example of practices that have served to maintain the Mediterranean as one of the deadliest bodies of water where economies of abandonment have tended to determine who lived and who died.

Such violent histories leave deep scars upon the lived experiences of generations to come. Yet, although individuals and communities will be deeply impacted by these traumas, there can also be examples of creative reckoning and resistance in their biographies and collective practices. In a lyrically written book, *Wayward Lives, Beautiful Experiments*, Saidiya Hartman (2019) maps the lives and mobilities – social, political, and cultural – of Black young women at the turn of the twentieth century who were likely to be seen as a problem by the social welfare and carceral agencies and socially constructed by them as wild, promiscuous, and wayward. They were subjected to surveillance, arrested, and punished, and pathologised as criminal. Yet, in their rebellion they inscribed a creativity not recognised by the criminalising agencies. Hartman represents them as "modernists, free lovers, radicals, anarchists", arguing that the 'flapper' – a term used for a generation of white women who flaunted with disdain the prevailing social and sexual mores of the time – was a pale imitation of the 'ghetto girl', though the latter were never recognised as such.

"By attending to these lives, a very unexpected story of the twentieth century emerges, one that offers an intimate chronicle of Black radicalism, an aesthetical and riotous history of coloured girls and their experiments with freedom – a revolution before Gatsby" (Hartman, 2019: xv)

She describes them as "innovators and social visionaries". One such woman, Mattie Nelson, travelled from Virginia to New York at the age of 15 to join her mother and make a new life. She was leaving behind "the oyster factory and the tobacco fields and the laundry baskets spilling over with soiled linens and dirty clothes" (Hartman, 2019: 45). Such travels by Black women and men were occasioned by the flight from terrible experiences of: "lynching, the white mob, chain gang, rape and servitude" (Hartman, 2019: 46). Although Mattie came to the North with optimism and hope in her heart, her working life was not much of an improvement on the drudgery she had been experiencing before. She now worked as a domestic at a boarding house with 23 rooms where she was the sole maid. There was some relief in her tough working life when she met a young man ten years older than her. In her relationship with him she sought to reconstruct a life of caring and intimacy inscribed within dreams of freedom. But this dream did not last and she was abandoned when she became pregnant and gave birth to a dead baby girl. She continued to chase after a better life in such pursuits as cabaret but was confined by the brutalities of racism. She had a second child with a man she regarded as her husband, but when the baby was just a month old, he disappeared and was presumed drowned at sea. Her life carried on until she was detained in the New York State Reformatory for Women of 'Immoral Conduct', although there was no evidence to confirm this. It was sufficient that she was a young Black woman so that it was assumed that she needed a better supervision than could be offered by a "lax Negro mother". She was tortured and abused inside the reformatory but it was a long time before "anyone ever questioned whether young women should be incarcerated for having children out of wedlock or staying out overnight or having serial lovers or intimate relations across the colour line" (Hartman, 2019: 74). Mattie's letters were not found in the case file, so we can only surmise what course her life may have taken. She is one of many whose struggles echo the practices of refusals, resistance, rebellions, and contestations that mark formations of Black radicalism.

As the examples above show, mobilities take various forms. Today, different categories of people in the world are on the move. These include migrants in search of jobs, refugees, asylum seekers, international students, entrepreneurs, mobile professionals, commuters, and holiday makers. It is evident that not all mobilities are equally facilitated. Some groups can travel without much hindrance, whereas others encounter inordinate obstacles on the way, especially many residents of the global South when they try to cross borders into countries of the global North. Visas, passports, residency and citizenship papers, and other documents are central in regulating different streams of movements. At the same time new technologies, especially the Internet, have had a very major impact on regulating virtual mobilities. An inquiry indicates that there were 4.66 billion users of the Internet at the end of 2020 (Chaffey, 2021). As Sheller and Urry (2006: 207) suggest, new forms of 'virtual' and 'imaginative' travel are getting "combined in unexpected ways with physical travel". The development of such information and communication technologies are permitting new coordination of people and events. They mark new identities and subjectivities. Sara Ahmed critiques an overemphasis on mobile forms of subjectivity and argues against a romantic understanding of mobility: "idealisation of movement, or transformation of movement into a fetish, depends on the exclusion of others who are already positioned as *not free in the same way*" (2004: 152, original emphasis). Access to different types of mobility is a function of power. As Beverley Skeggs has argued, "Mobility and control of mobility both reflect and reinforce power. Mobility is a resource to which not everyone has an equal relationship" (Skeggs, 2004: 49). The complexities of mobilities and deterritorialisation are highlighted by studies that mounted a critique of colonial and postcolonial power dynamics, modes of knowledge production, dissemination, and circulation. Such studies offered analysis of migration, diasporas, and transnationalism, and emphasised dislocation, disjuncture, multiplicity, globality, and a non-reductive 'homing desire' (Bhabha, 1994; Brah, 1996; Clifford, 1997; Gilroy, 1993; Hall, 1990). They foreground a complex and complicated relationship between moving and staying put or dwelling.

Tim Cresswell (2006) makes a helpful distinction between movement and mobility such that movement is understood as abstracted mobility, whereas mobility is seen as empirically embedded in contexts of power. Hence, if movement is the dynamic equivalent of location, mobility is the dynamic equivalent of place. Mobilities, like place, are, therefore, socially produced. Mobile people are not just people in the abstract – through movement they become dancers, athletes, refugees and citizens, tourists, and so on. It is in this sense that questions of mobility become politicised. Time and space are central vectors of mobilities around which life revolves. When we move, we become agents in the production of time and space, in the constitution of social time and social space.

Mobility is at the heart of Western modernity. Mobile technologies, mobile people, new developments in science and philosophy, and changing social relations are all central to the modern conception of time and space, foregrounding the interconnections between movement, mobility, and the social. Indeed, migration and border studies, in various shapes and forms, are constituted around the very idea of movement and mobility. Migration is a key dynamic of contemporary modern and postmodern worlds. We speak of time-space compression in the context of major developments in communication and modes of transportation in the world and in deep space. As noted above, the figure of the traveller is constitutive of multiplicities ranging from captains of transnational corporations, wealthy tourists, through labour migrants, to refugees and asylum seekers. It is in the last three instances that this figure is assumed to take on the appellation of the 'migrant' proper. In other words, mobility is not invariably positive, although it is often seen in that light. Indeed, words associated with mobility in contemporary social thought are likely to be positive such as dynamic, progressive, modern, enlightened, and forward looking.

The social outcomes of mobilities are dependent upon the nature and type of the socio-economic and political context within which mobilities are embedded. Texts such as *Undoing Border Imperialism* (2013) by Harsha Walia draw attention to the trials and tribulations of migrant lives, but, importantly, this book also charts the activities of an anticapitalist, anticolonial, and antiracist migrant justice movement, 'No One Is Illegal', designed to challenge 'border imperialism'. Walia's text combines academic discourse, lived experience of displacement, and movement-based practices to foreground a deeply political beacon of hope. Drawing on the author's experiences in the 'No One Is Illegal' movement, Walia reformulates immigrant rights movements through a critical analysis of transnational capitalism, settler colonialism, and racialised formations. Inter alia, the text highlights the ways in which "Colonial and capitalist interests continue to expropriate Indigenous lands, dispossessing Indigenous nations of their territorial base and livelihood, particularly within but not limited to settler-colonial states" (Walia, 2013: 47). This point is especially critical as the issues pertaining to Indigenous peoples tend to slide off the scale of debate. However, it is important here to remind ourselves that some racist discourses by right-wing organisations also valorise the notion of indigeneity as against the rights of immigrants, and we need to be vigilant against them.

Following Tim Cresswell (2006), we may distinguish between a 'sedentarist metaphysics' and a 'nomadic metaphysics'. The former inscribes mobility in terms of conservatism, rootedness, place, and belonging. According to a sedentarist worldview, mobility may be treated with a degree of suspicion and associated with threat and a somewhat negative valence. Nomadic metaphysics, on the other hand, valorises flux, movement, and not standing still. Movement is seen as synonymous with dynamism. It is likely to be coded as freedom, and considered as a harbinger of the new, the novel, and of exciting social change. This perspective gained ascendency in subject disciplines over the recent decades. In sociology, for instance, its traditional object of analysis, the 'society', has been reconstructed to take account of global mobilities, which often means the use of the term 'social' is more likely to be deployed than a bounded notion of 'society'. Similarly, metaphors of travel, translation, and migrancy have increasingly become the mainstay of studies in such subjects as anthropology, geography, and cultural studies. As scholars such as Edward Said (1994) have reminded us, the world has seen more refugees, migrants, exiles, and displaced persons in recent decades than ever before in the aftermath of imperial and postcolonial conflicts. As we have already seen, in 2020 there were some 80 million forcibly displaced people worldwide with 30.5 million refugees and asylum seekers. The analysis of such mobilities has drawn, inter alia, upon the 'nomad thought' of Deleuze and Guatarri (1986) and Rosi Braidotti (1994). The nomad is often seen as a figure of resistance, although there is a sense in which the term 'nomad' tends to be construed as undifferentiated by factors such as race, ethnicity, gender, class, and sexuality. The power dynamics underlying the intersections of these vectors have a critical bearing on the usefulness of nomadic analytics. As Cresswell argues,

So, in addition to the critique that nomadic metaphysics is overly abstract and universalizing in its allocation of meaning to mobility, its advocates often overlook the colonial power relations that produced such images in the first place. Indeed, the use of the nomad is often nothing more than a form of imaginative neocolonialism.

(Cresswell, 2006: 54)

Hence, the nomad is a figure of deep ambivalence in Western imaginary, one which is romanticised as well as treated with suspicion. Nomad is simultaneously feared, othered, admired, and desired. It is a figure of multiplicity and contradiction, constructed in multivariate modalities. As far back as 1996, Caren Kaplan drew attention to the intense and avid interest with which Gilles Deleuze and Felix Guattari's notion of 'nomad thought' was taken up in poststructuralist theory especially as it was deployed in Euro-American literary criticism. She cautioned against the use in these texts of 'nomadic' and the associated concept of 'deterritorialization' in ways in which cultural hegemony may be reinforced when the nomad is romanticised without attention to underlying power relations. Her caution and that of Cresswell are important to heed.

Deleuze and Guattari offer a politically committed theorisation of power relations that aims to construct alternatives to capitalist commodification of social relations. One of the metaphors they use for displacement and dispersion, especially in regard to the performitivity of subjectivities of deterritorialisation, is that of the 'rhizome'. This concept is attractive to them because "A rhizome has no beginning or end; it is always in the middle, between things, interbeing, *intermezzo*. The tree is filiation, but the rhizome is alliance, uniquely alliance"(Deleuze and Guattari, 1986). Although this conception is compelling in terms of emphasising interconnection and association, for signalling horizontal rather than vertical relations, and for valorising intermezzo rather than purity, the rhizome metaphor is rather curious in that it does not immediately bring to mind images of movement and mobility even when it is closely affiliated with the metaphor of nomad. Kaplan points to Deleuze and Guattari's penchant for likening the desert to border or margin, to 'underdevelopment' and 'third world', and their comparing of the nomad to an 'immigrant' and 'gypsy'. But these comparisons remain problematic because

European gypsies and ... Third World immigrants share the same theoretical space not through structural relations of historically specific diasporas but through a kind of generalized poetics of displacement... This kind of "othering" in theory repeats the anthropological gesture of erasing the subject position of the theorist and perpetuates a kind of colonial discourse in the name of progressive politics.

(Kaplan, 2000 [1996]: 87–88)

As a somewhat undifferentiated category, the figure of the nomad does not, as already pointed out, inherently highlight the workings of differentiations such as class, race, ethnicity, gender, sexuality, and debility. However, some of the authors using this theoretical framework do extend its reach to some of the above axes. For example, the feminist philosopher Rosi Braidotti attempts to address questions of gender in relation to nomadology with the aim, inter alia, to interrogate fixity and essentialism. Her project is concerned with developing theoretical and political practice that undermines binarism, maintains a focus on women, and that facilitates the emergence of alternative forms of agency. She is attracted to the figure of the nomad because it refers to:

> The kind of subject who has relinquished all idea, desire, or nostalgia for fixity. This figuration expresses the desire for an identity made of transitions, successive shifts, and coordinated changes, without and against an essential unity.
>
> (Braidotti, 1994: 22)

I would argue that the operative words here are 'against an essential unity' because a politics of solidarity is very much about that which is similar, which is common, which is shared among feminists.

In a critical text, Irene Gedalof (1999) discusses the undoubted strengths of Bradiotti's analytical framework but at the same time also draws attention to the analytical moves in this work, which undermines somewhat the veracity of Braidotti's claims. Gedalof finds it helpful that Braidiotti is concerned with using models of identity which construe identity in terms of rhizomic multiplicity so that differences are respected; that there is an emphasis on becoming rather than being; and there is a desire for non-hierarchical relationships of deterritorialisation that resist notions of authenticity, stability, and fixity. However, Gedalof finds Braidotti's figuration of the nomad as someone 'who has no passport – or has too many of them' a significant problem. This is partly because the question of a passport in the context of *the* unequal regimes of global inequality is hugely fraught: the passport both in terms of its material and metaphorical meanings differentiates and 'keeps out' or expels groups of people regarded as 'outsiders', 'aliens', or 'undesirables' to be feared and othered. Gedalof also highlights the fact that there is too much importance given to movement and transgression at the expense of the centrality of attachment to place:

And to downplay the question of place makes it particularly difficult to engage seriously with the kind of differences that race, nation, and ethnicity can make for women. To be marked by one's race or ethnicity, as are women of colour and 'postcolonial' women in a world which takes whiteness and Western-ness as the invisible unmarked norms, is to be 'placed' in ways that Braidotti's nomad never is.

(Gedalof, 1999: 128)

Gedalof acknowledges that Braidotti is aware of this problem with her framework in that she attempts to ameliorate the difficulties by bringing into the orbit of analysis feminist concepts of 'politics of location' and 'situatedness', which are not in themselves nomadic concepts. Gedalof continues:

But these always remain general statements, and Braidotti never follows through on her commitment to a politics of location that involves a specific 'attention to and accountability for differences among women' (1994a: 21) by actually engaging in any detail with, for example, the ways in which black or postcolonial feminists work with notions of place in the constructions of gendered-raced-national identities.

(Gedalof, 1999: 129)

In a sense, therefore, the relationship between feminism and nomad thought remains undecided. But the nomad, as a figure of resistance against controlling institutions of the state, may still resonate with affirmative connotations.

As I noted at the beginning of this chapter, questions of mobilities are inherently linked to those of 'rooting' since migrations are likely to be closely associated with histories of settling down. In the previous section I have discussed how the concept of mobilities has tended to be theorised. Here I wish to address how formation of Black feminism in Britain emerged out of histories of movement and settlement. My focus here is upon Black feminism that was produced and developed through the activism of African-Caribbean and South Asian heritage women who from the late 1970s to the present have mobilised the figure of Black as a political colour rather than skin tone. Their biographies or those of their parents or grandparents are likely to be marked by histories of migration. Their/our kinship and other social networks may be spread across the globe so that the complex relationship between globality and locality becomes a hallmark of their/our emerging subjectivities and identities.

Decolonial Feminisms

In 2019, I was involved in the 40th commemoration of two memorable anniversaries of political projects. The first was the anniversary of the events of 23 April 1979, when the far-right group, the National Front, marched into Southall, West London, to hold an election rally in the town hall. They had obtained permission to do so by the Ealing Council, against the protestations of the local people who came out in force to demonstrate against the National Front. There was a massive police presence on the streets of Southall, an area with a long history of migration ranging from that of Irish groups to South Asians and now Afghan, Sri Lankan, and Somali people. What started out as a peaceful protest by the residents of Southall and their supporters turned violent in the midst of a very large-scale police operation – involving some 3,000 police deployed to protect white supremacist National Front's 'right to assembly' in one of the most ethnically diverse areas of London. Approximately 700 protestors were arrested, 345 were charged, and 11 were convicted. Blair Peach, a New Zealand teacher from East London who had come to the area to express solidarity with the local people, was killed when he was struck on the head as police charged at him and the protestors. I attended his funeral, which attracted thousands of mourners. The other major casualty of violence that day was Clarence Baker, the manager of the Southall band Misty in Roots, who was beaten unconscious by the police. He had a fractured skull and was hospitalised for two months. What happened that day left deep political scars yet there was resilience and pride in having mounted strong resistance. In the process there was inscribed a living history of antiracist and anti-fascist local activism with a national, even a global, resonance and echo.

1979 was also the year when a group of young women with pre-dominantly African-Caribbean and South Asian heritage formed the resolutely feminist and secular organisation which we called Southall Black Sisters, using Black as a political colour. We had been meeting as a women's group for some time and were very active in the defence campaigns for protestors who were charged on 23 April. But it was in November that we formally constituted ourselves. With a radical history of struggle and achievement, Southall Black Sisters remains a vibrant political presence both locally and nationally. It is now a funded organisation with its own premises but in the early years we were a collective and used to meet in one another's homes. It changed from being a collective in 1998. I was a member until 1982, when I moved to Leicester. Our main emphasis in this early period was campaigning. We picketed a beauty contest and attracted the ire of local councillors; we were involved in a number of antiracist campaigns, including those providing support to families harassed by racist neighbours. We held advice sessions for women at a local law centre; went on the picket line of a women's strike at Chix factory in Slough; worked with women's refuges in Ealing and Acton; and campaigned against racist and sexist dimensions of immigration law. We campaigned against the notorious policy of 'virginity tests', which were administered to young Asian women arriving in Britain from the South Asian subcontinent to get married. These extremely invasive and demeaning investigations were used to establish whether or not the women were 'virgins'. These investigations were based on a stereotype that held that Asian women were required to be virgins at marriage so that if the women coming from the South Asian subcontinent were not virgins, the arranged marriage they claimed they had come to contract in Britain could not be genuine and the claim in reality was their passport to the UK. In addition, we addressed issues of forced marriages, co-habitation, and questions of queer identities.

Apart from political projects such as the above, we also mobilised popular culture as a vehicle for developing connection with the local population through the use of political theatre. In this regard, we staged our own feminist version of Ramlila, a term that refers to any popular dramatic enactment of the ancient Hindu epic Ramayana. One of the 'innovations' we used was to borrow from Shakespeare the figure of the jester, who delivered a comedic commentary with a decided feminist content on the story of Ram and his 'dutiful' wife Sita. We wrote our own script, and collectively produced it. The event was a great success (Richman, 1999). Ten years later, as an academic at London University, I received a grant to develop an educational project with adults in the community. I decided to base it in Southall, where together with researcher Jasbir Panesar and film teacher Vipin Kumar we decided to work with a group of older adults on a video project. As a result, the film *Aaj Kaal* (1990, translated Today, Yesterday, and Tomorrow) was made by the older adults themselves. Nirmal Puwar (2012) wrote an evocative article about the project. She notes that while the use of multimedia in participatory research became de rigueur ten years later, reflexive peda-gogic participative processes in which the adults, especially Asian older adults, actually made a film themselves in Panjabi as an educational oral history tool, was rare in 1990. As she says, "While Asian elders fea-ture in research-based films, often in a testimonial mode, they are less likely to have been granted the training and encouragement of learning some of the basic skills for actually crafting a film amongst each other" (Puwar, 2012: 127). Our aim was to help create a non-competitive, non-threatening, supportive environment in which the older adults would feel able to take responsibility for both the technical aspects of film making and content of the film that, in the event, covered topics such as caste, inter-faith co-existence, racialised discrimination, par-tition of the Asian subcontinent and associated sexual violence and suicide, women's position in society, and cultural change. However, the film is not just about discussion of 'social issues' but shows women performing 'bolian' (reciting oral verses and couplets) and 'giddha' (singing, clapping, dancing) with a good dose of banter and humour. These examples of popular theatre and videomaking highlight the point that culture and politics play a symbiotic role in maintaining community identity and politics.

With regard to the ongoing activities of Southall Black Sisters, some years later there was internal dissent in the group. While some members of the Collective wanted the organisation to be entirely committed to the political struggles of Black women, others wished to focus on case work. This contestation resulted in a split in October 1986, and in March 1987, a new centre was established (Southall Black Sisters, 1990; Gupta, 2003). Gender-related violence was a central concern from the beginning of our organising within Southall Black Sisters, but in time it acquired growing prominence. Over the years, Southall Black Sisters have helped thousands of women facing violence and abuse. Such work entails, inter alia, securing places at refuges for the women and their children; helping with legal battles for custody of children; negotiating the benefits system on their behalf; dealing with immigration cases; providing support to children who may themselves have been abused; and, when necessary, assessing English language assistance. Apart from case work, the organisation has maintained its campaigning work, pursuing ground-breaking legal actions. For instance, Southall Black Sisters campaigned on behalf of Kiranjit Ahluwalia who killed her husband after ten years of physical, psychological, and sexual abuse. Initially, she was convicted of murder and sentenced to life imprisonment, but after the intervention of Southall Black Sisters her conviction was overturned in 1992 on grounds of inadequate counsel and replaced with voluntary manslaughter. The case changed the definition of 'provocation', and in the same year her appeal led to the freeing of Emma Humphreys and Sara Thornton. Southall Black Sisters supported Zoora Shah, an Asian woman who poisoned her abuser after suffering 12 years of violence and sexual slavery. She was convicted with a term of 20 years, which, after their appeal, was reduced to 12 years. She was released in 2006. In addition, activism in relation to the organisation Women Against Fundamentalism was central to the work of Southall Black Sisters. Women Against Fundamentalism was set up in 1989 by Southall Black Sisters, Voices for Rushdie, the Iranian Women's Organisation, Brent Asian Women's Refuge, and individual women. They came from a diverse range of ethnic, national, class, and religious backgrounds. Women Against Fundamentalism was formed at the height of the 'Rushdie Affair' when Rushdie's book *Satanic Verses* was published and attracted strong opposition from some Muslim organisations. There were strident attempts to get the book banned including public burnings of the book, and in the process the Supreme Leader of Iran, Ayatollah Khomeini, issued a fatwa authorising the killing of Salman Rushdie. Established as a women-only organisation, and challenging fundamentalism in all religions, and in all its forms, Women Against Fundamentalism differentiated fundamentalism from religious observance, defining fundamentalism as "modern political movements that use religion to gain or consolidate power, whether working within or in opposition to the state" (Dhaliwal and Yuval-Davis, 2014: 8). As a feminist and antiracist social movement challenging authoritarian religious practices, it left an important social and political legacy.

These fragments of antiracist and feminist socio-cultural and political history highlight how new political formations emerge in, through, and out of complex political articulations. Over the years there has been vibrant Black feminist writing and activism. Texts such as *Finding a Voice* (Wilson, 1978), *Heart of the Race* (Bryan et al., 1985), *Charting the Journey* (Grewal et al., 1988), *Black British Feminism: A Reader* (Mirza, 1997), *Other Kinds of Dreams* (Sudbury, 1998), and *Feminist Review* Issue No. 17 are now classics of the archive. British Black feminism has from its inception been an anti-imperialist, anti-colonial/decolonial, antiracist feminism. A number of texts from the archive mobilised Black as a political colour, which is still a point of convergence for political activists, although there are those who wish to reserve the term 'Black' to refer to people of African heritage in Africa and the diaspora (Swaby,

2014; Abbas, 2020). In 1984, four Black feminists, namely Valerie Amos, Gail Lewis, Amina Mama, and Pratibha Parmar, guest edited a Special Issue 17 of the journal *Feminist Review* evocatively titled 'Many Voices One Chant: Black Feminist Perspectives'. The lead article in this publication was titled 'Challenging Imperial Feminism', and it charts the critical importance of historical struggles against imperialism to contemporary feminism. It maps the history of Black feminism, paying attention to the specificity of Black women's experience in terms of, for instance, class location, workplace struggles, questions of sexuality framed against the shadow of heteronormativity, contemporary manifestations of homophobia, and insurgent political avowal of Black lesbian experience.

Black feminism was not just 'against' various modes of oppression and exclusion, important though this was, but equally it was 'for' collectively creating a self-affirming, confident, constructive, optimistic 'presence' highlighting "a new cultural politics of representation" (Gunaratnam, 2014: 1). Thirty years later, in 2014, *Feminist Review* published another Special Issue dedicated to Black feminism, titled 'Black British Feminisms' and edited by Joan Anim-Ado, Yasmin Gunaratnam, and Suzane Scafe. While the previous Special Issue spoke of one chant, the Introduction here speaks of 'Black British Feminisms: many chants'. There is an emphasis on plurality and multiplicity here that, though it was far from absent in the previous Special Issue, did not carry the same resonance, perhaps because 'Many Voices, One Chant' was one of the first projects of its kind, and emphasising unity must have seemed a first priority. Some of the concerns of the two projects overlap but the latter text is not a repeat exercise. Issues addressed in 1984 had reconfigured with the passage of time and now stood against a new historical context of austerity, shrinking of the welfare state, Brexit, devolution, religious fundamentalism, and growing impact of neoliberalism (Gunaratnam, 2014). The impact of neoliberal consumer culture on feminism has been significant but this is not to view earlier projects as necessarily more progressive, especially as there is much progressive feminist dynamism today with new developments in trans feminism and queer feminism, for example, pointing to new directions in theory and practice. Also important is the turn to the study of interspecies that takes on board the relationality between human and non-human life-forms such as animals, plants, and microbes (Livingstone and Puar, 2011). Such emergent strands provide exciting, novel formations. Recent theorisations of affect, for instance, destabilise humanist notions of the body and the politics of voice (Puar, 2017). During the last decade, new organisations in Britain such as Black Feminista UK and Manchester Black Feminists have also worked under the mantel of political blackness, defining this to include women "who originate from or have ancestry in Africa, Asia, the Middle East and Latin America, as well as women of Indigenous and bi-racial backgrounds" (Swaby, 2014: 12). This feminism has had an active life on the Internet too. Swaby points out that alongside politics of solidarity there have also been challenges to the concept of political blackness, with some women questioning whether political blackness was a useful organising strategy. Charting the critical moments in the history of organising around political blackness, Swaby describes political blackness as an intersectional modality that was best addressed as an "analytic sensibility" articulating a "diaspora consciousness" which is "performative and dialogic" (Swaby, 2014: 13–15). What are the prospects for politics of solidarity today? What form do they take? What activities do they prioritise? Of course, such questions cannot be decided in the abstract but through political dialogue and activism.

Black feminism has had to struggle against exclusionary practices relative to hegemonic forms of feminism and other political projects. This is a question not only of stereotypic representations but also concerns how Black women's lifeworlds are made invisible. In two important recent essays, Gail Lewis helps us unpick the complexity of "the ways in which 'the Black woman' as both representation and embodied sentient being is rendered visible and invisible and to link these to the competing ways in which she is made present and declares her presence otherwise" (Lewis, 2017: 3). In dealing with the issues involved, she engages three overlapping conceptualisations of 'presence': as conceived and contested in performance studies; as worked within the British School of psychoanalysis; and as figured in terms of decolonising political practice among Indigenous communities. In foregrounding the multiple modalities of social violence to which Black women are exposed, Lewis addresses the figure of Sarah Reed, a young Black woman brutalised by the police and found dead in London's Holloway Prison in 2016, another 'ungrievable life' that lacerates with the enormity of violence as she is brought into 'presence' through repetition of her name and that of countless other Black women brutalised throughout history. The violence is challenged and disabled by this 'presence'. As Lewis says:

> If the impress at the top of the palimpsest represents presence and absence of black women through deficiency, what form of presence and being-ness might be revealed if, with precision and delicacy of hand, we bring to the fore the layers to be found in the depths? What other histories might be inscribed in the cross currents of triangular space in which black women reside and craft their presence and lived and ancestral connection?
>
> (Lewis, 2017: 13)

There is then the possibility of addressing the figure of the Black woman "not as abject figure of absolute alterity, but as separate from, equal to and essential to the self" (Lewis, 2017: 15). Drawing together theoretical and political insights from Black women's writing and that of psychoanalyst Donald Winnicot's theorisation of 'object use' and 'play', she elaborates pathways to "ethical relating based on the detoxification of racism's effects on 'self' and 'other', and the intersubjective field that the space between these constitutes" (Lewis, 2020: 1). In other words, she addresses the question as to what kind of an 'object' Black feminism is, both psychoanalytically and socially, and how might it be used in transformative politics centred around democratic, feminist, and antiracist practice. For the new generations of Black feminists today, the problematic of structural racism, the impact of the effects of whiteness, and the necessity to combat its manifold manifestation still remains critical (Eddo-Lodge, 2017). Muslim women have been singled out as the object of stereotypic representations in Britain for decades culminating in contemporary Islamophobia and anti-Muslim racism. A recent collection of essays – *It's Not About The Burqa* by Mariam Khan – poses a resounding challenge to such negative portrayal, documenting instead lives marked by complexity that women in most communities would be likely to recognise and identify with. Women speak frankly about such issues as love and divorce; feminism; queer identity; hijab as an emblem of self-affirmation and contradiction; community pressures; women interrogating and standing up to gender and other intersectional oppressions; and racism. The women are at times funny, charming, warm, vulnerable, sad, and, at other times, strong and resolute, angry, and poised to struggle against social injustice. It is the stuff of lives lived in and through multiplicity rather than stereotypes.

I have used the term racism above but recently there have been attempts to differentiate between racism and 'migratism'. Alyoxa Tudor has coined the term 'migratism' in order to refer to the "power relations that construct the ascription of migration" (Tudor, 2017: 30). In contexts where 'being settled' is the norm, the incoming migrant may assume a deviant positionality as the figure of the 'migrant' becomes pathologised. Tudor argues that migratism in Europe is likely to be a strategy of racism, but not all forms of migratism are racist. These constructions of migratism are presumed to be performative in the sense that Judith Butler uses the term (Butler, 1990, 1993). Tudor emphasises that this concept of migratism is not designed to privilege the discrimination experienced by white migrants but rather it is to sharpen the understanding of (post)colonial racism in Europe. But does the concept of migratism render Black Europeans as 'migrants'? Tudor argues that it does not, although "racism can work through migratising strategies, for example, when Black Europeans are asked where they 'actually' come from" (Tudor, 2017: 31) implying a sense of not belonging. Do we speak of racism or migratism when a Black European is referred to as an immigrant? Clearly the answer would be 'racism'. But what if the Black European were actually an immigrant? Would that be a case of 'migratism'? In other words, does a Black migrant/immigrant (as opposed to Black European) get migratised or racialised? How, in such cases, would racism and migratism be distinguished? Thus the problematic of migratism – its utility and reach – remains open to discussion and debate.

Predicaments of Locationality

In the previous sections I have explored mobilities and feminist groundings. Here I wish briefly to further pursue the importance of space and place with the use of the feminist concept of 'politics of location.' Politics of location is about situatedness within and across intersecting axis of differentiation, resisting the binary 'difference/sameness' and foregrounding multiplicities produced in and through such intersections and the power dynamics underlying them. Locationality through intersection is what is today referred to as intersectionality (Crenshaw, 1989). In later chapters I will analyse intersectionality in some detail, but here I wish to revisit 'politics of location' as the precursor of intersectionality. As a term, 'politics of location' was coined by Adrienne Rich, but it was elaborated through ten years of coalition work on her part with Black and other women of colour in the United States (Rich, 1984, 2018). Though authored by one person, it has the imprint of collective ideas, conversations, discourses, and practices of feminists such as Audre Lorde and Barbara Smith. Rich highlights the limits of a feminism that does not take account of racism and homophobia in the women's movement in the United States in the 1980s and 1990s. It is a deconstruction of the hegemonic notion of 'woman' as a monolithic, undifferentiated category, which can be oblivious to the power relations between women, and between women and men and other categories of gender such as trans gender. It emerged from over a decade of contestation about defining feminism in the face of the interrelationship of such vectors as racism, disability, homophobia, heteronormativity, and class privilege. It would seem that Rich's travel as a delegate from the United States to a Sandinista-governed Nicaragua made a deep impact on her in terms of raising awareness about global inequalities and the effects of United States imperialism. She realised that feminist priorities at the time in the United States such as free contraception and abortion were, while important in Nicaragua, somewhat secondary to the need for the basics of food, health, and literacy. Importantly, the workings of global colonialisms or imperialisms rendered whole countries subject to unequal relations vis-à-vis other nations. US feminists, Rich argued, had to resist imperatives of US imperialism and called on white women to challenge the privilege of 'whiteness.'

Caren Kaplan suggests that, partly because the concept of 'politics of location' was first elaborated by Rich in relation to a trip abroad instead of conversations inside the US, it would seem in its early articulation to suppress differences between white women and women of colour in the US. It also created a new binary between US white women and women who are victims of US foreign policies. Overall, the specific experiences of women of colour arising from histories of slavery, genocide of Indigenous people, colonialism, and diaspora were likely to be repressed. Questions of accountability that are presumed to be central to Rich's work can be hijacked if the term 'politics of location' is treated as a mere synonym for multiple differences and as such becomes an alibi for cultural relativism. Such danger is avoided, however, when careful political theorisation is undertaken by feminist scholars such as Chandra Talpade Mohanty. Working through questions of difference, she defines 'politics of location' as follows:

Specifically I ask the following question: How does the politics of location in the contemporary USA determine and produce experience and difference as analytical and political categories in feminist cross-cultural work? By the term "politics of location" I refer to the historical, geographical, cultural, psychic, and imaginative boundaries which provide the ground for political definition and self-definition for contemporary US feminists.

(Mohanty, 1992: 74)

She is critical of ahistorical conceptions of experience, and of notions of universal sisterhood, which fail to take account of histories and contemporary effects of colonialism, imperialism, and monopoly capitalism.

Feminist solidarities are built on working through and struggling with differentiation and heterogeneity, and not on the basis of the idea that because we are feminists, interconnections will emerge simply as a 'process of osmosis'. Following Bernice Johnson Reagon, she argues that the experience of being a woman can give the illusion of unity when in reality it is the meanings attached to vectors such as gender, race, class, or age at different moments in history which are of 'strategic significance'. Mohanty endorses Reagon's emphasis on histories of political struggle as the basis of a global perspective. She argues that the politics of location become crucial when trying to create a collective vision out of individual "experience of the self which is often discontinuous and fragmented... In other words, experience must be historically interpreted and theorized if it is to become the basis of feminist solidarity and struggle" (Mohanty, 1992: 89).

Like Mohanty, Sara Ahmed provides pointers towards hopeful futures by mobilising the figure of 'wilful subjects':

Feminists are often judged as wilful women because we are unwilling to participate in sexist culture; more than that, we are willing to critique the very requirement that women be willing. To be unwilling to participate is to have too much will.

(Ahmed, 2014: 154)

Wilful, assertive, resolute! And, in the process, exploring the variety of 'uses' to which feminism can be mobilised: "To make use a question is to inherit a feminist and queer project of living differently..." (Ahmed, 2019: 223). Finally, with Audre Lorde (2017), we may envision a world in which "unity does not mean unanimity" but "we can each flourish" and "relate within equality".

Overall, then, there are many complexities of mobilities and locatedness. I have discussed these in terms of how these complexities are worked through by black feminisms both in terms of oppressions and resistance. Some of these aspects will be taken up and further discussed in the next chapter.

Chapter 3

Borders, Boundaries, and the Question of Commonality and Connectivity

The globalised world in which we live today is marked by multifarious borders and boundaries. Despite the ubiquitous discourses about the world having become a global village, borders and boundaries are very much in evidence. It is often argued that transnationalism has served to undermine the nation state, but although some of the functions of the nation states may have become somewhat less central, nation states retain very significant importance in articulating state sovereignty. Indeed, during September 2020, the workings of boundaries of the nation state were clearly visible on our television screens, as we witnessed scenes of migrants from the global South attempting to gain a toehold in Europe, in overcrowded dinghies which have on several occasions sunk resulting in drowning and death. In the coastal town of Dover, in the UK, supporters of the asylum seekers and refugees crossing the channel from France were opposed by far-right extremists. In 2016, a far-right demonstration against refugees and asylum seekers and a counter-demonstration by anti-fascist campaigners resulted in a number of injuries and arrests. In cases of death, borders and boundaries make their lethal power felt literally on people's bodies but there are many other ways in which they operate. In this chapter I address some of the forms these operations take as well as examine how borders might be conceptualised and theorised.

Conceptualising Borders and Boundaries

It is understood that borders take many and varied shapes and forms depending on the context. They are not simply territorial, but are also social, cultural, political, psychological, psychic, and experiential (Anzaldua, 1987; Brah, 1996). It is important, therefore, to specify the sense in which a particular concept of the border is being invoked. I suggest that it is necessary to make a distinction between two uses of the concept of the border: as a *mode of cognitive differentiation*; and as a delineation of *a form of social division*. This distinction becomes particularly relevant when we consider the possibility of eliminating borders and boundaries as when political borders change or when propagating a utopian vision of a future borderless world. We also speak about 'going beyond borders' when we aim to abolish specific social divisions such as class or racialised divisions with the aim of securing egalitarian social relations. But it would be problematic to talk about 'abolishing borders' if the task is to theorise psychological and psychic processes of differentiation or categorisation because these are necessary for the integrity of one's sense of self. In other words, it is clearly important to dismantle and combat social divisions of, say, class, gender, racism, or homophobia, but 'undoing borders' would be problematic when speaking of the psyche since psychic operations are inherently involved in inscribing cognitive processes, which are essential if we are to avoid psychological anomie. The question of the sense in which the concepts are used is then crucial.

Borders are arbitrary constructions. But they assume specific meanings in relation to the history within which a particular border is inscribed. Each border enunciates its own narrative, its own story even as it may share common features with other borders (Nazir, 1991, 2007). Political borders can be abolished, as was the case between East and West Berlin in 1989 when the Berlin Wall, which divided East from West Berlin, came down; and new borders may be installed as was the case in South Sudan, when a new nation state was created in 2011. Each of these sets of events proclaims its own distinctive history. The question of how a border is maintained and policed and who is allowed in or, alternatively, kept out is embedded in the nature of the histories that underpin a given border. The socio-economic, cultural, and political conditions associated with the inscription of a particular border is central to the forms that border crossings assume. How are stigmatised groups of people – on the basis of race, gender, class, caste, ethnicity, or sexuality, for instance – treated across various borders? How are global mobilities negotiated within and across policies of immigration control? Histories of colonialism, imperialism, and contemporary neoliberal regimes have created many and various inequities and inequalities. As is well known, it is much easier for people from the global North to gain visas to travel and settle around the world than it is for groups from the global South. In other words, economic and political power relations are critical to the ways in which borders are negotiated.

Borders change and shift and with these changes emerge different senses of being a member of a polity. It is evident that borders are simultaneously meaning-making and meaning-carrying formations. Crucially, they are markers of identity. Border crossings are complex processes. They can be hazardous as, for instance, in a homophobic context when there can be legal, social, and psychological barriers to expressing queer identities. Similarly, discrimination, disadvantage, and exploitation may ensue when factors such as racism, class inequality, caste divisions, and disability/debility come into play. Borders between states may be easy to cross or quite impervious, depending on whether or not the countries in question are on positive terms and exercise good political relations. Borders signify the sovereignty of the state and as such signal if the relations between given states are friendly or hostile. They symbolise the ability of states to exercise control over the movement of people, goods, trades, capital, and information. On the other hand, friendly states may not even require visas of those of its citizens who may wish to travel between them. International politics is hence thoroughly enmeshed in the governance of border crossings.

Articulations between Borders and other Axes of Differentiation

When we speak of meaning-making processes, we are, in part, referring to cultural dynamics and practices that mark ethnicity and national identity. There has been longstanding debate concerning how to define concepts such as the 'nation', 'nationalism', and 'ethnicity'. It is not my intention here to engage this debate at length (but see Brah, 1996), but briefly, the term 'nation' is generally used to designate a broad category of persons with a common history and cultural heritage. At the same time, it may be used as a synonym for 'the people' with a shared destiny. In other discursive formations, it specifies a political entity embedded in a state. Famously, Benedict Anderson (1983) describes the nation as an "imagined community". An important issue to take into account, in my view, is whether these definitions encode essentialist conceptions of the term or uphold relational, contingent, and variable notions. When invoked in essentialist terms, they may foreground narrow, non-progressive, or retrograde nationalisms. Following Nazir (1986), I would suggest that it is not helpful to think of a general theory of nationalism. As he says, "...instead of identifying essences, we need to explore concrete sets of historical relations and processes in which these ideologies become meaningful" (Nazir, 1986: 501). It bears reminding that nationalism can be mobilised for very different purposes. It may construct and embody a variety of contradictory political and cultural tendencies and the outcome may be progressive or reactionary, depending on the historical and contemporary contingencies. This may be considered a contentious point by those critics who might view each and every form of nationalism in a negative light. For instance, Valluvan (2019) argues against the idea of a progressive nationalism, suggesting that nationalist movements, say, the twentieth-century anti-colonial struggles for independence, might organise on the basis of a radical political agenda but after independence the actual outcomes could well be different from what was originally envisioned. In this I agree with him. But my point is that anti-imperial and anticolonial nationalist struggles for independence entail progressive mobilisation practices. I regard nationalism as a process. This means that there is no essential inevitability that the outcomes would definitely take one particular form rather than the other. In other words, the whole point of having a political 'agenda' is that it signifies intent; it provides certain aims and objectives; but it cannot categorically predict that a specific outcome would definitely ensue. Political mobilisation is a risky business where the outcomes are desired and struggled over but there are no final guarantees. The outcomes of such processes can be intersectionally complex with variable impact on different categories of people. This means that we need to remain vigilant against those nationalist sentiments that may inscribe racialised and ethnicised ideologies, not least because, in extreme cases, such ideologies and associated practices may lead to murder and bloodshed.

There is a close relationship between the concepts of nation, nationalism, and that of ethnicity. As Stuart Hall points out, ethnicity is constructed historically, politically, and culturally (Hall, 1996b [1989]). His position on ethnicity challenges essentialist constructions of group boundaries as follows:

The term ethnicity acknowledges the place of history, language and culture in the construction of subjectivity and identity, as well as the fact that all discourse is placed, positioned, situated, and all knowledge is contextual.

(Hall, 1996b [1989]: 446)

He further argues that ethnicity must be retrieved from racialised nationalist discourses:

The fact that this grounding of ethnicity in difference was deployed, in the discourse of racism, as a means of disavowing the realities of racism and repression does not mean that we can permit the term to be permanently colonised. That appropriation will have to be contested, the term disarticulated from its position in the discourse of "multi-culturalism" and transcoded, just as we previously had to recuperate the term "black" from its place in a system of negative equivalences.

(Hall, 1996b [1989]: 446)

Hence, ethnicity inscribes historically specific socio-cultural commonalities underlying signifying or meaning-making practices. It is a concept that came into usage in scholarship in the USA in the early 1970s, referring largely to the condition of belonging to an ethnic group. But, 'ethnic group' has not been a neutral term, being largely used in the USA to define minoritised ethnic groups. In Britain, it was deployed in the 1960s and 1970s to speak of racialised groups such as African, African-Caribbean, and South Asian heritage people who had migrated to Britain. It is worth remembering that the term 'immigrant' assumed notoriety when, for quite a long period after the migration of the 1960s, there was a tendency in Britain to use it to refer even to British-born children of immigrants. Following a history of struggle and contestation, the terminology has now changed and the above groups are most likely to be addressed as 'Black British' or 'British Asian'.

One influential non-essentialising approach to the study of ethnicity has been that of Fredrik Barth (1969), who views ethnicities as categories of self-identification as well as ascription by others. Instead of emphasising the cultural content of a boundary, he lays stress on the process of its construction, arguing that ethnicities are socially constructed and their boundaries are fluid and shifting. In thinking about boundaries of ethnicity, a key question relates to how, why, and in what ways such boundaries are produced, maintained, or eroded. Ethnic boundaries may be constituted around a range of signifiers configuring in varying combinations under designate socio-cultural, political, and economic circumstances. These signifiers may include a belief in common ancestry or in a notion of shared destinies; they may valorise attachment to a 'homeland'; or they may foreground a sense of belonging on the basis of language, religion, or culture. These boundaries constitute the borders of 'us' and 'them'. Barth critiques those concepts of ethnicity, which regard it as a pre-given, already existing cultural difference. Instead, he emphasises context and process in and through which a specific signifier of difference assumes distinctiveness.

It will be evident from the above that processes of ethnicity are relational and they are historically produced, rather than eternally given. Ethnic bonds may vary in strength, being strong in one situation and weak in another. They may even dissolve at different historical junctures or phases of a particular biography. The point is that they are not primordial ties, although in particular nationalist discourses they may come to be represented as such. Ethnicity and nation are heterogeneous categories, differentiated across intersectional axes such as class, gender, or religion, but nationalist discourses may conceal these differences, emphasising instead commonalities that might be constructed in essentialist terms. For instance, discourses of 'kith and kin' are often invoked within nationalistic rhetoric, and can be highly emotive, which explains their deeply mobilising power. Nationalisms are likely to be constructed around racialised discourses that valorise inherent difference. They may invoke desire for 'racial purity', speak of 'common destinies', and raise fears about 'racial contamination' that in turn may stir heteronormative-patriarchal fears about women's sexuality. Not surprisingly, women feature centrally in racist and nationalist significations. Women are crucial to the construction and reproduction of nationalist ideologies. The figure of the woman is often used to symbolise the nation and the honour of the nation (Yuval-Davis and Anthias, 1989; Yuval-Davis, 1997, 2011). Women become the ground on which male honour is contested and non-binary identities are concealed or represented as pathological or deviant. The defence of women and children is often a rallying slogan of men going to war, yet women may fall prey to rape and other atrocities from opposing factions of men at war.

As Jasbir K. Puar (2007) shows, nationalist discourses and practices can be utilised in deeply contradictory fashion. For instance, they can be deployed by groups on the right of the political spectrum as they express support for LGBTQ communities while seeking to justify racist, xenophobic and, especially, anti-Muslim positions. They do so through mobilising stereotypes and prejudices against 'migrants' and Muslims and other such categories of people, arguing that they are sexist and homophobic while Western groups are constructed and signified as egalitarian and committed to sexual diversity. In order to describe this phenomena, Puar uses the concept of homonationalism as a "field of power" (p.231) and says that:

I challenged the hegemonic "queer outlaw" through the concept of "homonationalism" which named the "acceptance" and "tolerance" for gay and lesbian subjects as the barometer by which the legitimacy of and capacity for national sovereignty is evaluated.

(Puar, 2007: 226–227)

She further points out that:

Thus my interest in theorising U.S. national homosexuality, or homonationalism, is to map out the intersections, confluences and divergences between homosexuality and the nation, national identity and nationalism – the convivial, rather than antagonistic, relations between presumably nonnormative sexualities and the nation.

(Puar, 2007: 49)

On a similar note, Sara Farris uses the concept of femonationalism to foreground the paradoxical and contradictory convergence among three very different and diverse political actors – nationalists, feminists, and neoliberals – to push for a common agenda of anti-Islam campaigns in the name of gender equality. These political figures invoke women's rights to stigmatise Muslim men as one of the most dangerous threats to Western social formations. Why, Farris asks, this seeming consensus among groups with such different political affiliations? And, why, at the same time, are Muslim women being presented with offers of 'rescue' from their supposed dire predicament, especially given the context of rising Islamophobia and anti-immigration climate? Farris defines femonationalism as follows:

Short for "feminist and femocratic nationalism", femonationalism refers both to the exploitation of feminist themes by nationalists and neoliberals in anti-Islam (but, as I will show, also anti-immigration) campaigns and to the participation of certain feminists and femocrats in the stigmatization of Muslim men under the banner of gender equality. Femonationalism thus describes, on the one hand, the attempts of western European right-wing parties and neo-liberals to advance xenophobic and racist politics through the touting of gender equality while, on the other hand, it captures the involvement of various well-known and quite visible feminists and femocrats in the current framing of Islam as a quintessentially misogynistic religion and culture.

(Farris, 2017: 4)

Farris analyses femonationalism in term of its three dimensions, namely, as convergence (of diverse political interests), as ideological formation, and as neoliberal political economy.

There is thus a highly significant complexity of configurations mapping the interrelations between nation, ethnicity, and nationalism.

How individuals or groups relate to, identify with, or repudiate particular borders and boundaries vary significantly. While some may identify with and adopt a politically conscious stance in relation to how social boundaries operate and impact, others may remain oblivious to their effects. It is, for instance, not unknown for a subaltern group, say women, to deny the existence of sexism or a racialised group to not acknowledge the prevalence of racism. This may be partly due to a complex interplay between the social and the psychic, which may result in contradictory impact on individuals and groups. Such articulation between the social and the psychic means that some aspects of experience would be available to consciousness, whereas others would be concealed or repressed due to the workings of the unconscious. The functioning of social and cultural borders and boundaries is subject to processes of internal identification and social categorisation. As Richard Jenkins (1997: 23) claims, it is important to "distinguish between two analytically distinct processes of ascription: group identification and social categorisation. The first occurs inside... the boundary, the second outside and across it". He argues that scholars such as Fredrik Barth elide this distinction between group identification and social categorisation.

As already noted, nation states retain their importance despite the ascendancy over the decades of discourses of globalisation which portray the image of the world in terms of a global village. In other words, the nation state remains a critical entity to take into account when discussing processes of globalisation. It is necessary therefore to consider the implication of state borders and boundaries for global migrations. Migration, as is well known, is a key phenomenon in the contemporary world. According to the United Nations Department of Economic and Social Affairs report of 2020, there were over one billion migrants worldwide, of whom an estimated 281 million were international migrants living outside their country of origin. Nail (2015) argues that the migrant has become the political figure of our time. He analyses the figure of the migrant through 'Kinopolitics', a theory of motion and a politics of movement. This perspective posits that "Instead of analyzing societies as primarily static, spatial, or temporal, kinopolitics or social kinetics understands them primarily as 'regimes of motion'" (Nail, 2015: 24). Kinopolitics relies on three associated concepts of flow, junction, and circulation. In giving primacy to movement, this framework permits us to acknowledge that far from being a secondary phenomenon between states, "contemporary migration is the primary condition by which something like societies and states is established in the first place" (Nail, 2015: 236). Second, it draws attention to the fact that "the social conditions of migration are always a mixture of territorial, political juridical and economic types of expulsion. All four are operative at the same time to different degrees" (Nail, 2015: 236) and finally, it pinpoints that there are "alternatives to the contemporary conditions of migration being developed by migrants today" (Nail, 2015: 237). In other words, migrant is an agential subject. Other factors with a bearing on migration include new technological development in transportation, and in communication; major economic and political transformations in the world; and environmental changes. In addition, there are growing social, friendship, and family networks which mark the local and global migration dynamic. It is widely acknowledged, and it is evident, that migrants differ in their movement. For some movement promises adventure, exciting new opportunities, recreation, profit, and/or elite occupations. For others, movement can be dangerous, constrained, exploitative, involving employment at the lower rungs of job hierarchy and possible poverty, or it may entail positionality as a refugee or asylum seeker. As such the migrant negotiates a multiplicity of new borders and boundaries.

The Local and the Global

It is common to imagine territorial borders to be at the edges of a nation state. But this view is challenged today when it is argued that borders, rather than stopping at the edges of territorial boundaries, permeate the national, even global space. Importantly, Etienne Balibar (2002, 2004) draws attention to what borders *actually do*, that is, how they function, at particular historical moments. He regards the borders as 'instruments of differentiation'. It bears repeating that capital can move freely around the globe, but this cannot be said of people who may face all manner of obstacles or hinderances to entry. Passports and visas are one instrument that serves to impede or facilitate entry. Borders, as we have already noted, are not static, but "mobile and dispersed"(Rumford, 2006: 159). Borders may be understood as enacted practices that operate within the national or global space. As enacted practices they may be viewed as located on the body (Whitley, 2015), as for instance when immigration legislation permits fishing raids at places of work, or when some immigrants find themselves as having to live under the constant threat of deportation. In these circumstances, bodies come to carry borders on them.

Much contemporary migration has been underpinned by economic deregulation and neoliberal globalisation. Processes of globalisation breach a variety of borders and boundaries. Globalisation entails widening and deepening of interconnected networks in and through entanglements of the local and the global. These changes occur at the level of the economic, cultural, social, and the political. The past decades have witnessed a vast communication and information revolution resulting from such technological developments as the microchip, variety of digital devices, and the Internet. These are seen to usher what has been called 'time-space compression' (Harvey, 1989). For those who have access to these technologies, the world is indeed shrinking and information can be gained at the touch of a button. Neoliberal globalisation is marked by free market trade, deregulation of financial markets, a focus more on the individual than the group, and a tendency towards minimalist state intervention so that there is a shift away from state welfare provision. These were the ideals upheld in the late 1980s by Margaret Thatcher in Britain and Ronald Regan in the USA. But, faced with the current coronavirus (Covid-19) pandemic on a global scale, even the Conservative government of Boris Johnson in Britain made a very significant financial contribution in March 2020 when setting up and maintaining the government-led job retention scheme. Furloughed workers on this scheme received 80 per cent of their current salary, up to £2,500. In other words, this created a very significant enlargement of the public sector. It has already been extended twice, the last one being in November 2020.

Neoliberal globalisation means that certain places and territories such as large cities and particular regions, and segments of the political economy have an advantage over others. Overall, social change is not uniformly in one direction but rather, it is multidimensional, contradictory, and complex. In an important recent study, Nira Yuval Davis, Georgie Wemyss, and Kathryn Cassidy (2019) point to the centrality of neoliberal globalisation in shaping the multiscalar processes of bordering. They detail the many and varied bordering practices operating both at the edges of the state as well as in everyday life – in schools, hospitals, workplaces, and so on, thereby offering analytical insight into the multiplicity of forces that mediate and condition bordering processes at different levels of the social formation. They summarise their arguments as follows:

First, rather than operating at the margins of state and society, contemporary borderings, working as they do in the context of neoliberal globalisation, itself in (multiple) crisis, are central to and constitutive of multiscalar political, economic and social processes.

Secondly, within their local, regional and global context, the constructions, reproductions, and transformations of bordering processes are shaped by, and in turn shape, different shifting and contesting political projects of governance and belonging.

Thirdly, both locally and globally, contemporary multiscalar bordering processes have been a major axis in the development of intersectional social, economic, and political inequalities.

Fourthly, in order to understand contemporary bordering fully as social, political and economic phenomena, we need to encompass, in a dialogical and epistemological manner, the gazes of differentially situated social agents.

(Yuval Davis et al., 2019: 160)

This study, based on original research, provides an important framework within which the complexity of questions of bordering may be apprehended and understood. Thus, bordering is constitutive of social processes; it is underpinned by political projects of governance, governmentality, and belonging; it is both an outcome and a cause of inequalities; and it draws on the intersectionally situated gaze of differentially located social agents.

An intertwining of the local and the global is illustrated by the operations of immigration control (cf. Jones, 2021). Borders and boundaries are inscribed, governed, contravened, or infringed as control is exercised. A cornerstone of state-centric discourses and practices is that they legitimise the policing and protection of state boundaries against those regarded as outsiders, as for instance, foreigners or those with the legal status of an alien. Such groups are likely to be portrayed as a threat to social cohesion and immigration laws serve to regulate their entry. In Britain, the history of immigration law is instructive in thinking through how socially constructed boundaries of 'us' and 'them' are played out. Before the nationality law was introduced in Britain, all those who owed allegiance to the crown were subjects of the crown. There was a differentiation between alien and subject rather than between citizen and migrant. The 1707 Act of Union between England, Northern Ireland, Scotland, and Wales was paralleled by the death of Aurangzeb, the Mughal emperor, which marked the decline of Mughal power in India and the ascendance of the British East India Company. British people did not regard Britain's ventures abroad, or its propensity to colonise, explore, make war, or conduct trade as something to be viewed negatively. Rather, this was seen by the British and other colonisers as an important plank of the 'civilising mission' by the West. The arrival in Britain of the formerly colonised workers to fill labour shortages in the post-World War II period, on the other hand, was not seen in a favourable light (El-Enany, 2020). These members of the former empire came to perform mainly low-skilled work, and they were socially treated as inferior. Their legal position was governed by the British Nationality Act of 1948, which was a relatively lenient piece of legislation compared to immigration control that followed it. It divided the population into five designate groups. Two of these were not subjects: they were categorised as aliens and British Protected Persons. Three groups were subjects: Citizens of the United Kingdom and Colonies (CUKC); Citizens of Independent Commonwealth Countries (CICC); and the residual group of British subjects without citizenship (Anderson, 2013). This legislation continued effectively open borders, though there is evidence that even at this stage both the Labour and Conservative governments were concerned and worried about the arrival of immigrants from the New Commonwealth who predominantly were not whites. Overall, immigration from countries such as Australia, Canada, and New Zealand of mainly white groups was welcomed and it was assumed, indeed hoped, that immigration from the New Commonwealth, consisting predominantly of people of colour, would not be on a large scale. Moreover, growing racism led to the racialisation of the immigration debate during the late 1950s and early 1960s and resulted in the introduction of the 1962 Commonwealth Immigrants Act. The terminology of the 'New Commonwealth' that was widely used was not merely a descriptive term but rather it represented an ideological code for immigrants defined in the language of the time as 'coloured people'. It was during this period that a linkage was established between 'race' and immigration in policy debate and

popular political and media discourses (Solomos, 2003). The introduction of the 1962 Act was preceded by anti-immigrant rhetoric both
within parliament and the media. There was a noticeable resurgence
of right-wing groups. The immigrants were demonised as 'taking away
jobs from white workers'; were seen as a 'drain on welfare resources',
and were socially constructed as 'a threat to the British way of life',
themes that still remain with us today (Bhambra, 2017).

During the years following the Africanisation policies of East
African countries, there was an increase in the arrival in Britain of white
and Asian groups, particularly from Kenya. The incoming white population was not regarded as a problem, but there was an attempt to
keep out East African Asians by the introduction of the Commonwealth
Immigrants Act 1968. The Bill went through parliament in three days,
such were the panics about 'coloured immigration' of Asians. The Act
held that British passport holders retained their right of entry to Britain,
only if they or at least one of their parents or grandparents was born,
naturalised, or registered in Britain. This clause de facto excluded
Asians, as few Asians could claim that ancestry. Subsequently, this
clause formalised the category of 'patrial' (that is, permitting entry to
mainly white applicants) and non-patrial (read non-white applicants).
Although the numbers involved were not very large, Margaret Thatcher,
the then prime minister of Britain, spoke of the British people feeling
"swamped by people with a different culture". Thus 'culture' became a
signifier of undesirability of Asian groups. For example, Asian women
marrying men from abroad had to prove that the relationship was not
contracted 'for the primary purpose of' obtaining British residency,
implying that such relationships were likely to be 'bogus'. As we saw in
the previous chapter, there were cases of invasive and humiliating 'virginity tests' conducted on Asian women arriving at the ports of entry
into Britain. There was such strong opposition to this practice that it
was soon discontinued. Asian children coming to settle in Britain were
likely to be subjected to X-ray examinations to establish that their age
was within the guidelines for gaining entry. Again, the assumption was
that they could be lying about their age. In other words, such practices

were designed to confirm whether or not the applicants were genuine candidates.

The government has now introduced a points-based system, which is designed to be non-discriminatory. But so long as what is now referred to as an 'ancestry visa' (which is issued by the United Kingdom to Commonwealth citizens with a grandparent born in Britain) remains, there is bound to be discrimination against Commonwealth citizens without a grandparent born in Britain as a climate of suspicion persists. These applicants are likely to be mostly citizens from the New Commonwealth or mainly people of colour. For a period, before Britain left the European Union (EU), the largest number of immigrants arriving into Britain were from the EU countries. But now that, since 31 January 2020, Britain is no longer a member of the EU, EU citizens have to apply to remain in the UK. Evidently, as of 11 June 2020, over 3.5 million EU citizens had applied to remain in UK (schengenvisainfo. com – updated 11 June 2020). There was much anti-migrant clamour during the Brexit period, highlighting racialised hierarchies within Europe whereby Eastern Europe is not considered on par with Western or Northern Europe. Such discursive representations draw upon long-standing perceptions of internal hierarchies among differentially stereotyped categories of Europeans. Many borders and boundaries – territorial, juridical, cultural, political, and psychic, to name the most central to policies of differentiation – come to the fore when marking such social hierarchies.

Desperate Journeys

One of the most devastating consequences of the enforcement of territorial borders was witnessed in the plight of persons who were popularly defined as 'boat people'. They were fleeing intolerable conditions in their countries of origin, but found themselves in equally dire conditions, stuck in overcrowded dilapidated boats, trying to gain access to those nation states where they hoped to have better life chances. One such arena, where a vast human tragedy was played out, was in the Mediterranean Sea, where a large number of men, women, and children were drowned waiting to cross from Libya to Southern Europe. They have been at the mercy of political machinations of a Europe driven by anti-migrant sentiment where, for instance, a columnist, Katie Hopkins, for the British daily newspaper, *The Sun*, wrote on 17 April 2015,

No I don't care. Show me the pictures of coffins, show me bodies floating in water, play violins and show me skinny people looking sad. I don't care. Make no mistake, these migrants are like cockroaches. They might look like a bit 'Bob Geldof's Ethiopia circa 1984', but they are built to survive a nuclear bomb.

(Jones and Jackson in the *Guardian* newspaper, 25 April 2015: 6)

Sam Jones and Jasper Jackson indicate that this column was published hours before a fishing vessel carrying 800 migrants capsized off the coast of Libya. While this comment might be seen as an extreme case, it is part of a trend in the British tabloid press of regularly attacking and vilifying migrants. Not only is this language disrespectful and inflammatory in the extreme, it plays its part in the construction of the Gramscian 'common sense' (Gramsci, 1971), which in contemporary Europe seems to blame all major ills of society on 'migrants', 'foreigners', and all manner of 'outsiders'.

As we have previously noted, such migrant journeys often begin in the impoverished, sometimes politically unstable and conflict-ridden or war-ravaged parts of the world, such as Chad, Eritrea, Somalia, Sierra Leone, Syria, Iraq, and other parts of the Middle East and North and West Africa. The refugees, asylum seekers, and economic migrants are likely to reach the staging post of Libya, from where a growing number make desperate attempts to reach Italy or Greece. Sometimes 600 may be squeezed in vessels designed to carry 200, and the boats left to float in the Mediterranean in the hope that they might be picked up by, say, Italians. Some drown and never reach the other shore at Lampedusa or Sicily and the Mediterranean becomes a watery grave. In 2014, nearly 4000 bodies were recovered from the Mediterranean, while others were not found, according to newspaper reports. Between 2014 and 2019, the Mediterranean has claimed the lives of at least 19,164 migrants (International Organization for Migration, 2020). These migrants/ refugees are compelled to leave home due to a variety of factors – war, religious and other insurgencies, authoritarian and repressive political regimes, climate-change related drought and famine, lack of jobs and employment, and endemic poverty. They come with hope but they are knocking at the doors of a Europe singularly reluctant to let them in. For a time, even Italy's Mare Nostrum search and rescue programme was suspended and European Union "replaced it with a more limited border security operation run by its Frontex agency" (*The Observer*, 2015: 36). Evidently, monthly funding for its Triton programme was less than a third of the Mare Nostrum budget. Over the last few years, European nations have been proposing to help set up 'migrant' processing centres in North Africa, thereby displacing the problem elsewhere. What is needed, of course, is for Europe to create legal, safe options for migrants/ refugees to avail of instead of having to turn to people smugglers. On the contrary, plans were mooted to bomb empty fishing vessels that could potentially be used by people smugglers, although it was likely that such strategies might not be successful in deterring smugglers, whose capacities to make large profits from smuggling were such that the option of losing some boats was not too costly. While it was announced that the target boats would be empty, there was concern that some innocent people may still die. So desperate have European countries been to keep refugees/migrants/asylum seekers out that the European Union has paid billions to keep refugees from crossing to Greece. It has funded the Libyan Coast Guard to catch and return the boats to North Africa. It has also set up centres in distant Niger to process asylum seekers (Matina Stevis-Gridneff, *The New York Times*, 8 September 2019). This report notes that tens of thousands of asylum seekers remain trapped in Libya where they can be so packed that there is little floor space to sleep, and where they are sometimes sold into slavery and sex work. There would seem to be lack of a well-coordinated approach to deal with the issues at hand. According to Shoshana Fine (2019), the European Union's approach to migration has created a crisis of solidarity. While the numbers of migrants/refugees/asylum seekers have declined quite considerably, so has cooperation and responsibility sharing within the European Union (Fine, 14 October 2019, European Council on Foreign Relations).

It is by now well known that migrants make an important economic and social contribution to European countries. But as the playwright Anders Lustgarten argues,

Forget the fact that this society (Britain) wouldn't work without migrants, that nobody else will pick your vegetables and make your latte and get up at 4am to clean your office. Forget the massive tax contribution made by migrants to the Treasury. This is not about economics... This is about two things: compassion and responsibility.

(*The Guardian*, 18 April 2015: 30)

But it is crucial that compassion and responsibility are not seen as an act of charity. Europe itself plays a role that emerges as a contributory factor underlying these migrations. For instance, Lustgarten cites a report published by the International Consortium of Investigative Journalists, which shows that

the World Bank displaced a staggering 3.4 million people in the last five years. By funding privatisations, land grabs, and dams, by backing companies and governments accused of rape, murder and torture, and by putting $50 billion into projects graded highest risk for 'irreversible and unprecedented' social impacts, the World Bank has massively contributed to the flow of impoverished people across the globe.

(Lustgarten, *The Guardian*, 18 April 2015: 30)

He argues that by bombing the Middle East, the West destroyed the infrastructure of countries such as Libya, without paying attention to what would replace it. Hence, we find a social and political vacuum in which in-fighting factions collide and the broken state cannot prevent these places becoming the centre of activities such as people smuggling. In other words, it is critical to take into account the impact of Western foreign policies in fostering conditions that provide impetus for global migrations. We are faced with a global displacement crisis involving inter and intra state displacements. The majority of the displaced people move to neighbouring countries and are settled in the 'developing world'. At present, more than 80 per cent of the refugees are hosted by 'developing countries', yet the stereotypic representations in the West suggest as if the opposite were the case, namely, that it is the Western countries that are faced with supposedly enormous numbers of people from the global South. In contemporary regimes of globalisation, capital, as already noted, is free to move wherever it chooses to go, but there are likely to be restrictions on entry of certain categories of people, most notably the less well off. The wealthy, on the other hand, are likely to find it much easier to acquire exemptions from such restrictions.

Politics of Interconnectivity

The global inequalities that we witness today have a long history embedded within ideologies and practices of colonialism and imperialism, which assume new forms in today's 'postcolonial' world, marked by the emergence of contemporary neo-imperialisms (Bhattacharya, 2018; Gopal, 2019). These inequalities are underwritten by twenty-first-century modes of capitalism. That some parts of the world are rich and others poor is therefore not due to some accident. Our futures are intimately interconnected, by socio-economic and political processes on a local and global scale. For instance, the global environmental calamity affects us all though we are differentially positioned in relation to it, depending on such factors as where in the world we are located, our social class, and gender. The plight of the refugees and migrants is a symptom of the economic, political, and territorial divisions that underly interrelationships between contemporary societies. At the time of the acute Mediterranean crisis during 2015–2016 when refugees had to negotiate perilous journeys into Europe, there was considerable controversy about imposing refugee quotas on the then 28 countries of the European Union, under a distribution system set by Brussels. This action was proposed in response to the request by Italy and France that Europe should share the responsibility for handling the influx of refugees and asylum seekers arriving at the shores. But to many member states these proposals were controversial. Britain refused to accept a European Union mandatory refugee quota system. The Home Office indicated that not only would it refuse to accept any refugees under the proposed emergency settlement programme, but it would not take part in any such future permanent European Union system. A number of other countries, including France, Spain, Hungary, Poland, Estonia, Latvia, Lithuania, and Slovakia, also refused compulsory quotas. François Hollande, the then French president, stated that although he supported a fairer distribution of refugees, he could not accept quotas. All purely economic migrants, he insisted, should be deported. Such toxic debate continued for a period. In time, due partly to the operation of increasingly stricter immigration policies, the number of migrants arriving through the Mediterranean into Greece and Italy declined. Reporting on this, Jennifer Rankin quotes Frans Timmermans, the European Commission's first vice-president, as saying that "Europe is no longer experiencing the migration crisis we lived in 2015, but structural problems remain" (Rankin, 2019). Rankin continues that in 2018, 116,647 people were counted by the UN refugee agency UNHCR, as crossing the Mediterranean, an 89 per cent reduction on those who made this journey in 2015, when the crisis was at its height. Thus, in March 2019, the EU declared the 'migrant crisis' to be at an end, though of course, as the above figures demonstrate, the movement of refugees across the Mediterranean, while reduced, was not halted. By September 2020, there were still scenes of small boats filled to overcapacity with individuals trying to cross the English Channel from continental Europe to the UK.

In a social climate that is rife with divisive political debate and practice, the importance of developing politics of connectivity and solidarity becomes paramount. How do we transcend social borders that inscribe processes of 'Othering'?

The state-centric discourses of the nation that provide a lens through which events such as the global migration crisis are likely to be filtered tend to marginalise those features of the debate that go beyond the nation state. This points to the ongoing importance of continuing to think through the relationship between the particular and the universal. What kind of planetary consciousness (Pratt, 1992; Gilroy, 2006) do we still need to nurture so as to develop interconnections with, and responsibilities towards, one another and to non-humans? Feminists, anti-colonialists, anti-imperialists, antiracists, and postmodern thinkers and activists have all taken issue with meta-theoretical solutions and universalising truth claims of grand narratives of history, which place the 'European Man' at its centre. Western 'universalisms', it is generally acknowledged, have often served as a guise for claims to particularism. It is a major problem that few canonical texts of postmodernism have dealt with questions of postcolonialism, neo-imperialism, or antiracism despite their regular invocation of the 'crisis' of the 'West'. As Frantz Fanon has argued:

Leave this Europe where they are never done talking of Man, yet murder men everywhere they find them, at the corner of every one of their streets, in all the corners of the globe... That same Europe where they are never done talking of Man, and where they never stopped proclaiming that they were anxious for the welfare of Man: today we know with what suffering humanity has paid for every one of their triumphs of the mind.

(Fanon, 1967: 251)

Of course, there are reams written today that challenge scholarship, which has the effect of marginalising large parts of humanity. These critiques underline the central importance of analysing exclusions, injustices, inequities, and inequalities created by power dynamics ensuing from the intersections of such factors as class, gender, racism, sexuality, and disability/debility. These studies have, directly or indirectly, interrogated narrow and self-serving notions of universalism. But the adoption of a critical stance towards problematic discourses of universalism does not mean that there are no global principles that need our respect and, even, allegiance. The point is that we need to take issue with essentialist conceptions of universalism and instead seek to imagine non-essentialist ways of conceptualising universalism. As I have argued elsewhere (Brah, 1996), this may be done with the help of a conceptual clarification between:

1. essentialism as referring to a notion of ultimate essence that is seen as transcending historical and cultural variation; and
2. 'universalism' reworked and understood as a commonality derived from historically variable experience and as such remaining subject to historical and cultural change.

My use of the term 'universal' in the way described above is something of a departure from its general usage. I am arguing the case for a non-essentialist 'universalism'; that is, a concept of 'universalism' as a historical product. But, in the light of the complicity of the discourse of universalism with imperial projects, it might be worth substituting universalism with the idea of 'transversalism', following Foucault, Deleuze, and Guatari (Penfield, 2014) and Yuval-Davis (2011) or 'pluriversalism' (Mignolo and Walsh, 2018). At the same time it is worth bearing in mind that, as David Harvey (2009: 8) suggests:

all universalising projects be they liberal, neoliberal, conservative, religious, socialist, cosmopolitan, rights based or communist run into serious problems as they encounter the specific circumstances of their application... This gives us pause before we rush into define any alternative universalizing project, such as that proposed through a revival of cosmopolitan governance or some international regime based on universal human rights.

(Harvey, 2009: 8)

It is important to take this caution on board. Hence, not surprisingly, Seyla Benhabib (2004) notices a tension between the universality of human rights theories and their application, in different cultural situations. But on cosmopolitanism she is relatively more optimistic, arguing that "Cosmopolitanism, the concern for the world as if it were one's *polis*, is furthered by such multiple, overlapping allegiances which are sustained across communities of language, ethnicity, religion, and nationality" (Benhabib, 2004: 174–175; see also Benhabib, 2008). Cosmopolitanism does not relate only to elites, as is sometimes suggested, but rather it is rooted in real experiences of, for example, working classes, migrants, and subordinated ethnicities. The discourse of cosmopolitanism has varied over time. There have been periods when the term 'cosmopolitan' was used pejoratively. During the early twentieth century, for instance, the notion of cosmopolitanism was associated with the 'outsider' and was epitomised by the Jew who was socially constructed as the 'outsider within'. But today the meaning has shifted in a positive direction as a result of cultural pluralisation and multiplicity arising from migration, interculturalism, and diversity of various kinds, encompassing relationality, polyvocality, and multilayeredness of interconnections between peoples, communities, and formations of public culture. Public culture here is understood as communicative and dialogic, something akin to what Gerard Delanty (2009) calls 'cosmopolitan multiculturalism' that is centrally opposed to racism and addresses wider issues of citizenship and social inclusion. Importantly, he argues for a cosmopolitanism that is simultaneously post-universal and post-Western because Western versions of cosmopolitanisms are but one form. There are alternative cosmopolitanisms in the world, which cannot be subsumed under the Western varieties. This, he argues, is an important corrective to the received notion of modernity as a Western condition that was transported to the rest of the world. Similarly, Ben Rogaly affirms de Sousa Santos's notion of 'subaltern cosmopolitanism' with its emphasis on cosmopolitan solidarity, which critiques top-down cosmopolitan projects (Rogaly, 2020). Likewise, Steven Vertovec and Robin Cohen's (2002) edited collection on the subject highlights the complexity and variability of different forms of cosmopolitanism (see Chapter 10 for further consideration of the subject).

Discussions of cosmopolitanism and universal human rights raise the question of global citizenship. But is the talk about global citizenship another grand narrative whose truth claims are a ruse for articulating an appropriate ideology for the 'global village' of the neo-liberal international/managerial capitalist class? The point is, what is contemporary cosmopolitanism about? Is it a non-essentialist historically specific mode similar to 'universalism' as I have defined it above, or is it, instead, little more than an ethical or humanitarian mask for hegemonic neoliberal practices of domination? In what ways, Harvey asks, can a cosmopolitan project of opposition to cosmopolitan neoliberalism be formulated? For an answer he quotes from de Sousa Santos who argues that we must amplify the voices of "Those who have been victimized by neoliberal globalization, be they indigenous peoples, landless peasants, impoverished women, squatter settlers, sweatshop workers or undocumented immigrants" (cited in Harvey, 2009: 94). But even a subaltern cosmopolitan must deal with the demand of particularity. Hence, cosmopolitanism must always be rooted, as Appiah (2007) suggests, viewing cultural change as an ongoing process of construction rather than a finished product. Overall, it is clearly important that we do not endorse neoliberalism, whatever form it takes. Questions of interconnectivity are complex but perhaps best addressed through politics of care based on mutuality, equality, and respect.

Chapter 4

Reflections on the Postcolonial: A Conversation between Avtar Brah and Katy P. Sian

KPS: How did you first get into the field, and what was the journey that led your work to where it currently is?

AB: Actually, my move into the field of race, ethnicity, and postcoloniality was partly accidental. I came to Britain for a visit from the United States where I had been a student from Uganda. While in Britain, I became a refugee when Idi Amin, the then president of Uganda, expelled Asians from Uganda in 1972. I had never actually planned to settle in Britain, but suddenly, when I became a refugee, I started looking for a long-term job. It just so happened that there was a post going at Bristol University for a project exploring ethnicity and youth identities, and they were looking for someone who could speak Panjabi and Urdu. I had those language-skills so I applied for that job and got it. Subsequently, that post, which was initially based on interviewing, developed into a research assistant position and then into research associate position. So, I walked into this field rather accidentally.

KPS: How did you develop your sense of political consciousness?

AB: Well, this really goes back to my teenage years in Uganda. My family was not particularly political, but I had a family friend, a young woman, who introduced me to the work of a Panjabi male novelist, Nanak Singh,[1] and a female poet,

---

[1] Nanak Singh (1897–1971) was a prolific Punjabi poet, novelist, and essayist whose work was critical of British colonial rule in India. Key texts include *Pavitar Paapi* (Saintly Sinner, 1942) and *Chitta Lahu* (White Blood, 1932).

Amrita Pritam,[2] and these were radical intellectuals. Amrita Pritam was a feminist who, among other things, wrote a very famous poem about the position of women during the partition of the South Asian subcontinent in 1947. Nanak Singh wrote novels that provided a window into the social inequalities that existed within Panjabi society, so he looked at questions of caste, class, and gender; he was very concerned about women's equality. I read a number of his novels at a very young age and became strongly influenced by his work so that by the time I went to California as an undergraduate, I was already fairly politicised.

When I arrived in America, it was the late 1960s, a period of student radicalism, as well as Black politics and the Black Power movement. That experience really galvanised my political sensibilities, and later, when I came to Britain in the early 1970s, the feminist movement was in ascendancy, and I became involved in feminist politics. So that, by the time I started working around race and ethnicity at Bristol University, I was already involved in various social movements. In America, there was a lot of racism against African-Americans and other groups, but during my time in America, there were not that many so-called 'foreign' students of colour at the University of California at Davis. Davis was a small university town, and the racism I encountered in Britain was quite different from the kind of racialised 'exoticism' that I experienced there in the late 1960s. Racism really politicises you, and my experiences carried me forward and further into my political activism.

KPS: Which thinkers would you say have most influenced you and your work?

AB: At different stages, different thinkers have influenced my intellectual trajectory. Malcolm X's autobiography was quite formative in my undergraduate days in the USA when I was a science student. I

---

[2] Amrita Pritam (1919–2005) was a prominent Punjabi poet and novelist. Her important poem on partition is titled *Aj Aakhaan Waris Shah Nu* (Today I Invoke Waris Shah). Other works of significance include her novel *Pinjar* (The Skeleton, 1950).

did my PhD in Education in Britain during the late seventies, and the seventies and the eighties were crucial years when Marxism was a strong intellectual and political presence in the academy. During this period, I was influenced by Marxist thought, particularly by Gramsci's concepts of common sense and hegemony. Importantly, Gramsci offered me a methodology for thinking about the ways in which common sense becomes racialised. Louis Althusser was also influential, particularly his notion of ideology and interpellation. Those aspects were quite important in the early stages of my work.

Then, of course, there was a lot of internal critique within Marxism, as well as critique from outside, and for someone like me, who was interested in questions of racism and gender alongside class, Marxism was too class-centric. It was very difficult to think about these other axes of differentiation within classical Marxist frameworks, and at that time, there were also many debates among socialist feminists that really helped me develop my thinking. I still find Marxist insights important because you can't really understand capitalist structures without some recourse to Marxism. Moreover, Marxism's commitment to equality and social justice remains compelling. But there were other ways of addressing questions dealing with 'race', gender, class, and sexuality through which feminist thinkers influenced me greatly. Feminist debates were hugely productive in ushering new intellectual and political agendas.

KPS: Who shaped you in terms of postcolonial thinking and Black feminism?

AB: Stuart Hall has been a huge influence on me, as were figures such as Edward Said and Foucault, and of course the Black Power movement in the seventies and eighties, when it was quite strong. That's how I first became involved in Black feminist politics in Britain: because it was a movement that enabled people to say, let's look at colour, not as shade of skin, but rather, as a political colour. This movement deconstructed chromatist discourse and injected the word *Black* with a different kind of meaning, a positive meaning. We felt that if you are subjected to racism on the basis of colour, you can be

Black, irrespective of the hue of your skin. I was one of the founding members of Southall Black Sisters, and we actually called the group Black Sisters back in 1979,[3] although it included African-Caribbean origin Black women as well as women of South Asian heritage. We used 'Black' as a political colour.

Poststructuralism has also had a significant impact on my thinking, especially in relation to dealing with questions of subjectivity and identity, though my work on 'difference' combines insights from both poststructuralism and materialist analysis. Black and postcolonial feminist debates have influenced me greatly, and I think my work is centrally located within these debates. Feminist work has played a crucial role in helping me along my intellectual and political journey.

KPS: Did your Sikh heritage impact your intellectual trajectory and a way of thinking? Is that important to you in terms of the kind of work you engage in?

AB: I think my Sikh heritage has been important in relation to my politics. I think we are lucky that we have a heritage where, at least in theory if not in practice, there is a commitment in Sikhism to gender equality, social justice, class equality, and anti-caste politics. I was strongly influenced by such ideas and notions within Sikh tradition, although I found that, in reality, that wasn't always the case on the ground. I remember when I was quite young, I used to have arguments with the Sikh priest in our gurdwara (temple) about why what was said in the scriptures was not actually practised. My Sikh background and my Sikh heritage have both certainly marked my understanding of ethical issues, but I have had a troubled relationship with organised religion. In terms of the relationship between religion and state, I am quite secular, though simultaneously, I am attracted to spirituality. Of course, questions of religion and secularism remain very complex, especially in the contemporary world.

---

[3] Southall Black Sisters (SBS) was established in 1979 and based in Southall, London. It is a non-profit Black organisation, and its politics remain committed to antiracism and gender equality.

In terms of my research, I have worked on the overall category of Asians in Britain, rather than Sikhs *per se*, although when I was working on my PhD in Southall, a substantial number of my respondents were Sikh because when it came to the composition of Asians in the area, Southall at the time was predominantly Sikh. But I didn't look at them as Sikhs; rather, I saw them as Asians, and that again has to do with the politics of the time because the category 'Asian' actually had a political purchase. It was based on solidarity among different Asian ethnicities. Sadly, the category has since fractured across different religions.

KPS: What were your main aims and goals in *Cartographies of Diaspora*? What did you hope to achieve with this book?

AB: I didn't have a clear-cut plan as to what I wanted to achieve with the book; it gradually developed. I had empirical as well as theoretical concerns, and I wanted to produce a book in which theory, empirical work, and political practice came together. So that was one aim. And, of course, theoretical and political debates around 'difference' were pretty central in framing the book.

I think another aim was to address gender because, in general, a lot of the work on class, racism, and ethnicity in those days didn't look at issues of gender, and work on gender didn't much look at issues of 'race' and ethnicity. That, I think, has changed now, but at the time, there were all those exclusions, and so I wanted to produce something that would examine closely questions of gender, class, 'race' and ethnicity, nation and nationalism, sexuality, belonging, identity, and culture. These were some of the themes that attracted my attention, and I worked around them as they developed. I didn't actually have any grandiose idea about *Cartographies of Diaspora* as such. The concepts of diaspora and diaspora space provided a theoretical and political grounding and generative theme for these concerns. Diaspora and diaspora space as a theoretical framework provided a critique of racialised, essentialised, and nation-centric work.

KPS: In much of the literature on South Asians in Britain, readers are still confronted with the recycling of frameworks such as the 'culture clash,[4] yet you broke away from reproducing these tropes. How dominant were these themes during the early period of your research?

AB: Yes, this paradigm of 'culture clash' was dominant in the academy and the media as well as in political discourse. There were all kinds of newspaper articles and television programmes that focused on this theme, and I wanted to disrupt such a narrative. This was one of the first things I really came to grips with when I was writing my PhD thesis. Questions of culture were of great interest to me, although when I was finishing my PhD thesis in the late seventies, the study of culture was not as yet such a big element in the 'sociology of race' then commonly termed *race relations*. There were, of course, anthropologists working in this area for whom the concept of culture was central. However, there was a tendency in some of this work to be 'culturalist'. For me, the work that came out of the Centre for Cultural Studies at Birmingham University, especially after Stuart Hall took over as the director, was exciting and greatly influenced me.

On the whole, 'sociology of race' in Britain was focused on class; class was the big axis of analysis, and I was among a minority who were foregrounding culture and identity within the field of 'race' and ethnicity. When you analyse culture, there are some very complex issues to be handled, and it wasn't always easy to articulate certain non-culturalist perspectives. Debates on ethnicity and culture were highly politicised and polarised. The important book *Empire Strikes Back*, produced by scholars from the Birmingham Centre for Cultural Studies, provides a glimpse into the charged politics of the debate. Overall, it was difficult to challenge and disrupt the dominant paradigms and to think about these issues critically and differently.

KPS: What makes your engagement with diaspora distinctive, and why does it play such a big role in the work you do?

---

[4] The belief that South Asians in Britain have to navigate between distinct cultural formations and this navigation informs and explains much of their behaviour and outlook. Cultural conflict then is inscribed in the body and circumstances of South Asian settlers and is continuously mobilised to give an account of their experiences (Anwar, 1998; Sian, 2013).

AB: My engagement with diaspora emerged out of my research agendas. I was doing research in relation to British South Asian, Caribbean, and white groups, and I was interested in understanding the ways in which social relations between differently marked ethnicities were impacted by questions of migration and globalisation: What kind of lifeworlds are constituted in and through the encounters between dominant and minoritised ethnicities in postcolonial Britain? What kind of power dynamic would be entailed? What effects would positioning along various social axes have on social relations on the ground? I began to consider how migration might be thought of in new and different ways, and diaspora was a concept that attracted me. It seemed to offer new possibilities for making sense of mobilities in the late twentieth century.

When I went to the University of California at Santa Cruz for a sabbatical (1992–1993), I spent my time thinking about diaspora and how to theorise it: on the one hand, diaspora is about movements of people, cultures, commodities, capital, and technologies; and on the other, there is the question of how to tackle issues of borders, home, and location in relation to mobilities. So, there were global mobilities, but I didn't want to privilege movement at the expense of questions of belonging and questions of 'staying put'. I started exploring these concerns through the concept of diaspora and diaspora space and attempted to differentiate between diaspora as a concept and diaspora as historical movement. I also brought into play the relationship between time and space in the formation of diasporic identities. I am always grappling with and trying to explore non-essentialist ways of constructing politics, which is a difficult but essential task. So, the concept of diaspora, diaspora space, 'homing desire', and intersectionality – of location and borders, changing temporalities and spatialities – all came together in my work on diaspora.

KPS: You also talk about your East African-Asian background in *Cartographies of Diaspora*. How does your African experience interact and interplay with the British Asian experience?

AB: Well, the East-African experience is very important in my life trajectory. Uganda was home throughout my childhood and teenage years. It was an experience of racial and economic privilege compared to that of Black Africans, and it made me very uneasy. I was already reading things about inequality, so although I didn't know theories about colonialism as a system, I could see that there were inequalities in Ugandan society, particularly in relation to the Africans and the way in which the society was divided largely into white people at the top, Asians in the middle, and then Africans at the bottom, although there were groups such as the Ugandan royal families who were high status and wealthy. A growing understanding of these aspects of society was an essential element in my politicisation. I saw myself as a Ugandan of Asian heritage, and my relationship to India, the place of my birth, has always been marked by this.

Coming to England was such a different situation because, among other things, it involved an encounter with Asians from the subcontinent with whom I didn't have much previous contact. I had visited India once or twice as a child, but I didn't actually have any kind of longstanding experiences with Indians from the subcontinent. East African-Asian culture and social life had its own specificity. In time, I found myself becoming part of a broader British Asian scene, and that was a new diasporic reality.

KPS: Could you elaborate on your specific use of intersectionality? And to what extent do you think it is an important category for the social sciences?

AB: Understanding intersectional processes is important, although we didn't use the term *intersectionality* until the late eighties and nineties. I became engaged with the idea through feminist debates around the category of 'woman'. These debates challenged the notion that 'woman' could be addressed as a homogenous category. We argued that it was not possible to talk about 'woman' in the singular as there were many different groups of women. So, questions of intersectionality – of 'race', class, gender, sexuality, age, disability, and so on – are essential in thinking through the multiplicity of power dynamics in and through which differentiated bodies are produced.

I do not see these axes of differentiation as identity categories but, rather, as modalities of power implicated in the historically specific processes – economic, political, and cultural – that underpin the constitution of what we name as a specific category or a specific identity. Intersectionality is not, in my view, a grid on which you can map different subject positions. It might rather more appropriately be construed as a continually shifting, interchanging, kaleidoscopic constellation of multiple flows of power.

Cartographies of Diaspora is an attempt to try to think about these different processes of power. Intersectionality threads throughout *Cartographies of Diaspora*. The book is less about theorising intersectionality than about one way of *doing* intersectionality. Intersectional analysis, in my view, can be done in many different ways, depending on the nature of the problematic to be addressed and the subject-specific disciplinary analytical tools at hand. I would suggest that there is no single, overarching research method that is relevant to all situations. I like Nirmal Puwar's designation of intersectionality as 'analytic sensibility'. Intersectionality has become a very significant feature of analysis within feminism, though probably not so much outside feminism. Within feminism there are a number of critiques of the concept of intersectionality, some of which are productive and others not. It remains a contested terrain.

KPS: Poststructuralism has clearly been influential to you and your work. What do you think poststructuralist thought offers, and why do you think those of us exploring postcolonial identities are increasingly drawn to ideas of poststructuralism?

AB: Stuart Hall has been especially influential in Britain in this turn to poststructuralism. This theoretical, political, and analytical perspective is attractive because it raises certain important questions that, in part, relate to the debates on intersectionality in that it actually critiques the power regimes through which subjects and bodies are produced and differently marked. The 'European subject' has often been seen as being at the centre of the universe, and I think poststructuralism puts forward a convincing critique of this idea, and so, for postcolonial thinkers that is really quite important.

Foucault's notion of discourse has been rather productive in this regard and allows us to rethink in creative ways the play of power and constellation of identifications, as has been Derrida's concept of *différance*. I found poststructuralist ideas and concepts helpful in enabling me to analyse certain problematics. Located as I am within feminist politics and, more specifically, within Black feminist politics, I realise that some feminists do not favour poststructuralist perspectives, partly because people tend to assume that such an approach might be apolitical, and that in such analysis the human subject can disappear. But I would say that it is not necessarily the case. To critique particular hegemonic discursive practices that underpin subject and meaning formation is not to undermine the importance of the subject or the body. So, politics remain central for me. But I respect the reservations of the critics.

My work is multidisciplinary, and I use ideas drawn from different epistemological traditions. I have found poststructuralism quite productive in many ways, but I also know that there are questions raised from within Marxism, for instance, and other materialist feminist perspectives that are equally central to address, especially the ones about local and global inequities and inequalities. And, so I don't want to locate my analysis within just one theoretical framework. I prefer to draw on and integrate the range of different subject disciplines, theoretical frameworks, and political movements to help me work through the various concerns that have come to inform my work. I have called this 'creolised theory' in the book *Cartographies of Diaspora*.

KPS: Feminism is central to your work and activism. How do you think Black and/or postcolonial feminism challenges and unsettles conventional white feminist thought?

AB: I think this is a very important question. Just to give you a terminological context – postcolonial feminism and Black feminism, particularly in America, concluded that it was perhaps better to use the term *women of colour* rather than *Black* to refer to the coalition of different categories of non-white women. Here in the UK, we used the term *Black* to refer to women with African, Caribbean, South Asian, and other postcolonial racialised heritage. Subsequently, these politics fractured somewhat along different ethnicities. I understand that there are currently efforts being made by a new generation of feminists to revive politics around the signifier *Black* along lines developed during the seventies, eighties, and nineties. I watch these developments with great interest, although I have started using the term women of colour alongside Black. The latter remains important as a signifier of two related but distinct Black feminisms: one is a historically specific feminist project that used Black as a political colour; the second, current today, may or, perhaps, more likely, may not organise around Black as a political colour, so that it may not have South Asian heritage women as its members.

I think both postcolonial and Black feminism offers us a way of thinking not only about racism, which is very important, but also about the global power relations. Black feminism and postcolonial feminism critique the global system as a way of looking at structures of authority and power that continue to govern unequal relations between countries and between regional blocks. This type of feminism plays a very important role in that sense: they foreground and challenge the machinations of neo-imperialisms that stalk the globe today. This is not to say that these questions are not important to white feminist thought, which is not homogenous at all. Many white scholars tackle these issues, but Black and white human subjects and subjectivities are different and differently positioned within and across racialised networks of power. Everyday social experiences are different, and these differences matter.

In the earlier years, there were a lot of debates around the question of white feminism and Black feminism. Hazel Carby's influential article 'White Woman Listen!' in the book *Empire Strikes Back*, and the Special Issue 17 of the British journal *Feminist Review* epitomise central tenets of this debate. There were also questions of how racism was understood and how the Black experience was understood and theorised. So, all those issues were discussed and debated, and the question of subjectivity then became very important, the argument being that racism was not simply just an epistemological dimension; rather, there is a very deep psychic investment in particular ways of *being* and particular ways of relating to the world. Recognition of this is important to the politics of coalition and solidarity across ethnicities, religious groups, and class fractions.

KPS: When you were first in the academy, was there a space for Black thinkers to engage within and unsettle that space?

AB: It was difficult for us; it was a struggle to introduce different ways of thinking about issues of 'race', ethnicity, and feminism. Black academics could tell stories about difficulties faced when, ironically, working with white academics in the field of 'race relations'. Leaving aside individuals such as Stuart Hall, the most support I got was from feminists. Overall, we had a huge struggle initially to foreground the ways in which racism was deeply implicated in all forms of social relations. A smile, a look – those things can convey a lot of racialised sensibilities and meanings, so it was difficult; yes, definitely. It has been, and I believe to an extent continues to be, a struggle about the very nature of knowledge produced in our universities.

To an extent, the hegemony of certain forms of knowledge production that supported the status quo probably continues to persist in the social sciences and humanities, though positive changes have undoubtedly taken place, not least that there are more scholars of colour now in the academy and that the course content has shifted in some universities. We were able to introduce some important curricular changes at Birkbeck College, and I know colleagues who have done the same in other universities.

KPS: What do you hope to see developing in the social sciences around questions of 'race', ethnicity, and the postcolonial?

AB: Sometimes I worry that these topics or areas of study might disappear from the curriculum, so I would like to see the study of these subjects continue in schools and universities, partly as a way of challenging the idea that we are somehow already 'post-racial', if by this there is a suggestion that we no longer have racism. We do not as yet, unfortunately, live in a post-racial world in that sense, though we may hope for post-racial/non-racial futures.

I would also like to see teaching around 'race' and ethnicity to be approached differently. These topics should be studied across the range of courses and modules offered, or mainstreamed, as they say, although it is still important to look at specific topics and themes separately and in-depth. So, for example, if you are doing a course on gender, it should be axiomatic that you integrate throughout the entire course the experiences and contributions of persons of colour and how discourses of 'race' have marked Western knowledge formations. But on the other hand, it is essential to maintain the specialist study of such subjects. These issues can no longer be neglected in the social sciences or humanities. There is a major imperative to address questions of postcoloniality, neo-coloniality, and new imperialisms if we are to have better worlds.

KPS: Do you consider yourself to be a postcolonial thinker, and what do you think has been your main contribution to the field?

AB: I've never actually thought about that. My work is multidisciplinary, as I said earlier, and I'm certainly trying to address questions of postcoloniality as well as those of new colonialisms and new imperialisms in the current global order, so I suspect that my work could be situated within postcolonial studies. My specific approach to feminism as a field of study and activism, as well as my theorisation of diaspora and difference marks my contribution. These are the three main areas, and within these, there are my specific analytical frameworks, and sets of critiques relating to postcolonialism, ethnicity, and 'race', which I hope have made an impact.

Interviewer Biography

Dr Katy P. Sian is a Senior Lecturer in Sociology at the University of York. She completed her PhD in 2009 at the University of Leeds in the School of Sociology and Social Policy. In 2013 she was awarded with the Hallsworth research fellowship from the University of Manchester. Katy has held visiting research posts at the University of California Humanities Research Institute (UCHRI) and the Centre for Studies in Religion and Society (CSRS) at the University of Victoria, Canada. She has pioneered critical debates on Sikh and Muslim relations in the diaspora and continues to work on issues related to critical race theory and decoloniality; Islamophobia and the war on terror; and culture, migration, and identity. Katy is the author of *Navigating Institutional Racism in British Universities* (2019); *Conversations in Postcolonial Thought* (2014); *Unsettling Sikh and Muslim Conflict* (2013); and co-author of *Racism, Governance, and Public Policy* (2013). She serves on the steering committee for the Northern Police Monitoring Project, which campaigns against police brutality and racism.

Chapter 5

Diaspora in and through Feminist Inflections

As we saw in Chapter 2, the UN World Migration Report 2020 demonstrates that there are currently 281 million people in the world who are 'migrants', a figure that, although it constitutes a tiny proportion of the world's population at 3.6 per cent, nevertheless is substantial. These global migrations are creating new displacements as the persons involved either join existing diasporas, or in the fullness of time, form new ones. In this chapter, I focus on the ways in which the concept of diaspora has been developed, theorised, and studied in a range of contexts and research analysis. I address processes of bordering and border crossing and explore issues associated with politics of locationality. The concept of diaspora is elaborated through its inflection by feminist conceptual frames including intersectionality. I discuss the play of heteronormative bias in research and writing on diaspora and explore aspects of the emerging field of queer diaspora studies. These issues are contextualised within discursive and material practices of diasporic spatiality.

Defining Diaspora

In its historical manifestations, the term diaspora referred to religious groups, in particular, to the forced dispersal of ancient communities of Jewish people, the Armenians, and the Greeks. Over the last few decades, however, the concept of diaspora has become much more widely used to refer to present-day global migrations of people, which result in the formation of multiple diasporas. Foregrounding the concept of displacement, the term diaspora is widely used to describe a phenomenon of dispersion from a place of residence to elsewhere. Until recently, a connection with a place of 'origin', real or imagined, has been regarded as one of the defining characteristics of diasporas. Such a place is often defined as a 'homeland', although, as I have argued before, this conceptualisation is problematic. While identification with a presumed place of dispersal may be apprehended through the workings of a 'homing desire', such a place may or may not be construed as a 'homeland' (Brah, 1996). Moreover, in some current definitions of diaspora, the notion of a 'common origin' is altogether absent. Fatima El-Tayab, for instance, argues that:

> In this study I extend the notion of diaspora to describe a population that does not share a common origin—however imaginary it might be—but a contemporary condition. Within this broadened understanding of diaspora, the concept is transformed from a temporal and spatial displacement focused on the past towards one of productive dislocation directed as the future—mirroring the potential of queering ethnicity as a nonessentialist, and often nonlinear, political strategy.
>
> (El-Tayeb, 2011: xxxv)

This is a fascinating departure from the generally accepted usage, one that promises radical revisioning of diasporic agendas. I am sympathetic to the main thrust of the argument and I am especially partial to a non-essentialist, non-linear political strategy. However, I wonder if 'sharing a common origin' and 'sharing a contemporary condition' are necessarily mutually exclusive modalities. Is it not possible that a group may both share a common history *and* a contemporary social condition in the process of constituting a diaspora? I suppose I am suggesting that shared genealogies as well as contemporary social conditions are simultaneously important elements of the formation of diasporic lifeworlds. The problematic and tricky term perhaps is 'origins' as this can have essentialist connotations. Hence my personal preference for valorising the terms 'shared history' or 'shared genealogy' together with taking on board socio-cultural, economic, and political entanglements, as the basis for theorising diaspora.

There is some conceptual overlap between the twin terms of diaspora and transnationalism. While the former is an old concept, the latter is comparatively new, associated with our contemporary processes of globalisation. The term transnationalism first appeared in the Merriam-Webster dictionary in 1921 but as a process it expanded during the latter half of the twentieth century, its expansion being aided by the development of the Internet and wireless communication. At the same time, the notion of 'common origins' in describing diaspora continued to be used as one of its distinguishing features, but in newer definitions such as the above, this mode of specifying diaspora is considered far less important, if not irrelevant. The previous tendency in diaspora studies to emphasise the question of 'return', whether permanent, or temporary, actual or imaginary, is also currently not receiving much emphasis. Instead, a growing focus on circular exchange and transnational mobility is likely to further attenuate the boundary between diaspora and transnationalism. Yet, as Baubock and Faist (2010) argue, even in the multifaceted crossovers of meaning between these two concepts, there are distinctive imaginaries, research questions, styles of reasoning, and theoretical agendas which mark their specificities. The way forward, they suggest, may not be to settle the conceptual debate once and for all but rather to deploy the Wittgensteinian proposition that the meaning of transnationalism and diaspora must be inferred from their actual use. Transnationalism is a broader term than diaspora, connecting a wide variety of social formations including people's ties across countries, transnationally active networks of people, organisations, and social movements. In other words, transnational communities encompass diasporas, but not all transnational communities are diasporas.

As is widely known, 'diaspora' is a Greek term, derived from the word, 'diaspeiro', to scatter, which was used as far back as the fifth century BC by Sophocles, Herodotus, and Thucydides. During the second half of the twentieth century, it assumed new meanings. The 1931 edition of the *American Encyclopedia of the Social Sciences* included an entry on 'diaspora'. The author, Simon Dubinov, argued that the term should not be limited to the Jewish groups. This text led to the diffusion of the term and its secularisation. In 1939, Robert Park applied the term to Asians, and it was not until the 1960s and 1970s that the word came to be commonly used to refer to the 'Black diaspora'. Frantz Fanon, for instance, wrote of the 'Negro diaspora' in the 1961 text *Wretched of the Earth*, and subsequently other scholars followed (Dufoix, 2008). In the 1980s, definitions embedded in postmodern thought assumed currency. Postmodernist and poststructuralist analysis crystallised around the work of philosophers such as Michel Foucault, Jacques Derrida, Jean-François Lyotard, Gilles Deleuze, and Felix Guatari. Concepts of diaspora influenced by poststructuralist thought tended to express scepticism of modern reason, of grand narratives of science, truth, and progress, and instead came to foreground mixity, multiplicity, fragmentation, heterogeneity, fluid identities, and hybridity. In Britain these perspectives found a welcome home in British 'cultural studies', which addressed subaltern and postcolonial subcultures. An influential concept of diaspora marked by these developments is offered by Stuart Hall:

I use the term metaphorically, not literally: diaspora does not refer us to those scattered tribes whose identity can only be secured in relation to some sacred homeland to which they must at all costs return, even if it means pushing other people into the sea. This is the old, imperialising, hegemonizing form of 'ethnicity'... The diaspora experience as I intend it here is defined not by essence or purity, but by the recognition of a necessary heterogeneity and diversity; by a conception of 'identity' which lives with and through, not despite difference; by hybridity.

(Hall, 1990: 235)

Earlier Studies on Post-Second World War Diasporas

The studies discussed in this section do not always specifically address the questions of gender but they are important in laying the terrain of diaspora studies as a field of enquiry. They have been influential in setting the agenda for theoretical and political debate on the subject and are likely to feature as the formative texts on most courses in diaspora studies. Hence the need to discuss them in constructing feminist narratives in relation to diaspora.

In recent times, especially since the 1980s, the concept of 'diaspora' has gained growing currency to describe communities that have emerged from the migration and resettlement of people all over the world. As we noted earlier, there has been a long association of the word diaspora with the dispersal of the Jewish people after the Babylonian exile. The Jewish diaspora evokes a history of persecution and genocide, and occupies a central place within European cartography of displacement. It has a specific resonance in European narratives of trauma, especially in relation to the Jewish Holocaust during World War II. Yet, to analyse diasporas in the twenty-first century is to take such ancient diasporas as a point of departure rather than as models of ideal types. Safran (1991: 83) shows that diaspora was likely at the time and now to be deployed as a "metaphorical designation" to describe different categories of people – "expatriates, expellees, political refugees, alien residents, immigrants and ethnic and racial minorities *tout court*" – and it covers a wide variety of different peoples. The current usages of the concept of diaspora are likely to emphasise creativity and positive dimensions of diaspora, its cultural innovation and inventiveness, as much as its history of discrimination, disadvantage, and suffering. But, as Robin Cohen (1997) argued, creativity was a feature of ancient diasporas as well, though this fact has tended to have been overlooked by commentators. Emphasising the specificity of late twentieth-century valorisation of the term 'diaspora', James Clifford suggests:

> We should be able to recognize the strong entitlement of Jewish history on the language of diaspora without making that history a definitive model. Jewish (and Greek and Armenian) diaspora can be taken as non-normative starting points for a discourse that is travelling in new global conditions.
>
> (1994: 302)

Robin Cohen (1997) in his discussion of different diasporas provides us with 'typologies' of different kinds of diasporas. Typologies can be problematic if treated as hermetically sealed categories, but Cohen recognises that the histories they describe are much more complex and ambiguous than the typology suggests. This point is especially critical because typologies can be misread as standing for permanent and fixed mutual exclusions. Instead, he emphasises that there are no fixed boundaries between different types of diasporas, and the typology is a heuristic device to conduct an inquiry. His typology includes victim, labour, trade, imperial, and cultural diasporas. It is important to recognise that a given diaspora can take more than one form and others change their positioning over time in that a 'victim' diaspora, for instance, may in time become successful economically and politically and may no longer warrant designation as 'victim' as is the case of many Jewish communities and the Ugandan Asian refugees who settled during the 1970s in Britain and elsewhere.

There has been some considerable discussion of the criteria by which a group might be considered to constitute a diaspora. There is no final agreement on this except that a diaspora is not casual travel or short-term settlement of a few years but rather decades or more. Drawing upon some criteria identified by Safran, Robert Cohen lists nine common features of a diaspora as follows:

- Dispersal from an original homeland, often traumatically, to two or more foreign regions;
- Alternatively, the expansion from a homeland in search of work, in pursuit of trade or to further colonial ambitions;
- A collective memory and myth about the homeland, including its location, history and its achievements;
- An idealization of the putative ancestral home and a collective commitment to its maintenance, restoration, safety and prosperity, even to its creation;
- The development of a return movement that gains collective approbation;
- A strong ethnic group consciousness sustained over a long time and based on a sense of distinctiveness, a common history, and the belief in a common fate;
- A troubled relationship with host societies, suggesting a lack of acceptance at the least or the possibility that another calamity might fall the group;

- A sense of empathy and solidarity with co-ethnic members in other countries of settlement; and
- The possibility of a distinctive creative, enriching life in host countries with a tolerance for pluralism.

(Cohen, 1997: 26)

Although these criteria are offered as common features, they do not, of course, apply to all diasporas and not in the same fashion. For instance, not all diasporas sustain a desire to 'return' to the country of origin, other than perhaps for short visits. Nor do they necessarily start return movements. Similarly, I have reservations about using the term 'host', not least because populations in the country of settlement may be antagonistic rather than host-like to the diasporic groups. I also do not endorse an over-emphasis on attachment to the 'homeland' because diasporic persons do not always consider the country of 'origin' as their home but instead regard the country of settlement as one. This is not to suggest, however, that the question of home does not have a critical resonance in the diasporic lifeworld. In fact, home is a central trope in diasporic imaginary. I suggest that we need to think of a 'homing desire' that is not the same as a desire for the 'homeland' (Brah, 1996). Homing desire is in large part about a sense of belonging, a 'returning' that is also 'going forward'. And as desire it engages our deepest emotionality. It is marked by the unruly workings of the unconscious within conscious processes. Rather than the myth of return, homing desire poses a critique of fixed origins such that the question of homeland is indefinitely suspended. Home is a place of desire yet, equally, it refers to the materiality of lived experience. The two articulate and mark cultural creativity, hybridity, and innovation as well as all manner of contradiction. Recently, there has been a tendency in diaspora studies to place less emphasis on group solidarities and cohesiveness and a closer focus on internal complexities such as multi-faith, multi-lingual, and hybrid diasporas (Cohen and Fischer, 2019).

The theories that emerged from British cultural studies such as those of Stuart Hall and Paul Gilroy dislodged the concept from its emphasis on homeland, return, and exile. The emphasis here is on diasporic experience and the narratives of displacement of the postcolonial subject. Hall foregrounded a new theorisation of identity as "'production,' which is never complete, always in process" (Hall cited in Woodward, 1997: 51). He distinguished between two conceptions of identity. One regards shared history as something to be recovered that might mask a 'one true self' to be mined, excavated, and valorised. He argued that the colonial struggles, for instance, foregrounded such a conception of identity. It was a powerful notion of identity that reshaped the world even though it might be seen by some as an essentialist concept. The second view of identity is

as much about 'becoming' as 'being'. It belongs to the future as much as to the past. It is not something that already exists, transcending place, time, history, and culture... Far from being eternally fixed in some essentialized past, they are subject to the continuous 'play' of history... identities are the names we give to the different ways we are positioned by and position ourselves within, the narratives of the past.

(Hall, 1997: 52)

Hall points out that diasporic identities are constituted not just across similarities but equally within and through difference. Here he borrows Jacques Derrida's concept of *différance* – a simultaneous play of differ and deferral – so that meaning is always deferred. This continuous deferral might be a problem only if we see this "cut of identity as natural and permanent rather than an arbitrary and contingent 'ending' " (Hall, 1997: 55).

Working along similar lines, Paul Gilroy (1997) shows how diaspora poses a challenge to the "'family as building block' basis of the nation state, offering instead anti-national and anti-essentialist accounts of identity formation based on contingency, indeterminacy and conflict, and offering possibilities of different forms of political action" (Gilroy cited in Woodward, 1997: 339). Gilroy critiques essentialist authenticity and purity, challenges formations of ethnic absoluteness at the heart of nationalist projects and valorises identities that are seen as hybrid, creolised, and syncretic. Yet, these identities are not entirely arbitrary, embedded as they are in the social histories of the groups who live it. In the book *The Black Atlantic*, Gilroy charts diaspora cultural configurations and politics and argues that the Black Atlantic culture is not simply African, American, Caribbean, or British but all of these at once. It is a creolised formation. Inter alia, Gilroy foregrounds the centrality and prominence of music within the various Black communities of the Atlantic diaspora as a means of essential connectedness. He argues,

> But the histories of borrowing, displacement, transformation, and continual reinscription that the musical culture encloses are a living legacy that should not be reified in the primary symbol of the diaspora and then employed as an alternative to the recurrent appeal of fixity and rootedness.
>
> (Gilroy, 1993: 102)

My own analysis of diaspora (Brah, 1996), is refracted through an intersectional feminist optic. However, while it foregrounds intersections of power and differentiation, I was not familiar at the time that I developed the idea of 'intersectionality' with the concept of 'intersectionality' as deployed by Kimberlé Williams Crenshaw. I came to know of her theorisation at a later stage. My point of departure was to think through the distinction made by James Clifford between diaspora understood as a 'concept'; as 'diasporic discourses' and, as particular historical 'experiences' (Clifford, 1994). I tried to specify features that may be seen to distinguish diaspora as a theoretical concept from the historical 'experiences' of diaspora. I suggested that diaspora may be understood along the lines of historically contingent 'genealogies' in the Foucauldian sense. In other words, diaspora serves as

> an ensemble of investigative technologies that historicize trajectories of different diasporas and analyse their relationality across fields of social relations, subjectivity and identity. I argue that the concept of diaspora offers a critique of discourses of fixed origins, while taking account of a homing desire which is not the same thing as desire for a 'homeland.'
>
> (Brah, 1996: 180)

I wish to stress that diasporas are historically specific rather than trans-historical formations. Historical specificity is crucial in order to understand the relationality between distinct diasporas. Diasporas do not only signify the movement of people but are also associated with that of capital, commodities cultural processes, artefacts, and information. While the history of a specific diasporic trajectory will make for distinctiveness of social and cultural experience, diasporas may not, in my view, be theorised as inscribing some transcendental diasporic consciousness. That is to say that to acknowledge specificity is not the same as positing an essentialist notion of diasporic consciousness. Nor are diasporic politics invariably progressive, though this might emerge as a feature of some new social, cultural, and political transformations in the lifeworld of diasporics in a new location and context. It is worth bearing in mind that diasporas are heterogeneous, contested spaces as are the social formations in which they are embedded. Diasporic lives are lived through multiple modalities produced through the intersection of such vectors as race, class, gender, sexuality, disability/debility, religion, and generation. Construction of a common 'we', then, is not a straightforward process but involves complex cultural and political interaction and negotiation that may involve conflict and contestation as much as solidarity. In my approach to studying diaspora I have proposed a multiaxial performative conception of power that operates across multiple intersectional fields. The concept of diaspora in my frame emerges as:

an ensemble of investigative technologies that historicise trajectories of different diasporas, map their relationality, and interrogate, for example, what the search for origins signifies in the history of a particular diaspora; *how* and *why* originary absolutes are imagined; how the materiality of economic, political and signifying practices is experienced; what new subject positions are created and assumed; how particular fields of power articulate in the construction of hierarchies of domination and subordination in a given context; why certain *conceptions of identity* come into play in a given situation, and whether or not these conceptions are reinforced or challenged and contested by the *play of identities.*

(Brah, 1996: 197, original emphasis)

The concept of diaspora points to the importance of the notion of the border. As noted in Chapter 2, I have found Gloria Anzaldua's theorisation of borders particularly instructive and helpful. There are two insights that hold specific resonance. First, she uses the concept of border to reflect upon social conditions of life at the Texas–US Southwest/Mexican border where – using the terminology of the period in dividing the world into First, Second and Third World, the last being what is today referred to as the global South – she says, "the third world grates against the first and bleeds" (Anzaldua, 1987: 3). She also uses the concept of the border as a metaphor for psychological, sexual, spiritual, cultural, class, gender, and racialised boundaries. Metaphors are not simply abstractions of concrete reality, but rather they undergird the discursive materiality of power relations. A key question relates to how borders are policed and regulated. Who is allowed to cross a border with ease, and who is kept out? Who is considered outsider, alien, and as Other? How, for instance, will queer identities be policed in a context saturated with homophobia and heteronormative imperatives? How is the position of racialised groups, or 'economic migrants', regulated in and through immigration control?

Borders are arbitrary constructions but they hold particular meanings that vary according to the history within which a particular border is inscribed. Each border enunciates a distinctive narrative. Old borders may disappear under new socio-economic and political conditions, and new ones may be created. Thus power relations are crucial to the operations and workings of all borders. Borders signify the sovereignty of the state whereby they come to symbolise the ability of the state to exercise control over the movement of people, goods, capital, trade, information, and so on. Territorial borders are often assumed to be on the extremity of the nation state. Yet, it is increasingly recognised that they do not stop at the edges, but rather they permeate the national, even global space. As I have noted before, Étienne Balibar (2004) argues that what is important about borders is *what they do* at a given historical juncture. Borders may be conceptualised as enacted practices and in that capacity they will mark both the physical and the social body (Whitley,

2015). An example of this can be seen when immigration or nationality legislation comes into play. Such legislation will regulate the movement of suspected undocumented workers as they face the realities of life under constant threat of deportation. Here their bodies not merely carry but 'become' borders. According to Nira Yuval Davis et al. (2019), borders should be seen as a constitutive part of the world rather than understood as having the function to partition and segment a pre-given whole.

Global inequality and poverty run rife in our war riven world. These social and cultural conditions are at the heart of perilous journeys undertaken by migrants and refugees from the global South to the global North. They are trying to escape dire economic and/or political conditions or natural disasters such as famine and floods. Wars, religious insurgencies, authoritarian and repressive political regimes, climate change-related draught and famine, lack of jobs, and endemic poverty are all contributory factors in this tragedy. Though far fewer in number in 2020, hundreds of people are still dying in the Mediterranean. The International Organization for Migration (IOM) estimated in August 2020 that 554 migrants had died until that point in time. These journeys often begin in the impoverished, sometimes politically unstable, and conflict-ridden parts of the world such as Syria, Somalia, Sierra Leone, Iraq, and other parts of the Middle East, and North and West Africa. The difficulties of border crossing do not always disappear when one reaches the end of the first stage of the journey. In Europe, the refugees and migrants are faced with racism and xenophobia. Hopes of a coordinated European response to settle those arriving ran into difficulty such that, because of their geographical location, Italy and Greece disproportionately bore responsibility for the intake of newcomers. In 2017, for instance, the situation was dire. According to the editorial of the British newspaper *The Guardian* of 9 July 2017 ('Refugee Policy is Wrong and Short Sighted'), all hopes of a united European response to the refugee crisis seemed to have evaporated. There was still no network of commonly funded reception centres at that point in time. National leaders were likely to shun the idea of equitable resettlement quotas for EU states. The cornerstone of the European approach remained the hopelessly outdated Dublin Regulation, which insisted refugees must be processed by the first EU country they set foot in and could be sent back there if they journeyed beyond it. And so the injustice of two of Europe's poor nations – Italy and Greece – which had to struggle with large number of refugees. When some refugees tried to move up to north European countries, they would face incredible obstacles including razor sharp wired boundaries. Even countries such as Germany, which welcomed refugees for six months, gave in to internal anti-immigrant political pressure. Yet, it is ironic that, as noted earlier, 80 per cent of the world's refugees are hosted by developing countries. Moreover, migrants make important economic and social contributions to the receiving countries, and their labour is often crucial to many sections of the economy. At the time of writing in May 2021, the number of migrants crossing the Mediterranean has fallen quite radically by 90 per cent due primarily to the implementation of measures to control external borders by the EU. Evidently, there are currently plans for a long-term European Union policy 2021–2027 to control irregular migration for which there is to be a budget set up (www.consilium.europa.eu).

The cases cited above highlight the historical specificity of these particular journeys. They also place into relief why it is important to discuss them in relation to diasporas. These migrants arrive under difficult and specific material and psychological conditions. This makes their needs different and distinctive from long-term diasporics but in time they may create new diasporas or become part of existing ones. This, for example, was the case with Asian refugees to Britain from Uganda in the early 1970s. Over the last decades, they successfully made new lives in Britain and created a new diaspora.

Borders, Politics of Location, Diaspora, and Diaspora Space

A discussion of borders and boundaries, and of home and belonging, brings into focus issues of 'politics of location'. One early example of the use of the term 'politics of location', as seen in Chapter 2, is that by the feminist scholar Adrienne Rich. In her text Rich reflects upon the centrality of embodiment of feminist politics, and how the process of embodiment locates you across multiple axes of differentiation and power. She emphasises the importance of not transcending the personal but claiming it. She points to a time when she could quote without hesitation Virginia Woolf's statement, "As a woman I have no country. As a woman I want no country. As a woman my country is the whole world." But she could not do so anymore because, as she says:

As a woman I have a country; as a woman I cannot divest myself of that country merely by condemning its government or by saying three times, 'As a woman my country is the whole world.' Tribal loyalties aside, and even if nation-states are now just pretexts used by multinational conglomerates to serve their interests, I need to understand how a place on the map is also a place in history within which as a woman, a Jew, a lesbian, a feminist I am created and trying to create.

(Rich, 1994 [1984]: 212)

She speaks of how as a white middle-class woman, she was simultaneously 'located' by her gender, colour, and class. Indeed, she refers to 'whiteness' as a politics of location which places her in a position of power vis-à-vis people of colour.

Another autobiographical account that interrogates the shifting positionalities of whiteness and the simultaneous articulation of position of power with that of subordination is that of Minnie Bruce Pratt entitled 'Identity: Skin, Blood, Heart' (1984). She is committed to unpicking power geometries entailed when she, as a white, middle-class, Christian raised in Southern United States, decides to come out as a lesbian, and her family and friends 'back home' react negatively. She explores how she realised that her sense of belonging and safety had been dependent on her taken-for-granted acceptance of the normative cultural and social codes of her social milieu. These were shaken when she sought to gain custody of her children and had to face the hostility and rejection of people she had understood were her 'community'. She examines the politics of racism in the United States, both in terms of its structural dimensions as well as its personal manifestations. In contrast, Angela Davis's autobiography (1990 [1974]) of growing up Black in southern United States invokes life in the segregated south and charts an experiential terrain from the opposite side of the racial divide, especially in terms of her experience of racism. Such accounts foreground the ways in which the same geographical space may come to embody different histories so that politics of location may emerge as a politics of contradiction. Politics of location is the site of 'difference', which I have theorised as a nodal point of confluence of four articulating axis of differentiation. Axis one refers to difference analysed as 'experience', which is viewed as a symbolically and narratively mediated practice of making sense; the second axis is understood as 'social relation' foregrounding systemic relations within, through, and across economic, cultural and political structures, discourses, and practices; the third axis marks 'subjectivity', which stands as a critique of the subject as unitary and unified and where the unruly practices of the unconscious play their part; and the fourth axis foregrounds 'identity' as a process, not a finished product, constructed through non-essentialist multiplicity which is both personal and group-identified, underpinning commonalities as well as antagonisms (Brah, 1996).

In my analysis of the concepts of diaspora, borders, and politics of location, these concepts together provide a conceptual grid for analysing historicised accounts of the movements of people, information, cultures, commodities, and capital. I have called the articulation of these three concepts 'diaspora space'. The concept of diaspora space is defined as follows:

Diaspora space is the intersectionality of diaspora, border, and dis/location as a point of confluence of economic, political, cultural, and psychic processes. It is where multiple subject positions are juxtaposed, contested, proclaimed or disavowed; where the permitted and the prohibited perpetually interrogate; and where the accepted and the transgressive imperceptibly mingle even while these syncretic forms may be disclaimed in the name of purity and tradition. Here tradition is itself continually invented even as it may be hailed as originating from the mists of time. What is at stake is the infinite experientiality, the myriad processes of cultural fissure and fusion that underwrite contemporary forms of transcultural identities.

(Brah, 1996: 208)

Diaspora space underpins conditions of contemporary transmigrancies, crossing borders, territorial and otherwise, and the multiple power geometries where the play of power is both coercive and productive, and where identities and a sense of belonging are produced and contested. In other words, diaspora space, as distinct from diaspora, highlights the *"entanglement of the genealogies of dispersal"* with those of *"staying put"* (Brah, 1996: 242, original emphasis).

Diaspora and Differentiation

Why is it important to discuss intersectionality in a chapter devoted to analysis of diaspora? It is essential because diasporas are not homogenous categories but rather are deeply marked and differentiated by such axes as those of race, class, gender, and sexuality. In other words, diasporas are inherently intersectional formations. The theorisations of intersectionality is a very significant development within feminist analytics. As discussed in Chapter 2, Black women and women of colour have played a central role in its emergence and elaboration in the 1960s, 1970s, and since. At base, intersectionality is about the fact that our experience is marked by a variety of vectors such as race, gender, class, and sexuality. One of the early statements of intersectionality was that produced by the Combahee River Collective, a group of Black lesbian activists in Boston. Written in 1977, this statement is a key document of women-of-colour feminism. Its incisive insights are as relevant to scholarship and activism today as they were 40 years ago. Although it does not use the term 'intersectionality', there is no doubt that the statement is one of the major forerunners to our current debates. Its argument that "we are actively committed to struggling against racial, sexual, heterosexual and class oppression, and see as our particular task the development of integrated analysis and practice based upon the fact that the major systems of oppression are interlocking" (Guy-Sheftall, 1995: 232) is singularly predictive of subsequent developments in the study of intersectionality. Its emphasis on 'simultaneous experience' of different formations of differentiation such as racism, gender, class, and sexuality provides a critical lens on the kaleidoscopic effects of articulating modalities of power. It prefigures later debates on analysing the concepts of 'embodiment' and 'experience'. As socialist feminists, the member of the Combahee Collective foregrounded their politics in a critique of capitalism, imperialism, and patriarchal social relations. This contextualises US Black feminism in the global context of transnational feminism.

Over the years, the concept of 'social division' and that of 'different axis of power' was also used by scholars along similar lines to intersectionality. For instance, Floya Anthias and Nira Yuval Davis (1992) use the concept of social division to analyse the interconnections of race, ethnicity, gender, and class, and Floya Antias (2002, 2020) introduces the concept of 'translocational positionality', which also resonates with the meanings associated with intersectionality. Similarly, Rosi Braidotti (2006) provides interesting insights into the development of the term intersectionality and its transpositionality with other vectors of difference in the constitution of subjectivity, identity, and structural domains. But the term intersectionality itself is said to have been developed by Kimberlé Williams Crenshaw. Collins and Bilge (2016) note that today the term is widely used by scholars, policy advocates, practitioners, and activists in many different contexts in the world. A definition of the term to which all may subscribe is not an easy task. In 2004, Ann Phoenix and I described the term as "signifying the complex, irreducible, varied and variable effects which ensue when multiple axes of differentiation—economic, political, cultural, psychic, subjective and experiential—intersect in historically specific contexts"

(Brah and Phoenix, 2004: 76). Collins and Bilge offer the following definition:

> Intersectionality is a way of understanding and analyzing the complexity in the world, in people and in human experience. The events and conditions of social and political life and the self can seldom be understood as shaped by one factor. They are generally shaped by many factors in diverse and mutually influencing ways. When it comes to social inequality, people's lives and the organization of power in a given society are better understood as being shaped not by a single axis of social division, be it race or gender or class, but by many axes that work together and influence each other. Intersectionality as an analytic tool gives people better access to the complexity of the world and of themselves
>
> (Collins and Bilge, 2016: 2)

Importantly, Collins and Bilge suggest that intersectional analys is is underpinned by six core ideas that appear and reappear when the concept is used. They are: inequality; relationality; power; social context; and social injustice. For a sympathetic, though critical, engagement with intersectionality see Nash (2008). She raises questions about a lack of defined intersectional methodology; the use of Black women as quintessential intersectional subjects; the vague definitions of intersectionality; and the empirical validity of intersectionality. I would say that intersectionality is a multidisciplinary project and as such cannot have a single methodology that is appropriate for all occasions. Of course, in the US, intersectionality developed with a focus on the positionality of Black women, but since then it has come to signify a wider range of women. There would seem to be considerable evidence by now of empirical applicability of the concept to the condition of different groups of embodied women. Finally, the criticism concerning a lack of a precise definition of intersectionality is somewhat problematic because exact and explicit definitions are rarely able to deal with the complexity of social phenomena signified by a given definition, especially one concerned with multiple axes of differentiation. These are just some brief points that Nash's important and thoughtful questions have prompted me to think through. I totally agree with Nash that there ought not to be a defensive and/or protectionist stance towards intersectionality. How valuable the analytics are depends on the extent to which their use actually takes theoretical and political agendas forward, constructs new intellectual vistas, and extends our analytical horizons. Nash's reorientation of intersectionality while underlining its generative impulse, its transnationalism, its highlighting of inequality, its sensitivity to human complexity, power and social justice, is critically important (Nash, 2019).

Jasbir Puar has used the concept of intersectionality for many years and still values its analytical reach but she has moved from its general deployment in favour of the concept of assemblage:

> As opposed to an intersectional model of identity, which presumes that components – race, class, gender, sexuality, nation, age, religion – are separable analytics and can thus be disassembled, an assemblage is more attuned to interwoven forces that merge and dissipate time, space and body against linearity, coherency, and permanency.
>
> (Puar, 2017 [2007]: 212)

She is critical of its take up as a "tool of diversity management and a mantra of liberal multiculturalism" and argues that it "colludes with the disciplinary apparatus of the state – census, demography, racial profiling, surveillance – ..." (Puar, 2017: 212). I am sympathetic to the reservations she holds but am not fully convinced, however, that the paradigm of intersectionality can be held responsible for the multiplicity of uses to which it has been put, both positive and negative, by different sets of users, though one should definitely be categorically critical of, and stand in opposition to, its negative usage in such practices as surveillance or racial profiling. Moreover, I view intersectionality and assemblage as complementary rather than as mutually exclusive analytics.

Scholars working in the field of diaspora studies do not always address questions of intersectionality. But my point is that diaspora studies and intersectional studies are intimately interconnected (see Chapter 7 in this volume). Diasporas are intersectionally heterogeneous categories and share a common focus on 'difference'. It is here that the two intersect and overlap.

Queering Gendered Diasporas

Work on sexuality in the field of diaspora studies has been limited. One of these studies is undertaken by Fataneh Farhani (2017), which examines the narratives on sexuality of first-generation Iranian women living in Sweden. Much early work on sexuality in the field of diasporas has been refracted through a heteronormative lens. More recently, however, this focus is increasingly being challenged by scholarship that interrogates the demands placed by heteronormativity on bodies, desires, subjectivities, and identities. This mapping of queerness onto diaspora decentres these regimes. This queer scholarship challenges nationalist ideologies by foregrounding the impure, inauthentic, and non-essentialist promise of the concept of diaspora. As Gayatri Gopinath (2005) argues, "The concept of a queer diaspora enables a simultaneous critique of heterosexuality and the nation while exploding the binary oppositions between nation and diaspora, heterosexuality and homosexuality, original and copy" (Gopinath, 2005: 11). In other words, "suturing 'queer' to 'diaspora' thus recuperates those desires, practices, and subjectivities that are rendered impossible and unimaginable within conventional diasporic and nationalist imaginaries" (Gopinath, 2005: 11). The term 'queer' is preferred by Gopinath to 'gay' and 'lesbian' as a critique of the globalisation of 'gay' identity that judges all 'other' sexual cultures and practices as premodern against a model of Western sexual identity. Queer diasporic scholarship also reframes questions of home, a preoccupation in studies of diaspora:

The resignification of 'home' within a queer diasporic imaginary makes three crucial interventions: first, it forcefully repudiates the elision of queer subjects from national and diasporic memory; second, it denies their function as threat to family/community/nation; and third, it refuses to position queer subjects as alien, inauthentic, and perennially outside the confines to these entities.

(Gopinath, 2005: 15)

Her text challenges discourses that "forget, excise and criminalise queer bodies, pleasures, desires, histories, and lives" (Gopinath, 2005: 187). In her more recent work, Gopinath extends her analyses to a study of diaspora and visuality, exploring a variety of cultural forms such as film, fine art, poetry, and photography, which she conceptualises as "aesthetic practices of queer diaspora". Here she interrogates fixed notions of both diaspora and indigeneity, and argues against those framings that position these two categories in opposition to each other, and regards them instead as co-constitutive rather than antithetical. In this way she reconfigures the normative ways of analysing the interrelationships between affect, archive, region, and aesthetics. The aesthetic practices of queer diaspora are theorised as archival practices that underpin minoritised histories which are not encompassed by nation-centred narratives. As she argues:

Through a sustained engagement with queer visual aesthetic practices, we can identify alternative ways of seeing and knowing capable of challenging the scopic and sensorial regimes of colonial modernity in their current forms. The aesthetic practices of queer diaspora, in other words, disrupt the normative ways of seeing and knowing that have been so central to the production, containment, and disciplining of sexual, racial, and gendered bodies; ...

(Gopinath, 2018: 7)

In a similar vein to Gopinath, El-Tayeb uses queer theory to analyse diaspora and ethnicity. She interrogates the 'national' through which exclusion takes place, exploring the means by which minorities are constructed as being outside the national politics, culture, and history and represented as not being British, German, Spanish, and so on. Her book focuses on Europe and delineates the ways in which racialised groups are externalised from Europe so that their histories of longstanding connections with Europe are concealed. For her, the alternative community building by a variety of groups she analyses such as the Black Women's Summer School in Germany might be best conceptualised as 'queering ethnicity'. The term would seem to refer to the mixing and matching of genres and styles in the cultural processes of performativity, which resists notions of purity, authenticity, and 'uncomplicated belonging'. The term diaspora is important here as it transcends such binaries as citizen and foreigner and defies linear models of movement from origin to destination. As we have already seen, El-Tayeb does not define diaspora in terms of a common origin but rather as a shared "contemporary condition". It shifts its gaze from a "temporal and spatial displacement" oriented towards the past to one "of productive dislocation directed as the future" (El-Tayeb, 2011: xxxv). This does, however, beg the question as to how one distinguishes diasporas such as South Asian from say, Armenian, without some notion of common background in so far as these terms stand for specific and distinctive genealogies. Does this distinctiveness not include some notion of a shared ethnicity that distinguishes them? Ethnicity is historical not essential. Yet ethnicity may include reference to some shared notion of common identification with a region or place. In other words, as I noted previously, it may be argued that diaspora can simultaneously reference 'a shared history and/or genealogy' and 'contemporary condition'. It is my hope that these discussions lead to productive lines of inquiry which, rather than enact finality and enclosure, introduce fresh insights and inject open mindedness in conversation and debate.

Chapter 6

Contemporary Feminist Discourses and Practices within and across Boundaries: A Conversation between Avtar Brah and Clelia Clini

Clini: Dear Professor Brah, first of all, thank you for agreeing to this interview. As you know, this issue of the journal *Genre, Sexualité et Société* is specifically focused on feminism and on the production, circulation and consumption of images (in the arts as well as in the media) related to gender and sexuality. As we are adopting an interdisciplinary approach to the analysis of feminism, our aim is also to expand the debate by bringing in feminist voices from different fields and locations, so to explore the 'boundaries' and the crossing of boundaries of feminist discourses and practices. We are thus interested in the 'wordliness', to borrow Edward Said's (1983) expression, of feminist discourses and practices as well as in the dynamics of power that shape feminist discourses as well as contemporary discourses on feminism. As a feminist scholar and an activist you could certainly help us in developing a debate on these issues.

For a start, we would like to ask about your own approach to feminism and feminist politics. Could you please comment on how your own experiences of having been born in Panjab and raised in Uganda, and your subsequent experience of studying in the US and the UK, have influenced your approach to feminism?

Brah: I was born in Panjab and went to Uganda at the age of about six. During my early school years Uganda was still a colony or a 'Protectorate' to be precise. Uganda achieved independence during my high school years so that I learned what it meant to live in a society in which White Europeans were at the top, Black Africans were at the bottom, and the South Asians were in the middle. You became tuned to what it means to view the world within and across this racial and class divide. At a personal level, I became aware of the social and psychological impact of the simultaneous positionality of dominance and subordination, and of the complex entanglements of colonial power hierarchies. Gender was inextricably linked with the workings of this coloniality as well as caste and religious differences. I remember that when Uganda became independent, I was sent to stay with an uncle and aunt's family in Tanzania because my parents had memories of the carnage at the time of Indian Independence from Britain in 1947, when Panjab was partitioned and during the mass movement of population across the borders of newly created Pakistan women were subjected to sexual violence and rape from all sides. This fear of sexual violence was transposed to the Ugandan case where in reality no such incidents, to my knowledge, took place. Anxieties about Black male sexuality together with those of men of different castes and religions were due to the South Asian practice of caste and religious exogamy. These prohibitions did not affect general everyday social interactions among South Asians but came to the fore whenever these boundaries were challenged by potential sexual or marital liaison across race, caste, or religion.

My consciousness as a child about anti-colonial politics was influenced by radio news bulletins about the Mau Mau struggles in Kenya, the tales of the struggle for Indian Independence, and some Indian films that provided progressive visions of society. On gender issues, the Panjabi poet and novelist Amrita Pritam and the novelist Nanak Singh, and the poet Sahir Ludhianvi were my guide. I was introduced to their works when I was about 12-years-old, and I was nurtured by their nuanced but trenchant critiques of patriarchal values.

I had a strong identification with Uganda as home. I stayed up late into the night to listen to the commentary on radio in Tanzania, as the Ugandan flag was raised at the Independence ceremony in 1962. I felt a sense of deep pride when the national anthem was played. Of course, I know now how such patriotic sentiments can also be mobilised in the name of nationalisms such as those that stalk Europe today. My identity as a 'Ugandan of Asian origin' provided me with a means of reflection on the nature of hybrid identities, and the power dynamics which underpin them.

When I went to the USA in the late 1960s, I became involved in student politics and became aware of the plight of African Americans. The Civil Rights Movement and The Black Power Movement prevailed as a potent political force. The grapes boycott with Caesar Chavez as its leader drew attention to the conditions of migrant labour in California. The interconnections between gender, race and class were now beginning to impinge on my consciousness though the language of race and class or patriarchal relations was not yet part of my everyday vocabulary. I was also attracted to the message of the peace movement, and was active in the anti-Vietnam war politics. At the same time, the flower power of the 'Hippy' groups was also attractive. All this made me question the relative merits or otherwise of militant vs pacifist political strategies and action. I felt ambivalent about the two sets of competing strategies, and that ambivalence still remains. After completing my studies in the USA, I came to Britain during the early 1970s for a short visit on my way back to Uganda but became a refugee when Idi Amin expelled Asians from Uganda and I could not return. In Britain, I came to be engaged in socialist feminist politics, initially through the Women's Liberation Movement (WLM) but later through the aegis of Black Women's groups such as the Organisation of Women of Asian and African Descent, and Southall Black Sisters. These feminist politics addressed patriarchal relations within their global context of colonialism and imperialism. We examined gendered class inequities and inequalities of the global South and North, interrogated their relationality, and attempted to develop strategies for change that were sensitive to these broader transnational interconnections.

Clini: You are often cited as a key figure of transnational feminism. Could you please tell us how you define transnational feminism and what do you think is its use nowadays?

Brah: Transnational feminism is about understanding how patriarchal relations are enmeshed within power geometries of global relations. Global inequities and inequalities underpin, construct, and position different patriarchal formations in relation to one another. That is to say that in order to address gender relations today we need to examine how and in what ways they are impacted upon by imperial/ neo-imperial and colonial/postcolonial power dynamics. Contemporary global socio-political, economic, and cultural configurations have a critical bearing on inscribing gender relations. For instance, to speak of Pakistani Muslim women in Britain means we must address the history of the partition of India and the creation of Pakistan, the emerging postcolonial relations between Pakistan and Britain, and the resonance of these in the postcoloniality of Britain in its global context today. The life experiences of these women are impacted upon not only by patriarchal relations prevailing within Pakistani groups (with all their class, regional, and linguistic internal differences) but also by gender relations as they exist in British society as a whole. These patriarchal relations are refracted through the prism of racism. Britain's role in the wars in the Middle East and its fall out, especially in the emergence of Islamophobia, is highly relevant to understanding the lives of Pakistani women. The discourse of 'Muslim woman' is singularly orientalised and racialised. There have been instances of Muslim women being subjected to racial abuse, attacked on the street, and some of their items of clothing, especially the hijab, being pulled off their heads. The power of whiteness has its bearing on how Muslim women are discursively constructed and represented.

As feminists, we take it as a given that we critique and challenge patriarchal social formations. Yet we need also to be attentive to how different categories of people are 'Othered'. White women are 'Othered' but differently from women of colour and there are power relations inscribed in this relationship which need to be taken into account. Similarly categories such as trans, heteronormativity, and queer have their own specificity. There are global dimensions to all these. Transnational feminism keeps us attentive to these differentials and divisions.

Clini: You have been one of the strongest advocates of intersectionality. In *Cartographies of Diaspora* you discussed the condition of South Asian Muslim women working in the UK and the gendered and racialised discourses built around them. What do you think has changed in the past 20 years? How do you think dominant discourses tend to frame immigrant Muslim women in the UK, and Europe in general, nowadays?

Brah: Much has changed in the last 20 years – some things for the better and others for the worse. The 9/11 destruction of the Twin Towers in New York in 2001 ushered a new phase in global relations. Trust between different groups was replaced by suspicion. The 'War on Terror' unleashed polarised forces. The wars in Afghanistan, Iraq, Libya, Syria, South Sudan, and so on have devastated whole regions of the globe. Economically, neoliberal regimes have taken root globally and deepened global inequality. The proliferation of new information technologies and social media have nurtured new and instantaneous modes of communication bringing the world closer, but at the same time they simultaneously entrench technologies of surveillance and control. After the 1989 fall of the Berlin Wall there was hope for global peace, but this hope has been depleted and we seem to have a new 'cold war' between Russia and the West, which could pose a threat to world peace. Floods, tsunami, droughts, and other forms of environmental degradation exacerbate the conditions of world poverty, which can have the effect of setting new population movements in train. It is in this broader context that gender relations are currently played out. Muslim women have been orientalised in Western discourses for a very long time, but they are now subjected to a new racism called 'Islamophobia', and are represented as a threat par excellence to the very core of Western civilisation. They are socially constructed as the polar opposite of the Western woman. Of course, while many Muslim women remain one of the most disadvantaged groups in Britain, others have done well in all areas of life. There are journalists, Members of Parliament, entrepreneurs, academics, professionals, and so on. Intersectionality teaches us to analyse the interrelationship of such differential social and cultural location and discursive representation. It focuses on the interlinks between gender, race, class, sexuality, disability, and so on under such global geo-political scenarios.

Clini: How do you think an intersectional framework of analysis could be helpful in understanding the social and political events of our time? I'm thinking especially of the current 'refugee crisis', but also of the impact of Brexit on the lives of immigrant women – what do you think of the ways in which refugees are framed in dominant discourses (in the UK and Europe)?

Brah: Intersectionality, as Ann Phoenix and I defined it in 2004, signifies the complex outcomes when multiple axes of differentiation such as the economic, political, and cultural, intersect in historically specific contexts. Collins and Bilge (2016: 2) argue that "people's lives and the organisation of power in a given society are better understood as shaped by not a single axis of division, be it race or gender or class, but by many axes that work together and influence each other". These local and global contexts are intimately intertwined. Above I have described some of the key social and political events of our time. Indeed, the 'refugee crisis' is an outcome of the wars, political conflicts, global poverty, and environmental crisis. These factors work together and create conditions which make people flee their homes and become refugees. Of course, it goes without saying that the refugee is not a homogenous category. Different subjects and subjectivities emerge depending on the particular differentiations – such as gender, class, ethnicity, age, and generation – which articulate and come into play in specific circumstances. The 'refugee crisis' is in effect a crisis in global governance in which powerful nations and global political institutions play a central part. The recent and current arrival of refugees in Europe has unleashed virulent racism and xenophobia or xenoracism. In Brexit Britain this has attained levels rarely reached before. Individuals born and brought up in

Britain have been told to 'go home' by their fellow citizens. They are blamed for taking their jobs away, for competing with them for housing, education, and social welfare. Yet, evidence shows that immigrants and refugees are likely to do jobs locals do not wish to do, and that problems of inequality which affect those at the lower rungs of society are endemic to neoliberal regimes. They are underpinned by the government's social, economic, and political policies. There are as we know some critiques of intersectionality, one of which is concerned with whether or not intersectionality has its own methodology that differentiates it from that which pertains to other subject disciplines. I favour the view that methodologies derived from particular subject disciplines are important and that you frame the analysis using your own specific subject based methodology. I concur with Sumi Cho, Kimberlé William Crenshaw, and Leslie McCall that "intersectionality is best framed as an analytic sensibility" (Cho et al. 2013: 795). So, as they argue, you do not regard categories as inherently and completely different and distinct but always permeated by other categories. What is crucial is the nature of the intersection between categories and their outcomes at the level of social structure, subjectivity, identity, and experience, marked as they all are by dynamics of power (Brah, 1996). It is in this broader sense that intersectionality can help us make sense of problems today.

Clini: Connected to the previous question is the aftermath of the events of New Year's Eve in Germany (2015–2016), when Muslim men were alleged to have attacked white women. The ensuing debate saw the popular resurrection of issues such as: (1) the need to protect 'our' women from the 'Other'; (2) the competition of antiracism and antisexism, as feminists have been accused yet again of being silent on the attacks for the sake of anti- racism. Could you please comment on that?

Brah: Violence against women is endemic to most societies. In Britain, an incident of gender-based violence and abuse is reported to the police every minute, largely perpetuated by men against women (amnesty.org.uk). Apparently, seven women are killed every month by partners or ex-partners. Sexual harassment at work and in public places is common as a Trade Union Congress report demonstrates (10 August 2016). This is the context in which the New Year's Eve sexual assault needs to be understood. Without doubt we take a position against such assaults against women while at the same time draw attention to the violence against women perpetrated by men in general. We should not be silent on the attacks but we must simultaneously expose the 'rescue narratives' for what they are – an attempt to shore up what is mainly white male privilege. Moreover, we must challenge the way in which the actions of a few Muslim men are made to stand for all Muslim men, the seeming assertion being that they are more violent than non-Muslim men, which they are not.

Clini: What do these simultaneous attacks on feminists by several journalists and politicians (in Europe but the US as well) say about feminism in the twenty-first century?

Brah: Feminism in the twenty-first century is a beleaguered project. The intersectionality of gender, race and religion is a combustible mix. Understanding these issues demands complex and nuanced analysis which are irreducible to the conventional binaries of Right/ Left or secular/religious. But, by the same token, feminism is needed more than ever. We need to be mindful of all that potentially divides us so as to work through strategies to foreground all that we hold in common and that holds us together.

Clini: What about the state of feminism in the US? What have been the implications of Trump's election and the Weinstein scandal?

Brah: The election of Trump posed severe challenges for feminist politics. His embodiment of a sexist, aggressive kind of masculinity became normalised for some sections of the population, which is sympathetic to the neo-con values. As was the case with Thatcherism and Reaganism, a new common sense emerged in the wake of Trumpism, in which the values of the new right became commonplace, and his supporters have included many women. For feminists, the challenge is to dislodge and replace this common sense. This feminist project will have to operate at all levels of the social formation – economic, cultural, political, experiential, and subjective levels. It will involve the development of whole new sets of diverse practices informed by feminism. But, of course, women are already engaged in combatting this common sense and resisting sexism in general. The scandal of Harvey Weinstein in the film industry is part and parcel of a culture of violence against women. The hashtag #metoo represents a very significant fight back by women against such violence. It has shown how pervasive and acceptable this violence is across all sectors of society. The reluctance of some men in power to acknowledge the gravity of the situation also speaks of an enduring resistance to change. In a number of cases, there has been victim-blaming and it shows how difficult it is for women to come forward and disclose that they have been violated.

Clini: In the wake of the 2003 war against Iraq you and Ann Phoenix wrote, in 'Ain't I a Woman', that "that feminist dialogues and dialogic imaginations provide powerful tools for challenging the power games currently played out on the world stage" (Brah and Phoenix, 2004: 84). How would you apply this suggestion to current world politics?

Brah: Current world politics is an extremely complex ensemble. On the economic front, inequality persists both within and between nation states. Political strife and wars are converting large and thriving cities into rubble, making millions homeless. The 2003 war in Iraq was a watershed moment when, among other sites, the Middle East became a major focal point for the twenty-first century power manoeuvres for global hegemonies. We live in a strongly polarised world. Human security is under threat, not just from politics of radical extremism the world over but also from state machinations of various global powers through surveillance, control, and war. There is a serious question about the links between the foreign policies of some Western nations and the various wars waging around us, and the role in this of the new rather cool if not antagonistic relation between Russia and the West. At the same time there is violence by extremist groups which gives succour to those political actors who regard war as the only solution. Feminist peace movements pose radical challenge to militarised regimes. Yet, there are also divisions among feminists about these issues. There were feminists who supported the 2003 Iraq war, and there are others who remain in favour of the war in Syria. Then there are those of us who prefer political negotiation and peaceful solutions to violence and war. If we had to live in Europe with the everyday devastation of war that people, say, in Syria have to live through, what would our reactions be? We could not afford to be complacent then and would need to find peaceful solutions.

Clini: Despite the attacks it receives, feminism seems also to be experiencing a newly found popularity nowadays. What do you think are the most pressing issues feminists should focus on these days?

Brah: Struggles against global/local economic, political, and cultural inequities and inequalities remain paramount. Economic inequalities between men and women such as the gender pay gap are still rife. Women are the hardest hit by the austerity policies of governments. Women are underrepresented in the higher echelons of society. Violence against women must be combatted. Trafficking of women is a major issue to be addressed. Racism, xeno-racism and discrimination against migrants, refugees, asylum seekers, people of colour, Jewish people, Muslims, Gypsies, LGBTQ people is one of the most pressing issues to confront us today. The political Right is gaining strength throughout Europe, and is fuelling virulent nationalisms. Strategies to deal with these racisms and nationalisms is an urgent task for feminists. Degradation of the environment is at crisis point and must be addressed with great urgency. Campaigns to end wars through peaceful means, I believe, are a feminist priority. We have a very full agenda.

Clini: One last question about your involvement with the *Feminist Review*. As the longest-standing member of the collective, how do you think feminism and feminist politics have changed in the past 20 years?

Brah: As I noted above, I came to Britain from the USA in the early 1970s when the Women's Liberation Movement was getting off the ground. I became involved in a conscious-raising group in Bristol where I was working as a research assistant and doing my PhD at the same time. We were a predominantly white middle-class group. In fact, I was the only woman-of-colour member. We attended some of the early national feminist conferences. Again there were very few women of colour at the conferences. I remember that at one of the conferences, we tried to raise the importance of racism as a feminist issue, but this claim was largely ignored. Questions of sexuality and lesbian politics were also being raised. Gradually, I met other feminists of colour in Bristol and we formed a feminist group called Bristol Black Sisters. The term 'Black' was then being used as a political colour to bring about solidarity among African, Caribbean, and Asian people against colour-coded racism in the British context of postcoloniality. Later I moved to London and became one of the founding members of Southall Black Sisters, an organisation which is still active today. Nationally, we were part of the Organization of Women of Asian and African Descent (OWAAD), a body to which other local organisations were affiliated. Many of us were also socialists, so class politics was also at the centre of our concerns. The journal *Feminist Review* defined itself as a socialist feminist journal. Hence it was a kind of natural intellectual and political home for me and I became a member of the editorial collective. Some of the key debates of the time – around racism, ethnicity, class, sexuality, debility, 'the family', patriarchy, reproduction, domestic labour, subjectivity, psychoanalysis, and so on – took place on the pages of *Feminist Review*. Much of the early debates were centred on the binary male/female and the question of the indeterminacy of 'sex' as a category was yet to be addressed.

When, more recently, the question of 'third wave' feminism came to the fore, its advocates recognised the advances made by the 'second wave' but also critiqued some of its goals and assumptions. In some 'third wave' writings the 'second wave' appears mostly white and middle class, partly because the struggles of women-of-colour feminists tend to be written out of standard feminist accounts (Jonsson, 2016). As I have already said, we, women of colour, were present right at the beginning of WLM. Third wave also claimed that the 'second wave' was focused primarily on issues of economic, educational, and political access, which they considered rather narrow. By contrast, they regarded themselves as more inclusive and transformative in their goals. Of course, one could take issue with the claim that economic, educational, and political access are narrow concerns.

The point of inclusion was also raised way back in the 1970s by women of colour so that, although the term intersectionality was not deployed, questions of inclusion and the power relations underpinning them were firmly on the agenda. So what is new is the theorisation of the concept of intersectionality. Scholarship on sexuality too has developed and expanded in a hugely significant way, to the extent that now there are book titles such as *After Queer Theory*. The question of fluid sexual identities is not entirely new, but it has gained a very significant momentum now. There has also been much wider emphasis recently on the trafficking of women globally, as it is on the struggles of refugee and migrant women reaching the southern shores of Europe from perilous journeys by land and by sea, many drowning on the way.

How useful is the wave metaphor discussed above remains an open question and, in any case, different texts offer different chronologies of the development of histories of different 'waves' or 'formations' of feminism. Compared to the 'second wave, 'third wave feminism' has been seen as broader in vision, more focused on global issues and sensitive to factors such as racism. It is represented as inclusive and committed to transformative politics. These histories have, of course, been contested so that there is a destabilisation of standard chronologies. What is important is that we recognise the importance of working through differences if coalitions are to be built across variance, divergence, and dissimilarity. We need to address how economic, political, and cultural factors intersect and impact our daily lives. In the context of politics where figures such as Donald Trump as the then president of the USA championed Islamophobia, misogyny and virulent nationalism, the politics of resistance to this kind of toxicity are crucial. Such politics have been resoundingly opposed by women's protests, which took place all over the world. The recent election of Jo Biden as the president and Kamala Harris as vice-president of the USA seem to usher the possibility of a different kind of politics to that of the Trump era. Therein lies some hope but there is little room for complacency.

Interviewer Biography

Clelia Clini is a Research Associate at Loughborough University London, where she works on the project 'Migrant Memory and the Postcolonial Imagination: British Asian Memory, Identity and Community After Partition.' Her research interests lie at the intersection of migration and diaspora studies, South Asian postcolonial cinema and literature, race and gender studies, and cultural sociology. Before joining Loughborough University London, she was a Research Associate at UCL, where she worked on a project on forced displacement, creativity, and wellbeing. Clelia has taught Media, Cultural and Postcolonial Studies at John Cabot University and at The American University at Rome (2012–2016). She has a PhD in Cultural and Postcolonial Studies of the Anglophone World from the University of Orientale of Naples. This interview was conducted for a special issue of the French journal *Genre, Sexualité et Société*. It has also been published in 2017 in the journal *Feminist Review*, issue 117.

Chapter 7

Multiple Axes of Power: Interrelations between Diaspora and Intersectionality

It is evident that migrations form a key phenomenon in the contemporary globalised world. As we have already seen, the UN World Migration Report for the year 2020 shows that there are 281 million people in the world who are migrants, of whom 51.9 per cent are men and 48.1 per cent are women. This figure includes 26.3 million refugees and 4.2 million asylum seekers. In other words, global migrants range from economic migrants, through trafficked persons to refugees and asylum seekers (Braziel and Mannur, 2003; Braziel, 2008; Knott and McLoughlin, 2010). These migrations create a plethora of diasporas. Of course, not all migrations comprise diasporas. There has been considerable debate surrounding the criteria that may be used to define a particular migration as a diaspora. Our discussion in previous chapters shows that scholars such as William Safran (1991), James Clifford (1994) and Robin Cohen (1997) have been centrally engaged in such debate. At minimum, diasporas are not temporary sojourns; rather they are about settling down 'elsewhere', though the notion of creating a 'home' away from the place of 'origin' has been seriously problematised (see Chapter 5). According to scholars such as Fatima El-Tayab, it is the 'contemporary condition' of diasporicity rather than 'shared origins' that are important in defining diasporas. Over the decades, considerable effort has gone into theorising and analysing different formations of diaspora and there have been major shifts in conceptualising diaspora with dynamic conceptions acquiring greater salience over time (cf. Hall, 1990; Gilroy, 1993; Bhabha, [1994] 2004; Brah, 1996; Cohen, 1997; El-Tayab, 2011). The study of diasporas is largely a transdisciplinary endeavour based on the use of what I call 'creolised theory'. That is to say that analysis of diasporic projects calls for the use of conceptual tools and analytical insights from different subject disciplines, theoretical paradigms, and political movements.

Diaspora/Intersectionality Articulations

As I have noted in Chapter 5, diasporas are inherently intersectional and the study of diaspora and intersectionality is intrinsically connected. For instance, as an empirical trajectory diaspora cannot be understood as a homogenous category. A specific diaspora is differentiated according to factors such as gender, race, class, caste, ethnicity, and sexuality. As a concept too, diaspora is an articulation of diverse narratives enunciated from various 'situated' positions, or from a 'situated and embodied knowledge' to use the formulation posed by Donna Haraway (1988). This 'positionality of location' is one of dispersal along multiple axes of differentiation. And the situated knowledges and positions are the terrain upon which the embodiment of our specificity is constructed. We become a 'woman' or a 'racialised person', or a 'classed individual' in and through the social, political, and psychic effects that ensue through interplay of intersecting axes of differentiation. I have argued elsewhere that the concept of diaspora centres on the configurations of historically specific modalities of power which undergird, mark, and differentiate diasporas internally as well as situate them in relation to one another (Brah, 1996; see also Chapter 5). The concept of diaspora is a genealogical one, and it signals the historically variable analysis of economic, political, and cultural forms in their inter- and intra-relationality. That is to say, this genealogical analysis is intersectional. There is some concern in the field of diaspora studies that the concept of diaspora overemphasises mobilities, and the routes are foregrounded at the expense of roots. In my view the two aspects are not mutually exclusive: diasporas are simultaneously about 'space' and 'place', about movement as well as settling down and 'living side by side' as Bhabha (2013) puts it. It is important to pay attention to both features of diaspora. I have described articulation of the 'genealogies of dispersal' with those of 'staying put' as 'diaspora space'. Within this conception of 'diaspora space' multi-locationality, home, homing desire, and belonging are juxtaposed with historical temporalities and diasporic spatialities. How does a site of migration become home? How do we come to 'feel at home'? This is a complex question, one that brings the social and the psychic simultaneously into play. A home, whether in the sense of a dwelling in which we reside or a country or region in which we live, is often *assumed* to be a 'safe' place, but it is not always the case, something that physically and psychologically abused persons know all too well. In terms of a nation state, a region, or locality immigrants may reside in a given place but they may often be constructed and represented as the 'Other'. They may experience all manner of discrimination and made to feel as outsiders. They could be denied citizenship rights. Or, they may have legal rights but may not still be seen to belong to the larger community or the nation. There could well be terror on the streets directed against racialised, or ethnicised people who may or may not be immigrants. All this mitigates against 'feeling at home' on the part of the diasporic groups. Yet there are also the intimacies of everyday life – kinship bonds, friendships, relations of conviviality, neighbourliness, collegiality, interconnections of love – which make a place feel like home. Feeling at home is essentially about feeling secure and having a sense of belonging – but this cannot be taken for granted, may have to be struggled over, and for migrants (or even for the generations that follow them) remain an on-going project rather than a once-and-for-all established fact. The concept of diaspora space addresses the complexity of encounters between those who have migrated and those others who might regard themselves as Indigenous. Diaspora space emphasises the interactions between the psychic and the social, between subjectivity and identity, and between the material, the imaginary and the imaginative. As Kim Knott (2010) notes:

It is necessary, then, for scholars of diaspora to adopt and work with a multi-dimensional understanding of space and movement that does not restrict to actual physical migration but makes room also for imagined, discursive, material, cultural, virtual, and socially net-worked places and travels [...]. A key challenge for diaspora studies is to engage with the realities of settlement, the political contingencies and relationships of diaspora space, as well as the narratives of travel and circulation, and the location of diasporic subjectivity.

(79–83)

So far, I have been concerned with issues to do with diaspora. But how do vectors of differentiation play out in designate contexts? As regards this, the concept of 'intersectionality' is likely to be invoked in order to analyse how different social groups are socially and culturally situated in relation to one another. There are varying 'origin stories' in terms of how and where the concept of intersectionality first emerged. The most generally accepted narrative is that the concept was first 'named' in the US where it is associated with individuals and groups such as the Combahee River Collective, Kimberlé Crenshaw, and Patricia Hill Collins. As Jennifer C. Nash (2019) reminds us, the term is most closely linked with Crenshaw's two articles 'Demarginalizing the Intersections of Race and Sex: A Black Feminist Critique of Antidiscrimination Doctrine, Feminist Theory and Antiracist Politics' (1989) and 'Mapping the Margins: Intersectionality, Identity Politics and Violence against Women of Color' (1991). The emphasis here is explicitly on the experience of Black women and women of colour. But Nash (2008) raises an important question: she asks whether or not all identities are intersectional or does the concept only refer to marginalised subjects. Naomi Zack (2005) foregrounds the concept's reference to multiple oppressions experienced by women of colour and working-class/poor women but also points out that it is, at the same time, applicable more generally because additional factors including sexuality, disability/debility, and age are also sites of subordination and oppression. The concept of intersectionality, as is now widely recognised, has been mobilised first and foremost within feminist discourse and practice. It grew out of feminist critiques that sought to emphasise the heterogeneity of the category 'woman'. For instance, there are class differences among women. Different groups of women are differently and differentially racialised. Women comprise different ethnicities. They may be hetero-sexual, queer, trans, nonbinary, intersex. Such differentiations are politically relevant in terms of how individuals and groups self-identify as well as the manner in which they are socially positioned. There have been longstanding debates surrounding these factors, which remain relevant today not only because they highlight and signal diversity, important though that fact is, but because they raise the related issues in terms of how best to theorise and understand such differences. In what ways do we address the concept of 'difference' and what appropriate theoretical and methodological resources are necessary for analysing different intersecting axes? I have theorised 'difference' across four articulating axes, namely, those constituting social relation, and mapping experience, subjectivity, and identity (see below). Intersectionality is sometimes seen as another term for 'diversity' and 'inclusion', thereby deflecting attention away from intersectionality's emphasis on the workings of power. Each axis of intersectionality, say, class, stands for a specific modality of power that, in turn, interacts with formations of power surrounding other axes. As Sara Ahmed (2012) points out, feminists of colour have offered some of the most incisive critiques of the language of diversity, and have favoured the concept of intersectionality as a more useful alternative analytic. Chandra Mohanty (2003), for instance, conceptualises diversity as "benign variation" at best or in a more pejorative sense as "empty pluralism". To some people, the language of diversity tends to be more palatable, more easily acceptable, than that of equality/inequality which underpins the discourse of intersectionality, because the discourse of diversity is less likely to generate antagonism.

In 2004, Ann Phoenix and I wrote about the discourses on intersectionality, and we started with nineteenth-century debates which pre-empt what today goes by the name of 'intersectionality'. We started with the well-known nineteenth-century locution in the USA, 'Ain't I a woman?', and I believe it is helpful to begin with it again for it places questions of power into stark relief. Nineteenth-century contestations among feminists involved anti-slavery struggles and campaigns for women's suffrage, and they showed how untenable essentialist notions of the category 'woman'/ 'man'/ 'trans'/ 'intersex'/ 'nonbinary' are. These categories and positionalities are inscribed within and across such social divisions as racism, gender, ethnicity, sexuality, and disability/ debility. Ann Phoenix and I described the concept of 'intersectionality' in terms of historically specific, irreducible, and varied effects which emerge when multiple axes of differentiation intersect with one another. I still find this approach to theorising intersectionality useful, with an emphasis on historically specific socio-economic, cultural, and political effects arising from the articulations of a multiplicity of power dynamics. It challenges the additive models of discussions on the subject. There are those who argue that debates on intersectionality fail to take on board issues of colonialism, imperialism, and postcolonialism. But this patently would not be the case in the above definition. Historically, specific intersectional relations must, in my view, emphatically address questions of coloniality, postcoloniality, and imperialisms in their various varieties. There has also been some criticism that intersectional studies may not always attend to transnational and global concerns (Purkayastha, 2010; Anthias, 2012). This is an important point, yet when *diasporic* intersectional analysis is conducted questions of transnationalism become central. The discourse of intersectionality has also been taken to task for theoretical vagueness (Knapp, 2005), and that it underemphasises class and social relations of capitalism (Skeggs, 2004). Again these are vital issues to take on board. In my own thinking, class and questions of capitalism are central to theorising intersecting relations of gender, race, disability, and so on. These social formations are not disconnected but thoroughly imbricated. A critique of what is viewed as an over-emphasis on the concept of the 'subject' in much intersectional theorisation has been made by scholars such as Jasbir K. Puar who work on postrepresentional, posthuman, or postsubject conceptualisations of the body and thereby interrogate subject-centric discourses (Puar, 2012b; 2017). I am sympathetic to some aspects of her critique but would suggest that such alternatives as the discourse of 'postsubject' may usefully decentre the 'subject' but it would not be helpful to attempt to entirely replace the 'subject.'

It is worth reminding us that the question 'Ain't I a woman?' was first articulated by Sojourner Truth, a woman freed from slavery. She took this name instead of her original name, Isabella, when she became a travelling preacher. It is also important to bear in mind that the first anti-slavery society was formed in 1832 by Black women in Salem, Ohio, in the USA. Yet a decade later, Black women were absent from the Seneca Falls Anti-Slavery convention of 1848 where white middle-class women debated the motion for women's suffrage. Sojourner Truth campaigned for both the abolition of slavery and women's rights. Referring to the prevailing codes of sexualised chivalry among white communities, this ex-slave said:

> That man over there says that women need to be helped into carriages, and lifted over ditches, and to have the best place everywhere. Nobody helps me into carriages, or over mud-puddles, or gives me any best place! And ain't I a woman? Look at me! Look at my arm! I have ploughed and planted, and gathered into barns, and no man could head me! And ain't I a woman? I could work as much and eat as much as a man – when I could get it – and bear the lash as well! And ain't I a woman? I have borne thirteen children, and seen most all sold off to slavery, and when I cried out with my mother's grief, none but Jesus heard me! And ain't I a woman?
>
> (https://sourcebooks.fordham.edu/mod/sojtruth-woman.asp)

This speech had a resounding impact at the conference and it circulated widely among political activists and other opinion makers. What is particularly significant is that it embodies a powerful critique of patriarchal gender relations and racism in slave societies. Its powerful critique and searing imagination poses a challenge to hegemonic moves of all kinds, and its message remains relevant today. It pre-figures contemporary debates on the interlinks between such factors as racism, gender, pre-capitalist social relations, sexuality, and questions of embodiment.

Another definition of 'intersectionality', provided by Patricia Hill Collins and Sirma Bilge (2016), complements the one offered by Ann Phoenix and myself above. To rephrase, these authors note that the complexity of the social and political life cannot be understood as shaped by one factor but by multiple factors, and these social divisions entail the working together of these varying axis of differentiation: "Intersectionality as an analytic tool gives people better access to the complexity of the world and of themselves" (Collins and Bilge, 2016: 2; see also Chapter 5). However, Jasbir Puar, a long-term advocate of intersectionality, now valorises the concept of 'assemblage' to provide a different heuristic for her analytical project (Puar, 2017). For instance, she argues that "...the study of intersectional identities often involves taking imbricated identities apart one by one to see how they influence each other, a process that betrays the founding impulse of intersectionality, that identities cannot so easily be cleaved" (Puar, 2017: 212), whereas, following Deleuze and Guattari, assemblages are a confluence of multiplicities. Intersectional identities and assemblages, she stresses, must remain as "interlocuters in tension" with the former trying to stop or quell the perpetual motion of assemblages, to contain this threatening mobility. Differentiating the two dimensions further she adds, "Intersectionality privileges naming, visuality, epistemology, representation, and meaning, while assemblage underscores feeling, tactility, ontology, affect, and information" (Puar, 2017: 215). At one level, the two analytical modalities would seem to be complimentary rather than oppositional.

Within scholarly literature, intersectionality has been variously conceptualised as a framework, a metaphor, a paradigm, a concept, a heuristic device, as well as theory. In her most recent book, Collins (2019) evaluates whether intersectionality can be understood as a theory and concludes that it is a 'theory in the making'. In thinking through what makes intersectionality a critical theory, she addresses varying conceptions of what the term critical means, and, in so doing, places her analysis in conversation with critical theory of the Frankfurt School (1930s–1940s), strands of Francophone social theory (1950s and

1960s), and British Cultural Studies (1970s–1980s). Intersectionality is a project that mobilises knowledge of resistance which engenders oppositional politics in order to challenge the toxic effects of inequality, subordination, and injustice. Before the introduction of the concept of intersectionality, these multi-axial configurations of power were likely to be analysed as separate, even disconnected phenomena with the result that the interactions between them would be marginalised, if not erased. Collins describes intersectionality's multi-axial approach to thinking about the ways in which mutually constructed power relations shape social phenomena as producing a paradigm shift in analysis. In treating intersectionality as a paradigm, it is important to specify the core constructs and guiding premises that may be understood as its distinguishing features. According to Collins (2019), some of the core constructs that underlie intersectionality's critical inquiry include: relationality; power; social inequality; social context; complexity; and social justice. Although presented as discrete, they are in fact not so, working instead as enmeshed and articulating vectors. In other words, it is important to address how and in what ways these concepts function singly or in combination within a given intersectional investigation. Alongside these core constructs, Collins identifies the following four guiding premises that demarcate intersectional analytics:

i) Race, class, gender, and similar systems of power are interdependent and mutually construct one another.
ii) Intersecting power relations produce complex, interdependent social inequalities of race, class, gender, sexuality, nationality, ethnicity, ability, and age.
iii) The social location of individuals and groups within intersecting power relations shapes their experiences within and perspectives on the world.
iv) Solving social problems within a given local, regional, national, or global context requires intersectional analyses.

(Collins, 2019: 48)

Together, these core constructs and guiding premises provide a theoretical and political vocabulary and tools for addressing the particularity of intersectionality's operations. It is important that intersectionality is not cited as a mantra; rather, the problematic is to analyse the complexity of how and in what ways the articulations between specific axes take place. What theories and methods are deployed in a given analysis of the diasporic intersections? What multi- and interdisciplinary methodological frameworks are utilised?

On a similar note, Floya Anthias (2020) underscores the contribution that intersectionality has made to innovative theoretical and political analysis and practice designed to eliminate inequality and engender projects of social justice. She uses the concept of 'translocational intersectionality', by way of approaching dilemmas concerning the ways in which different forms of hierarchy interconnect. The notion of 'location' in translocation is understood as a broader term than place, figuring social location as social space defined by boundaries and hierarchies of difference where difference is understood as embodiment of power. As she argues, "... the notion of 'translocational' references the level of the *processual and the reinforcing or contradictory articulations of locations* across axes of difference *and* spatio-temporalities" (Anthias, 2020: 88, original emphasis). In other words, the emphasis is on the processual so that difference and inequality are understood as sets of processes with an emphasis on historicity and not defined in terms of characteristics of individuals. With its focus on gendered, ethnicised, and racialised relations at its core, translocational intersectionality makes it necessary to rethink traditional approaches to stratification.

The second half of the twentieth century witnessed a variety of social movements – anti-colonial struggles for independence, Civil Rights and Black Power movements, peace movements, student protests, and the workers' movements. Together, they expressed a serious disaffection with the vision of a centred universal subject of humanism. Within the academy, critiques of the self-referencing, unified subject of modernity flourished across academic disciplines. Within feminism, there was a systematic decentring of the 'normative subject' of other earlier phases of feminism. One of the first such critiques, as we have already seen, was mounted in 1977 by the Combahee River Collective, the Black lesbian feminist organisations from Boston, USA. They spoke against the many ways in which the experiences of women who were not white, middle-class or heterosexual were marginalised. Importantly for subsequent discussions of intersectionality, they argued against privileging a single dimension of experience as if it were the whole of life. Instead, they spoke of being "actively committed to struggling against racial, sexual, hetero-sexual and class oppression" and advocated "the development of inte-grated analysis and practice based upon the fact that the major systems of oppression are interlocking" (Combahee River Collective, 1977). This conceptualisation of 'interlocking oppressions' was one of the most productive insights of post-World War II feminisms. At the same time, while lesbian feminist activists were challenging the heteronormative focus of much feminist writing and politics, they were themselves being taken to task for treating some women's experiences as if they were mar-ginal. In the anthology, *This Bridge Called My Back: Writings by Radical Women of Colour*, Cherríe Moraga and Gloria Anzaldúa (1981) argued that lesbian feminism itself was enacting exclusions and overlooking the experience of lesbians of colour by not fully taking on board issues of racism. According to Kira Kosnick, there would seem to have been similar reservations about queer studies (Kosnick cited in Lutz et al., 2011), although increasingly queer studies is using intersectional ana-lyses of heteronormativity (Braziel, 2008). Queer intersectional studies, Kosnick argues, bring a deconstructive/post-structuralist perspective to bear upon intersectional modalities of subordination and privilege.

In Britain during the 1970s similar issues were raised by women who formed a coalition of Women of African, Caribbean, and Asian heritage under the common emblem of the 'Black'. As I pointed out in Chapter 2, we formed an organisation called OWAAD – Organisation of Women of Asian and African Descent. Its member organisations worked around a wide variety of issues such as wages and conditions of paid work, immigration law, fascist violence, reproductive rights, domestic violence, and many manifestations of racism and class inequality. It foregrounded unequal global relations between North and South in its postcolonial formations. It undertook 'integrated analysis' of racism, gender, and class while remaining sensitive to questions of cultural specificities. Yet it took little notice of lesbian and gay concerns. And when these concerns were raised at a conference, it created a huge controversy. During the 1970s and 1980s, the major contestation between what was then known as 'Black' and 'white' feminists prefigured later theories of 'difference' and those of intersectionality.

Thinking through Difference

The concept of difference is subject to ongoing debate. What are varying and variable meanings associated with different discourses of difference? Who has the power to define difference? What is the nature of normativities from which hegemonic difference is measured? By what processes is difference marked, constructed, challenged, maintained, or eroded? How are social groups represented in varying discourses of difference? How are hierarchies of difference instituted? What are the effects of social difference on the constitution of psychic and psychological structures? Such questions define the parameters within which questions of difference may be addressed.

Studies of diaspora and intersectionality share a common focus on difference. Much has been written on the subject of difference across different disciplines. In my own case, as I have said before, I have tried to work through this concept by suggesting that difference may be theorised along four axes: difference construed in terms of a social relation; difference understood as subjectivity; difference theorised as identity; and difference conceptualised as experience (Brah, 1996). Importantly, each of these axes is in turn marked by intersectionality. Although for analytic purposes these axes are presented as separate, they cross-cut and enmesh in practice. Experience, for instance, cannot be understood independently of social relations, nor do social relations exist without having a bearing on identity and subjectivity. Indeed, the four axes are centrally implicated in the constitution of one another.

As a social relation, difference is to be understood in structural terms along economic, political, and cultural discourses and institutional practices. Here it references the macro and micro regimes of power and status within and across which forms of differentiation are produced as structured formations. Social relations foreground systemic and systematic dimensions of social hierarchies and regimes of power. Structural features undergird our social positions and mark the many and variable ways that historical genealogies impact on everyday experiences. For instance, the life chances of barristers and doctors are different from manual workers. As a social relation this difference is expressed in different indices of quality of life such as health, education, residential environment, access to social amenities, and expenditure on travel. In other words, it is about access to differential resources and their use.

In terms of the second axis of difference, namely subjectivity, we need to explore the means by which the subject is socially and psychically produced. Here, the linguistic approach has been influential in analysing 'difference', though, of course, the question of affect and emotion and preverbal experiences remains critical even as language remains important in making verbal sense of these experiences. Within Saussurian and post-Saussurian linguistics, language represents a way of differentiating between things and relating them to one another. Meaning is understood as neither intrinsic nor referential but as relational and differential. In other words, each sign derives its meaning from its difference from all other signs in the chain. Since we develop our sense of ourselves in and through language, language is a major site of the formation of subjectivity. Issues of 'difference' have therefore figured prominently in debates about subjectivity. These debates have centred around various critiques of humanist conceptions of the subject. For example, as I have suggested before, "the notion of the subject as a unified, unitary, rational and rationalist 'point of origin' " (ibid.: 119) has been problematised, as is the view that emphasises conscious being while the workings of the unconscious are elided. Poststructural approaches question the view that consciousness is an origin, treating it instead as an effect of signification (Weedon, 1987; Belsey, 2002). Similarly, it is argued that the discourse of 'Universal Man' as the embodiment of an ahistorical essence is seriously flawed. Overall, there has been considerable contestation about the relative merits of critical discourse analysis as compared with psychoanalytic approaches to the constitution of the subject and subjectivity. I believe that both approaches are relevant. Psychoanalysis is important because it too disrupts the notion of a centred, unitary, rational self by foregrounding an inner world permeated by fantasy, conflict, non-rational and unruly responses, and desire. Difference as subjectivity, then, is neither unified nor fixed but fragmented, and continuously in process.

In relation to the third axis of difference, namely difference understood as experience, this is yet another arena of debate, as the concept of experience has been highly contested. It is now generally agreed that experience is not transparent. In other words, it does not transparently reflect a pre-given reality, it is not an unmediated guide to some pre-given transparent truth. Rather, experience is a cultural construction and it is the site of subject formation. Indeed, experience is a process of meaning-making which is the very basis of the constitution of that which we call 'reality'. Experience, as a signifying/coding practice, is embedded within symbolic and narrative means of making sense. It interrogates presumed essentialist truth claims, positing them as historically produced. This links with the idea of diaspora as a confluence of diverse and different narratives, both complementary and contradictory. The point is that experiences do not happen to a fully constituted subject; rather experience is the site of subject formation. That is, we are constituted in and through experiential processes and dynamics. Experience is mediated through intersectional social formations. As Joan W. Scott argues, analysing experience "entails focusing on processes of identity production, insisting on the discursive nature of 'experience' and on the politics of its construction. Experience is at once always already an interpretation *and* in need of interpretation. What counts as experience is neither self-evident nor straightforward; it is always contested, always therefore political" (Scott, 1992: 37). But experience is not only discursive in nature, it is, critically, also embedded in deep unconscious processes foregrounded by psychoanalysis. It is, therefore, not only consciously contested, but equally it is subject to unruly unconscious processes of suppression and repression glimpsed within dreams.

Finally, we consider 'difference' understood as identity. Indeed, struggles over identities are in part contestations over meaning. The problematic of difference and identity is relational. As Stuart Hall, drawing on Derrida's concept of *différance*, suggests, identity is always in process and not an established fact. He raises the question:

> If 'identities' can only be read against the grain – that is to say, specifically *not* as that which fixes the play of difference in a point of origin and stability, but as that which is constructed in or through *différance* and is constantly destabilised by what it leaves out, then how can we understand its meaning and how can we theorize its emergence?
>
> (Hall, 1996c: 5)

Although he is persuaded by the Foucauldian notion that the subject is constructed in discourse, Hall remains cautious in so far as this perspective fails to fully address how and why the subject identifies with some subject positions and not others. In an attempt to resolve this quandary, he opts for the use of psychoanalysis alongside the discursive approach. Identities are therefore not only what they seem on surface, rather they also resonate with the subconscious and unconscious subterranean modalities of affect.

It will be evident that the four axes of difference just described always interrelate and articulate. For example, identities are inscribed through experiences which, in turn, are culturally constructed within social relations. Subjectivity – our sense of ourselves and of our relation to the world – is the modality through which the precarity of the subject-in-process is experienced as identity. Identity, as is widely acknowledged, is neither fixed nor singular but rather it is a shifting multiplicity that assumes specific patterns in the context of given circumstances. But, I think that it is important to differentiate between identity as it pans out in its intimate relationship with unconscious process of subjectivity, and the highly conscious and reflexive acts of political identity. Political identity is a conscious avowal of specific positions and is part of the configuration of social relations. There is thus a constant inter- and intra-flow of conscious/ unconscious streams of processes in the play of identity. As such, there is an ongoing relationship between difference as theorised in terms of our collective 'histories' and difference understood as 'personal experience' codified in individual biographies. These domains constantly intersect but are irreducibly distinctive. How an individual subject relates to and experiences an event varies according to how he/she/they are culturally constructed; how the many and different and unpredictable ways these constructions are figured in the psyche; and the repertoire of political perspective and positionalities on offer. In other words, while personal biographies and group histories may be inherently interlinked, they are not reducible to one another. To theorise experience as subject formation means that the issue of agency is refigured so that, although the 'I' and the 'we' who act certainly do not disappear, they are refigured from being unified, fixed, fully-formed entities into multi-locationally inflected modalities marked by everyday cultural and political practices.

Intersectionality, Diaspora, and Policy

So far, I have argued that questions of intersectionality and diaspora have been directly or indirectly tied up with theorisation of the concept of difference. Here I explore intersectionality with regard to its workings within policy arenas. Over the decades, the discourse of intersectionality has come to be valorised not only within the academy, but it has also made a significant impact in policy circles. For example, during 2001, Kimberlé Crenshaw was invited to the World Conference Against Racism in Durban in South Africa to discuss her ideas. Nira Yuval-Davis (2006) notes that during the non-governmental organisation (NGO) session of the conference, Radhika Coomarswamy, the special rapporteur of the UN secretariat on violence against women, stated how the term 'intersectionality' had become extremely popular and used in various UN and NGO forums. Indeed, at the 58th session of the UN Commission of Human Rights on 23 April 2002, the resolution on the human rights of women in its first paragraph state that it: "recognised the importance of examining the intersection of multiple forms of discrimination, including their root causes from a gender perspective" (Resolution E/CN.4/2002/1.59).

Within the European Union, anti-discrimination policy was embedded in the legislation of member states. The process of the adaptation of the European Non-Discriminatory Directives into the national law of member states allowed for a discussion of multiple forms of discrimination and the intersectionality approach was debated for the first time. Hence, according to the European Commission Report of 2007, a certain notion of multiple discrimination is characterised as 'intersectional discrimination' (European Commission, 2007).

Within the academy, there has been a proliferation of discourses of intersectionality, especially within feminism. In recent years, an increasing number of special issues of journals, books, conferences, PhD courses, and programmes have been devoted to the study of the topic. But, as Collins and Bilge (2016) note, intersectionality frameworks are utilised not only within diverse academic disciplines, but also by human rights activists, government officials, grassroots organisations, bloggers on digital and social media, and practitioners in education and welfare. They discuss its global dispersion across these fields.

Despite its popularity in certain circles, intersectionality has not, as already seen above, been without its critics. In a similar vein, during a debate held at a conference at Goldsmiths College of the University of London ('Feminist Genealogies' conference held in May 2012) some scholars argued that the preoccupation with intersectionality can serve to deflect attention away from a focus on social class. I would suggest that this criticism is somewhat difficult to sustain given that social class is considered a crucially important feature of intersectionality. Furthermore, it is also alleged that intersectionality emphasises categories of identity at the expense of structures of inequality. But, as

I have suggested before, axes of differentiation may not be understood as identity categories but rather as modalities of asymmetrical power. Another criticism, which has some validity, has been whether the metaphor of 'intersection' – with its image of roads crossing – is adequate for the critical task of analysing power differentials, normativities, and identity formation across multiple fields of gender, racism, class, sexuality, and so on. But if intersection is understood as an '*articulation*', as I do, the term remains productive and analytically useful. There has also been some reservation as to whether or not there is a need for a specific theory and methodology of 'intersectionality' (Nash, 2008). Leslie McCall (2005) has developed a threefold clustering of approaches to the study of intersectionality: intercategorical complexity, intracategorical complexity, and anticategorical complexity. The intercategorical approach presumes the existence of intersections, and then attempts to map the relationship between different social groups and how these are changing. The intracategorical approach is alive to the shortcomings of existing categorisations and interrogates the way in which they mark boundaries of distinction. The anticategorical approach is concerned with a critique of the presumption that categories are pre-given. Rather it deconstructs the categories, paying attention to the regimes of power in and through which the categories are constituted in the first place. Here social categories are seen as historically, culturally, and linguistically produced. I am sympathetic to the anticategorical approach. This is not to suggest, however, that categories themselves are meaningless. Far from it. Rather, they are not already existing formations but take form and meaning through social-cultural, economic, political, and psychic processes. This broad categorisation of approaches by McCall is helpful but it does not provide a specific methodology. In my view, as I have suggested above, there cannot be a single methodology that all intersectional analysis may follow, not least because intersectional analysis is first and foremost an interdisciplinary endeavour. Different disciplines have varying methodologies. That which one chooses is dependent upon the problematic that one is addressing and the subject discipline(s) within which one is operating. It cannot by definition have a single, overarching set of methods as tools of analysis. My position gains support from the introduction to a special issue of the journal *Signs*, where Lily Cho, Kimberlé Williams Crenshaw, and Leslie McCall state that "intersectionality is best framed as an analytic sensibility" (Cho et al., 2013: 795).

Some analysts working with intersectionality locate their work within the feminist standpoint theory. Standpoint feminism argues that feminist social science foregrounds the standpoint of women, arguing that women are better able to understand certain features of the world. Because of their location as a subordinate group, it is argued, they hold a different type of knowledge from men, one that challenges male-biased conventional wisdom. This perspective has been characterised as being essentialist, and, in some measure, contrary to the demands of intersectionality in so far as women are not simply equivalent to their gender. In a much more nuanced perspective which does not fix knowledge construction along a single dimension, Donna Haraway, as already shown, has used the notion of 'situated knowledge', which is produced, circulated, and challenged via intersectional articulations. This concept is akin to what Chandra Talpade Mohanty, following Adrian Rich, calls the "politics of location" understood as "historical, geographical, cultural, psychic and imaginative boundaries which provide the ground for political definition" (Mohanty, 1992: 74). This debate also has a bearing on the processes of embodiment, in which I include the workings of the psyche. People are much more than an amalgam of subject positions – there are emotions, yearnings, unruly and precarious workings of the psyche, and the intersectional excess of 'experience'.

Another question that scholars of intersectionality have raised is whether perspectives informed by standpoint theory and others that take inspiration from poststructuralist theoretical formulations are mutually exclusive. Despite their major differences, I would suggest that there is significant overlap between these two in so far as both interrogate patriarchal social relations; posit that knowledge is socially and culturally situated; and, in the work of analysts such as Patricia Hill Collins, address the collective subject 'woman' through an intersectional lens.

In addition, both require us to integrate marginalised life-experiences as well as highlight the importance of understanding power and privilege in its manifold manifestations. Moreover, both perspectives caution against reciting the race, class, gender, and sexuality mantra without due attention to the complexity entailed when processes of social division, inequality, and subject formation intersect and articulate.

What are the prospects for the future of intersectionality? Nira Yuval-Davis (2011), for instance, sees the concept of intersectionality as having a great deal of potential. According to her, intersectionality is far better equipped to do justice to the analysis of complex relations of inequality than stratification theory in sociology. Floya Anthias (2020) argues along similar lines, and offers a critique of traditional stratification theories with an emphasis on a translocational lens. Kathy Davis (2011) finds that, paradoxically, the very vagueness and open-endedness of the framework of intersectionality is the secret of its success and this portends well for its future. One of its strengths lies in the way in which it demands that those engaged in theoretical work try to embed their meta-narratives in the concrete social and political contexts while simultaneously asking generalist researchers to appreciate the importance of theory in feminist inquiry. Nina Lykke provides a qualified assessment of intersectionality. She conceptualises intersectionality as a 'nodal point', and favours it only so long as it remains an "open ended framework for comparing different feminist conceptualisations of intersecting power differentials, normativities and identity formations – a discursive site where different feminist positions are in critical dialogue or productive conflict with one another" (Lykke, 2011: 208). Jennifer Nash reminds us that women's studies has tended to treat intersectionality and transnationalism as if they were mutually exclusive, ignoring that they are similarly constituted "regimes that are embodied and performed by particular racialized bodies" (Nash, 2019: 104). She suggests that it might be productive if the two approaches were sutured. This proposition holds a particular interest for me because it resonates with my work, which deploys these two analytics together with the postcolonial framework. In Chapter 6, Clelia Clini and I discuss the transnationalism, intersectionality, and postcolonial dimensions of my analysis. In using these three approaches, I do not in any sense claim a 'political or theoretical completion.' Far from it. Analytical approaches are as partial as regimes of knowledge formation. I live and work in Britain with its colonial and imperial legacies, which have a central bearing on the transnational dimensions of my writing on questions of 'race', class, and gender, for instance. Their intersections and interrelations produce social complexities that demand multiple approaches designed to address fluidity, exchangeability, and multiplicity.

It is important to bear in mind that from its inception, intersectionality has been an antiracist framework. But a travelling theory or practice may change during the course of its translocation to a different context. Gail Lewis (2013) addresses this question through an analysis of a conference held in Frankfurt in Germany, which was held in order to assess the achievements of intersectionality. She shows how such events may create deep anxiety and emotionality, underpinned by fears and anxieties about cultural multiplicity even though the concept of intersectionality is precisely about multiplicity. She points to the ways in which the "terminological category of race is disavowed as unspeakable in parts of Europe" (Lewis, 2013: 874), and feminists of colour become 'Othered' and positioned as outsiders in Europe. These outcomes are likely to be unintended but their effects are palpable. So even a highly inclusive project such as that of intersectionality could have exclusionary effects and this possibility calls for much vigilance.

In conclusion, we may reiterate that diaspora and intersectionality are mutually articulating formations. Diaspora – a dispersal of bodies, histories, cultures, imaginaries – is inscribed by the multiple modalities of power constituted in the play of different markers of difference. Such multiple modalities of power intertwine, and questions of belonging and un-belonging are inscribed in and through various subject positions, subjectivities, and identities. And this diasporicity is inherently permeated by intersectional differentiations.

Chapter 8

Formations of Citizenship: Articulations across Diaspora, Law, and Literature

Global migrations, as we have seen, are a key feature of today's world. They range from the movement of labour migrants to that of elites such as the personnel of multinational corporations, documented and undocumented workers, students, refugees, and asylum seekers. Some migrations are 'voluntary', whereas a significant number of migrants are 'trafficked' from country to country. At 281 million, international migrants comprised about 3.6 per cent of the world population in 2020, so that political discourses in some receiving countries about 'being swamped' grossly exaggerate the proportion of the migrants in the popular imagination.[1] In any case, the economic and social impact of global migrations is significant. I am concerned in this chapter not with migration in general, but rather with those groups that form diasporas. In contemporary debate the previous emphasis on 'common origins' in defining diasporas has shifted. It is now on the sharing of a 'contemporary condition' rather than on 'origins' (see discussion in Chapter 5). There are many different diasporas in the world, and the study of diasporas is now a well-established field. Diaspora can be a descriptive term delineating a historical diaspora such as that of the Jews, African-origin Blacks, or South Asians. But it can also be deployed as a concept that comprises a set of investigative technologies that theorise and analyse the socio-economic, cultural political, and psychic relationality within and across diasporas (Brah, 1996). I use the concept of diaspora here in both the above two senses: as a description of a historical diaspora and as a concept. My aim is to examine and explore interconnections

[1] See World Migration Report 2020, IOM, UN Migration.

between the field of diaspora studies, literature, and law. For decades now, law *and* literature as well law *in* literature has occupied an important place in the academy. Similarly, the study of diasporic texts is well established within literary studies. However, the links between these fields of study and diaspora studies is less well developed. How might this triangulation develop further?

One way of doing this might be by identifying common thematics, concepts, and theoretical perspectives across these distinctive fields. This, in my view, may prove fruitful in taking this objective forward. How might these areas be interconnected in and through these common threads? How might this specific type of transdisciplinarity be practiced? What are the linking elements? I list here some of these common elements that may be analysed in developing the triangulation of the three fields. They are as follows: citizenship is a concept central to all three areas; law, governance, and governmentality are themes that link law to literature and diaspora studies; the position of refugees and asylum seekers has a common resonance across all three areas; the feminist concept of intersectionality underpins all these areas; and questions of identity and difference feature across all three areas.

It is not my intention to address all the above aspects sequentially or in the same depth. Rather, I aim to examine a diasporic text and see how issues that link the three areas feature across this text. This is followed by a more substantive discussion of immigration law and citizenship in order to tease out the interconnecting themes. I begin with Mohsin Hamid's novel *The Reluctant Fundamentalist* where many of the above concerns are central.

This is a diasporic novel par excellence, set in Pakistan and the USA. It contains an incisive commentary upon personal and political experience forged within contemporary transnational social formations. It opens with the following words:

Excuse me, Sir, but may I be of assistance? Ah, I see I have alarmed you? Do not be frightened by my beard: I am a lover of America.

(Hamid, 2007: 1)

And so ensues an intricate narrative of love, anger, and ambivalence. The novel stages a contestation between male facial hair – which came to signify a 'terrorist' in the post-9/11 world of the US-led 'War on Terror' – and the mighty power of America. The Pakistani male protagonist is a migrant in America during the years preceding and following the 9/11 destruction of the Twin Towers, the symbol of corporate power in New York. In the aftermath of this attack, the sight of a beard grown by Muslim men produced fear because in popular imagination a beard came to stand for 'extremism'. The novel is about Changez, a young man of Pakistani origin who goes to America to study. He falls in love with an American young woman, Erica, who is described as inhabiting a fantasy world steeped in the memory of her dead boyfriend. From the beginning, the relationship appears to be doomed, as Changez could only be a poor copy of the boyfriend. In the course of the unfolding narrative, Erica falls ill and is taken into a care home where she gradually fades away with anorexia and depression, and eventually is presumed to have committed suicide, although this event is not witnessed by anyone. This fading away may be understood as a metaphor for the estrangement of Changez from America, which he had grown to love.

Changez is a brilliant student at Princeton University where he beats off stiff competition upon graduation, and succeeds in securing a prestigious job as a management consultant within corporate America. But his world of high life and social extravagance made possible by transnational capitalism crumbles in post-9/11 New York. He now faces racial discrimination. In this social climate, we witness the emergence of a new politicised identity on the part of Changez, although its precise features remain 'unknowable'. The novel describes an imagined conversation between Changez, and an anonymous American man who, according to Changez, might well be an undercover CIA operative, but this is never confirmed. Changez tells his life story to the American, in response to the latter's questions. The novel is many things, but at one level it marks an encounter between the power of global corporate capital and the formation of subjectivities or identities marked by asymmetrical power relations. These identities are produced within cultural difference, within 'dialogicity', which as Janet Wilson argues:

[...] informs the novel's narrative structure – a monologue that delineates a dialogue – and accounts for the impact of the enigmatic climax as Changez retains ambiguity of voice, incident, and character right up to the last minute.

(Wilson, 2012: 91–108)

Initially, Changez is an enthusiastic participant in the intricate workings of American capitalism, but later he becomes disillusioned and dissociates himself from it. He loses his job, because he can no longer be the keen member of staff that he used to be, and his colleagues begin to show suspicion and distrust towards him. He returns to Pakistan but he still carries fragments of America within him. He tells his American interlocutors:

I had been telling you earlier, sir, of how I *left* America. The truth of my experience complicates that seemingly simple assertion; I had returned to Pakistan, but my inhabitation of your country had not entirely ceased. I remained emotionally entwined with Erica and I brought something of her with me to Lahore – or perhaps it would be more accurate to say that I lost something of myself to her that I was unable to relocate in the city of my birth.

(Hamid, 2007: 195)

This quotation narrates the predicament of all diasporic identities. They negotiate multiple spatialities and temporalities. Different landscapes of memory jostle with each other as varying and variable modalities of 'homing desire' are juxtaposed within its realms. These identities are characterised by multiplicity and hybridity. The power of this novel, indeed perhaps all novels – resides in the way it can vividly portray the workings of subjectivity and identity alongside social and structural relations. This novel raises a number of issues, themes, and concepts that are pertinent to our discussion. One of these is citizenship in both its legal sense (Changez can only hold a visa so long as he has a job) and in terms of its wider meaning of a connecting motif across law, literature, and diaspora studies. In the most general sense citizenship is about membership of a political community. As such it involves a relationship between rights, duties, participation, and identity. Citizenship laws govern who belongs or does not belong to a nation state, or as is the case with the European Union, to a supra-national organisation. For instance, what rights do migrants have in a given context? Rights may be distinguished between civic, political, and social rights, and identity can refer to either political or cultural identity. In this broader sense citizenship is about economic, socio-cultural, and political issues as they impact upon individuals and groups. Legal issues are framed by wider concerns in a specific social context. The British Nationality Act of 1981, for example, was instituted amidst the circulation of massive anti-immigrant racialised discourses. Margaret Thatcher was at the forefront of anti-immigrant rhetoric when during a television interview for the Granada World in Action programme on 27 January 1978, she suggested that the British way of life needed special protection because she feared that the "country might be rather swamped by people with a different culture"[2]. Several decades later, such sentiments still abound. Overall, there is a close connection between immigration and nationality law in Britain and elsewhere. Hence, the circumstances under which migrants acquire citizenship or are refused it, and the ways these events are experienced hold interest for those working in diaspora studies, literary studies as well as the study of law. I begin by exploring how the development of British immigration law affects diasporic experience.

Rhetorics of Immigration Law

As is now well known, the post-World War II period witnessed an economic boom. There were labour shortages in Britain – especially in areas where the white workforce did not wish to be deployed because the jobs were low-paid and accompanied by poor working conditions.

[2] TV interview for Granada World in Action programme broadcast on 30 January, 1978.

Britain turned to its former colonies to fill these labour shortages. The workers came predominantly from the Caribbean and the South Asian subcontinent and found themselves doing low-skilled and semi-skilled jobs. There was a small fraction of professionals such as doctors, some of whom would be spread in isolated areas where the British doctors were less likely to want to work.

According to the 1948 Nationality Act, migrants from the former colonies had open entry into Britain where they had the legal right to work and settle. Although this period has been described by some as the 'liberal hour' of immigration, in actual fact both the Labour government of 1945–1951 and the Conservative government of the 1950s considered various ways of curtailing immigration from the 'New Commonwealth'. This terminology of New Commonwealth was a code for what was then called the 'coloured' immigration. As I discussed in an earlier chapter, it was during this time that a linkage was established between 'race' and immigration in policy debates and in popular political and media discourses (Solomos, 2003: esp. 48–56). It was against this racialised political climate that the riots of 1958 in Notting Hill and Nottingham took place. Although the riots involved attacks on Black people by white youth, the political and media commentaries made it seem as if it was the presence of Black people that was the problem. The riots served to bring to national prominence issues that had previously been mainly the subject of discussion in local areas or within government departments. The riots were used by the pro-immigration control lobby to support their arguments for the exclusion, even expulsion, of people who were considered by them to be 'undesirable immigrants'. The intro-duction of the 1962 Immigration Act was preceded by anti-immigrant rhetoric both within parliament and in the media, accompanied by a resurgence of right-wing groups. In these anti-immigrant discourses, people of colour who were technically citizens under the 1948 Act, were presented as taking jobs away from white workers, described as a drain on welfare resources, and socially constructed as a threat to the 'English way of life,' themes that are still familiar to us today. The legislation was introduced by the Conservative Party and was opposed by the Labour Party, but once in power Labour also gave in to what has been described by scholars as 'state racism'. Since the 1962 Immigration Act was placed on the statute as a response to the political campaign against the intake of people of colour, it was not surprising that many of its clauses sought to control the entry of these Commonwealth citizens into Britain.

One aspect of the 1962 Immigration Act was that it gave exemption from control to British citizens living in independent Commonwealth countries provided they held British passports. This included a large number of European settlers and a sizeable number of Asians in Kenya and Uganda. Between 1965 and 1967, some of these Asians started to migrate to Britain due to Africanisation policies of those countries. A section of the media and certain Members of Parliament began to demand action against this inflow of British citizens and a heated debated ensued. The Labour Party succumbed to this pressure and introduced the Commonwealth Immigration Act of 1968. This Act was specifically designed to control the entry of Asians from East Africa. Under this law any citizen of Britain and its colonies who held a passport issued by the British government would be subject to immigration control unless (and this is the key point) they or at least one parent or grandparent had been born, naturalised, or registered in Britain as a citizen of Britain or its colonies. This clause, as I have indicated before, institutionalised a racial underpinning to the legislation as most of the white citizens with a connection by descent were given the right of entry. Despite this, the continuing arrival of the *dependents* of New Commonwealth migrants kept the 'numbers game' high on the political and media agenda and the pressure generated resulted in the introduction of the 1971 Immigration Act, which qualified the notion of citizenship by differentiating between citizens of Britain and the colonies who were 'patrial' (read white) and therefore had the right of abode, and 'non-patrials' (read people of colour) without connection via descent who did not. There was now no automatic entry into Britain for Commonwealth people who were not white, yet the political discourses focused on the curtailing of immigration went unabated during the period of Margaret Thatcher and John Major.

Although the proportion of dependents of people of colour settled here and the fiancés from the South Asian subcontinent of British

Asian women was small, these groups continued to be seen as posing a threat to the British way of life. Cultural difference came to be used as a code for the undesirability of Black and Asian minority ethnic groups. As I have already shown, Asian women marrying men from abroad had to prove that their relationship was authentic, implying that these were likely to be 'bogus' marriages. There were cases of virginity tests that were conducted on Asian women, and Asian children arriving in Britain underwent X-ray examinations to establish their age. All these measures were instituted in order to prove that the applicants were genuine candidates under the Immigration Rules. While the government has now introduced a points-based system for potential applicants for entry into Britain, there still exists the Ancestry Visa according to which you can work in the UK if you are a Commonwealth citizen and you can prove that one of your grandparents was born in the UK, the Channel Islands, or the Isle of Man.[3] Clearly, white Canadians or Australians or New Zealanders are much more likely to have grandparents born in the UK than people from Asia or the Caribbean. While Britain has now left the European Union, it was not that long ago when during May 2014 European Parliament election, the party that got the highest level of popular vote, the UK Independence Party, ran specifically on an anti-immigration and anti-EU platform. This was the first time that a party other than the Labour Party and the Conservative Party had won the popular vote in a national election since the 1906 general election. It was also the first time since the 1910 general election that a party other than Labour or Conservative won the largest number of seats in a national election. The anti-immigrant sentiment was crystallised by Nigel Farage, the leader of the UK Independence Party, when he stated in an LBC radio interview in May 2014 that British people would be wary of Romanian families moving into their street. When pressed about the fact that his own wife was German, he said that people would know the difference between living next door to Romanians and Germans. There is thus a

---

[3] See "Ancestry Visa" (6 April 2015), GOV.UK www.gov.uk/ancestry-visa/overview (accessed 20 August 2015).

hierarchy in his view between Eastern and Western Europeans, where Eastern Europeans would seem to be considered comparatively inferior. During the 1990s, the treatment of asylum seekers and refugees was a major cause of political conflict across Europe and it remains one of the most controversial items of the political agenda with increasingly stringent controls on the entry of asylum seekers and refugees. The predicaments of being a refugee or asylum seeker interrogate the very notion of citizen, nation state, and nationality. As Giorgio Agamben notes:

If refugees (whose number has continued to grow in our century, to the point of including a significant part of humanity today) represent such a disquieting element in the order of the modern nation-state, this above all because by breaking the continuity between man and citizen, *nativity* and *nationality*, they put the ordinary fiction of modern sovereignty in crisis. Bringing to light the difference between birth and nation, the refugee causes the secret presupposition of the political domain – bare life – to appear for an instant within that domain. In this sense, the refugee is truly "the man of rights," as Arendt suggests, the first and only real appearance of rights outside the fiction of the citizen that always covers them over. Yet this is precisely what makes the figure of the refugee so hard to define politically.

(Agamben, 1998: 77, original emphasis)

In other words, "the refugee must be considered for what he [sic] is: nothing less than a limit concept that radically calls into question the fundamental categories of the national state [...]" (Agamben, 1998: 78).

The refugee is partially constituted in and through legal protocols. In contemporary Europe the refugee is the "new dispossessed" as Patricia Tuitt puts it (Tuitt, 2004). In many countries of Europe, there are racialised discourses that represent refugees and asylum seekers as 'bogus' economic migrants, who are intent on circumventing immigration law. These claims have led to the erosion of rights of refugees and asylum seekers, so that the persecuted in the country of origin face another form of persecution as they reach the place where they seek refuge. Interrogating these legal regimes of power is a critical mode of intervention today.

Formations of Citizenship Discourses and Practices

It is evident that there is a link between immigration and citizenship in terms of the ways in which citizenship is legally conceptualised as well as how it is understood more broadly. These conceptions interconnect diasporic concerns with legal and literary treatment of the subject. How do we think of citizenship in the current context of migration and global mobility? Who is included and who is excluded and under what circumstances? If citizenship is about membership of a political community, what does this membership consist of? Where do the boundaries of citizenship lie? How does immigration law impact on citizenship status? These are some of the questions that animate the following discussion of changing conceptions of citizenship.

As membership of a political community, citizenship involves a relationship between rights, duties, participation, and identity. In the classical liberal tradition of modern liberal thought there has been greater emphasis placed on rights and duties and much less on participation and identity. One may identify two distinct models of citizenship. First, there is the model that foregrounds market and state-centred conceptions of citizenship that represent a formal and legally coded status. On the other hand, there is a view of citizenship that focuses upon substantive dimension of participation in civic community. The first conception is primarily about nationality whereas the second notion is much more about active citizenship. Whereas the liberal tradition was focused on the issue of rights, the conservative tradition has tended to favour responsibilities of citizenship. The republican and communitarian forms of citizenship have given centrality to participation. A key debate in the discourse of citizenship is about the tension between citizenship as the pursuit of equality and the recognition of difference. As is well known, from the beginning the term citizenship involved exclusion. Exclusion could take the form of not being accorded the status of a citizen as was the fate of the enslaved, children, and women. In other words, no account of citizenship can avoid the fact that it was originally constructed on the basis of exclusion of certain categories of persons.

In a way, the history of citizenship has been an ongoing contestation for the removal of inequities and inequalities. Although all citizens are conceptualised as equal before law, there are differences in the life chances of different groups in society.

Famously, T. H. Marshall has distinguished between civil rights, political rights, and social rights. He suggests that these rights were achieved over three hundred years with social citizenship emerging with the development of the modern welfare state. The latter was not fully realised until the twentieth century. Importantly, Marshall recognised that equality in law and politics could easily co-exist with social inequality. Social rights took the form of social welfare covering housing, health, education, unemployment benefits, and pensions. These rights, together with those of civic and political citizenship, served to alleviate the impact of structural inequalities of capitalism. But inequality has not been eradicated due in part to deeper antagonisms between capitalism and the welfare state. As critics have argued (Offe, 1984; Delanty, 2000), the welfare state has not only not reduced inequality to the degree Marshall expected but in some ways exacerbated it. It might be argued that social citizenship has to some degree bought off dissent.

Gerard Delanty (2000) in his book titled *Citizenship in a Global Age* offers a fivefold critique of Marshall's theory, which is relevant to contemporary understanding of citizenship. First he points to the contemporary challenge of cultural specificities and rights. Following the work of scholars such as I. M. Young (1990) and Isin and Wood (1990; see also Young, 1990; Isin and Bielsen, 2008), he argues how the politicisation of the issues of gender and race, for instance, indicate that policies of universal equality will not be adequate to tackle these inequities and inequalities. Hence, a conception of 'difference' is necessary in the recognition of group rights. That is to say that we need a different model of rights if we are to take full cognisance of the rise of claims to cultural rights and group rights. Second, there is the challenge of globalisation, which signals major transformations in economy, culture, and the social formation. For instance, some aspects of the nation state have experienced erosion by global processes and global social movements have pointed to the limits of modern citizenship. Third, there is the challenge of substantive over formal citizenship. Marshall would appear to underplay the salience of participation as a key element of citizenship. Of course, the rights of citizenship did not come from a benevolent state but emerged as a result of centuries-long struggle and contestation through which various rights were achieved. The point is that citizenship is not merely a question of rights but also involves identification and commitment to the political community. A fourth element of Delanty's critique is that Marshall did not question the link between nation and state: that is to say, the state as the provider and guarantor of rights; and the nation as the focus of identity. Today this linkage cannot be taken for granted. In the context of globalisation, the state is no longer entirely in command of all the forces that shape it. This means that there is no perfect equivalence between nationality, as membership of the political community of the state, and citizenship as membership of the political community of civil society. This is clearly evident in the case of immigrants who, as we have seen above, can possess formal citizenship in the sense of nationality and yet be excluded from participation in the society in which they live. Fifth, Marshall took for granted the strict separation between the private and the public realm which has been radically contested, especially by feminists. These concerns have introduced critical reappraisal of citizenship (see for, instance, Isin and Nielsen, 2008).

There have been other pressures on citizenship too. The arrival of neoliberalism, for example, has had a major impact on discourses of citizenship. Neoliberalism has been accompanied by government policies such as decentralisation, deregulation, privatisation, and monetarism. The concept of citizenship in neoliberal discourse replaces the citizen with the consumer. Neoliberalism poses a very serious challenge to the liberal concept of citizenship with the return of citizenship to the market.

Other approaches to citizenship that have a bearing on a reappraisal of citizenship are: communitarian, social democratic and feminist approaches. The broad range of positions that can be termed communitarian locate civil society in community. Instead of a focus on rights and duties, it tends to emphasise participation and identity. It critiques moral individualism in favour of a collectivist conception of citizenship which is, however, distinct from socialist conceptions because the focus here is on culture rather than material conditions. Communitarianism construes self as always culturally specific and as such it may be seen as advocating cultural particularism against liberalism's moral universalism. Self is seen as socially constructed and embedded in cultural context. In this it has a shared vision with interculturalism. Communitarians accept that different cultural groups might have different concepts of the common good. While the liberal idea of 'difference' stands for individual freedom, the communitarian notion of 'difference' stands for the group's power to limit individual freedom (Bauman, 1993). Of course, Liberals such as Will Kymlicka (1989) believe that liberalism can be reconciled with interculturalism. There is, however, a tension between intercultural and the communitarian versions of citizenship in that the concept of community in communitarian discourse is not entirely an open one. In other words, minoritised and incoming groups must adapt to the dominant cultural community in order to participate in its political community. This is an assimilationist view of society. The communitarian perspective, especially in their conservative forms, tends to stress family, religion, tradition, and what in general might be called a culture of consensus. Those social divisions in society which signal conflict, as for instance gender divisions, may not receive adequate attention. As a consequence, social struggles, especially in the private domain, could be sidelined. Feminist theories of citizenship, on the other hand, tend to pay much greater attention to the relationship between citizenship and democracy. They reconceptualise identity and participation in a way that challenges the private and public divide.

But before considering feminist perspectives on citizenship, I wish to briefly comment upon *radical theories of citizenship and democracy* because these are intimately connected to feminist theories.

The various stances on radical democracy can be seen as carrying out advocacy of democratic citizenship whereby citizenship is re-politicised by democracy. There was a revival of civil society around the emergence of new social movements during the 1970s and 1980s, which served to concretise democratic citizenship. Of course, today movements such as Black Lives Matter are also reinvigorating democratic citizenship. These developments, which foreground radical democracy of participatory citizenship, could be seen to be somewhat different from civic republicanism. Here, for instance, the primary goal is the transformation of the relationship between state and society by initiating social change through transforming politics. It is significant that the new social movements cited above made democracy central to their political project and thereby made an impact on citizenship. Their extra-parliamentary nature and ability to mobilise large segments of the population is especially noteworthy. The idea of civil society is foregrounded as these movements valorise the political within the social. The politics of radical democracy are based on the formation of collective identity around a common goal which bring a more meaningful dimension to citizenship.

Feminist Citizenship

Feminist approaches to citizenship challenge the private–public dichotomy that is typical of liberalism. Feminist approaches interrogate the assumption that there is only one public, arguing that civic republican theories of citizenship from the point of view of women and other disadvantaged groups have not made a major advance over liberal theories. Feminist theories foreground the politicisation of the private sphere as well as underscore the pluralist view of the public domain. The point of departure for feminist theories of citizenship thus differs from conventional liberal and communitarian approaches.

The universality of liberal conceptions of equality together with the communitarian notion of a unitary ideal of community have been contested by feminists. Neither rights nor participation offer adequate models when issues of patriarchy are concerned. While communitarianism speaks of culture, its starting point is not an intercultural standpoint. Rather, it is a case of a dominant group trying to accommodate cultural diversity. In other words, the dominant group's values become universalised and hegemonised while those associated with marginalised groups are rendered secondary. In contrast, group difference is a starting point for feminism and thus there can be no unitary community but a plurality of cultural forms. Liberal and communitarian as much as civic republican theories assume that citizenship is the expression of already autonomous citizens. These autonomous subjects are deemed to be working within a broadly homogeneous society, which is patently not the case, as no society is homogenous. And subjects are not already constituted pre-givens but are produced in and through discourse together with the operations of the unconscious. Feminist theories of citizenship build upon notions of radical democratic citizenship. For theorists such as Iris Marion Young (1990), the homogenous ideal of universality must be rejected for a more differentiated notion of rights. Similarly, Ruth Lister (1998b) argues for what she describes as 'a differentiated universalism' or what we may today call pluriversalism. She highlights the need for interconnecting politics of solidarity with a politics of difference. The political subject is theorised as made up of multiple, fluid identities produced and marked by the workings of such vectors as gender, 'race', and class. Whether referencing the private domain or valorising a public notion of the common good, feminist conceptions of identity see it as process rather than fixed. In other words, identity is theorised as contested and always open to redefinition. According to Sasha Roseneil (2013), citizenship is attractive in its expansive, inclusionary promise, yet disappointing when it comes to its exclusionary imperatives. In discussing different constructions of citizenship, Nira Yuval-Davis (2011) draws attention to active vs activist citizenship. She reminds us of the Thatcherite notion of 'active citizen' as a voluntaristic actor of philanthropy, and contrasts it with 'activist citizen' addressed by Isin (2008) who engages in a variety of acts of citizenship which blur the boundary between, say, human rights and civil rights; and political and social rights. These writers also argue the case for additional categories of rights such as ecological and sexual rights, reproductive rights, and rights concerning intimate relationships, putting into practice the feminist slogan 'personal is political'. Intimate rights are also addressed by Roseneil et al. (2011) in terms, inter alia, of marriage and divorce (both same sex and heterosexual), recognition of same-sex relationships in immigration legislation, abortion, pornography, prostitution, and trafficking.

Theorists of citizenship also speak of *Cosmopolitan Citizenship*. Overall, as we have seen, the debate on citizenship has been dominated by two quite opposed positions – one predominantly liberal and the second largely communitarian. These positions have been challenged by radical democracy, feminist theory, and intercultural/antiracist positionalities. In contrast to approaches that use the nation state as the territorial reference point, cosmopolitan citizenship goes beyond the nation state. These developments are closely connected with processes of globalisation. We cannot, however, overlook the nation state, since citizenship is embedded in state protocols and many rights, including the right to settle in a country, are granted by the nation state. Migrants, refugees, and asylum seekers, for instance, know what it means not to have rights of a citizen when residing in a nation state. However, the concept of cosmopolitan citizenship requires serious consideration, not least because it pays attention to cultural rights, lifestyle rights such as consumer rights, and rights relating to new technologies and the environment. The European Union is a good example of a concrete kind of cosmopolitan public sphere. Although we know that the European Union can serve as 'Fortress Europe', it can also provide opportunities for solidarity across European countries designed to work against racism, sexism, homophobia, and so on. Cosmopolitan citizenship, however, ought not be understood as a rarefied status devoid of association with a notion of community where community is viewed not as one of descent but of residence. This distinction between descent and residence is important because we must bear in mind that the concept of community is likely at times to be hijacked by essentialist nationalist discourses. Cosmopolitan citizenship needs to foreground a notion of community, which feminists have prioritised: that is, community recognised as a heterogeneous ensemble underpinned by intersectional dynamics of power.

Citizenship and Multiculture

As we noted earlier, the main axis of citizenship defining the boundaries of inclusion versus exclusion have historically been based on intersecting social divisions such as class, gender, race, ethnicity, sexuality, and disability/debility. The history of citizenship can be viewed as an ongoing struggle on the part of the disenfranchised, the marginalised, and the dependent to be included in the ranks of the 'citizen'. Although there have been significant achievements, in some ways these struggles continue today. For example, women did not gain the vote in Switzerland until 1990. While millions of people are on the move globally, questions of citizenship become increasingly complex and questions of cultural diversity assume growing importance. Although 'multiculturalism' has been under attack in more than one country in Europe, it is important to note that as Kivisto and Faist (2007) point out, 'multiculturalism' has been a response to the demands on the part of marginalised groups for collective rather than individualistic solutions to exclusion, inequality and recognition. There are many reasons for these attacks on 'multiculturalism', especially in Britain. These include the changed political climate following 9/11 in 2001; the racialised riots in Northern English cities during 2001; the 7/7 bombings in London in 2005; the unleashing of Islamophobia since the Satanic Verses Affair of the 1980s; the Demark Cartoons affair of 2007, and, currently, the War on Terror; the global political and economic crisis; and the crisis in Iraq and Afghanistan. All this has made anti-immigrant politics mainstream from France to Germany, from Holland to Austria, from Sweden to Switzerland. It is worth bearing in mind that these onslaughts on 'multiculturalism' have come from both the right and the left of the political spectrum (Hesse, 2000; Rattansi, 2011).

The arguments of those opposed to 'multiculturalism' may be grouped in three broad categories:

The first argument that is likely to be put forward is that 'multiculturalism' is divisive and as such threatens national unity. But this argument assumes that there is at base a homogenous monocultural society when, in fact, all societies are heterogeneous, marked by social differentiations of region, language, class, gender, ethnicity, disability/debility, and sexuality. Such differentiations make for complex cultural variations within a social formation. Britain, for instance, is not 'multicultural' simply because of the presence of minority ethnic groups but because it is composed of four national cultures – English, Irish, Scottish, and Welsh – and many regional cultures over and above different gendered and racialised class cultures. I would argue that national unity is brought about by a commitment to equality, justice, and 'difference' in an atmosphere of mutuality rather than to a notion of homogenous culture. While a degree of national unity is necessarily desirable, an overarching focus on national unity may lead to the emergence of varying and variable forms of nationalism. Moreover, different social groups in Britain share enough in common to regard themselves as British albeit in ways that, at times, mobilise a hyphenated identity such as British Asian. In the context of the fact that Islamophobia is currently rife, it is sometimes assumed that Muslims do not identify with the British national identity, but evidence suggests that this is not the case and a majority of Muslims do indeed regard themselves as British. And, even the minority who do not consider themselves as British do fully participate in the socio-economic and political life as British citizens (Moosavi, 2012). Moreover, discussion of Muslim identities needs to be contextualised in the broader national and international context (cf. Ahmed, 1992; Lewis, 1996, 2004, 2015; Sayyid, 1997; Nazir, 2007, 2010; Khan, 2019). Such national identities may co-exist with transnational identities but they have palpable resonance in the national culture.

A second argument fielded by the opponents of 'multiculturalism' is that it serves to 'ghettoise' marginalised groups rather than assist them to integrate within the mainstream. The problematic of integration is a complex one since, to be effective, integration must take place at different levels of the social formation such as the economic, the social, the cultural, the political, and the juridical. But popular discourses rarely conceptualise integration in such differentiated terms and this can mean that patterns of inequality among minoritised groups become concealed. In other words, the talk about 'ghettoisation' has a narrower focus in that it invokes primarily the geographical location of minoritised groups. There are, of course, many reasons for the concentration of groups in specific localities and they are not always negative. People may decide, for instance, to live where they may share a culture or lifestyle or ethnicity with the residents, and they might feel secure in terms of numbers against possible racist attacks. On the whole, among majority ethnic groups, middle-class and upper-class residents live in different areas from working-class residents. But that process is rarely described as 'ghettoisation'. Minority ethnic groups may be concentrated in a given area not simply because of cultural reasons but also due to socio-economic ones. These groups are likely to be disadvantaged and as such they may congregate in low-income areas on the basis that they cannot afford to live in more prosperous areas. So, it would seem that cultural proclivity may not be the only reason for 'ghettoisation' but socio-economic conditions and discrimination might actually be a rather more significant factor. In order to assist these groups to enter the mainstream, it is the structures of inequality and discrimination that need to be dismantled, not 'multiculturalism'.

Third, there are criticisms of 'multiculturalism' from the left of the political spectrum. One such criticism has been that cultural diversity may undermine progressive alliances. However, this is to assume that cultural diversity invariably leads to cultural division. I would suggest that it is the social hierarchies and power differences that create cultural divisions rather than 'multiculturalism'. It is also argued on the left that politics of recognition may mean that the politics of redistribution are ignored. This would seem to be a weak argument because 'multiculturalism' itself cannot be held responsible for lack of attention to socio-economic inequality. Indeed, ethnic minorities tend to be one of the most disadvantaged groups in society and large sections of these are at the bottom of the social scale. They need politics of redistribution as much as, if not more than, the majority group. One of the arguments on the political left in Britain during the 1980s used to be, and I was a proponent of this position, that the discourses of 'multiculturalism' overemphasised cultural diversity and did not pay enough attention to structural questions of class and racism. This was a valid criticism, and people spoke of antiracism as a more appropriate means of tackling inequality as opposed to 'multiculturalism'. Hence 'multiculturalism' and antiracism came to be categorised as oppositional perspectives when, in fact, they were complementary. The two need to be joined together with equal attention to issues of culture and structural inequality.

It is important to emphasise that 'multicultural citizenship' is not defined only in relation to the state, crucial though this is, but also in relation to civil society. What is needed is a 'multicultural' citizenship that is undergirded by a commitment to equality and democratic citizenship. According to Charles Taylor, equality may refer to equal as in 'equal dignity' and equal as in 'equal respect'. The former appeals to people's common humanity and applies to all members in a uniform way. The latter, that is equal respect, refers to an understanding that difference is also important. As Tariq Modood (2010: 108) notes,

There is, then, deep resonance between citizenship and multicultural recognition. Not only do both presuppose complementary notions of unity and plurality, and of equality and difference, but the idea of respect for the group self-identities that citizens value is central to citizenship.

Some theorists such as Engin Isin have used the term diaspora citizenship instead of 'multicultural' citizenship. This is attractive to me as I have invested considerably in developing a diasporic framework for social analysis. However, there is an argument in favour of retaining the term 'multiculturalism' or interculturalism (which I prefer), partly because it is not just an analytical term but also part of the popular discourse and imagination. I am in favour of the concept of critical interculturalism and a concept of citizenship that takes on board intersectional axes of power. The point is that, unlike classic multiculturalism, interculturalism goes beyond mere celebration of diversity and urges the setting up of dialogues and joint activities. As Rattansi (2011) points out, interculturalism interrogates a potential essentialist tendency by emphasising connectedness and interaction between changing practices and lifestyles of different ethnic groups, including the majority group, as part of national cultures that are marked by technological, economic, political, and cultural factors including the Internet and the impact of globalisation. It also avoids the tendency to construct Western and non-Western cultural practices as if they are mutually exclusive when they are clearly connected. As we know, over the last three decades, feminists have deployed the discourse of intersectionality to focus upon the interrelationship between these different axes of differentiation and power (Crenshaw, 1989). I am in agreement with Nira Yuval Davis (2011) that citizenship must be understood in terms of its articulation with different axes of intersectionality.

In debates about intercultural citizenship, there are those who assume that interculturalism is in conflict with gender equality. Here a picture of allegedly stereotypic patriarchal treatment of girls and women in minoritised communities is invoked as a way of discrediting interculturalism. For instance, the question of arranged marriages is often raised when in fact the problem is not with arranged but forced marriages. I am against forced marriages as are many other members of Asian communities. But a great many arranged marriages are not forced marriages. It is ironic that patriarchal practices among minoritised groups are castigated and typecast when there are many patriarchal practices that are still prevalent in many Western societies but they are not used to stereotype these societies. Feminists have long argued against the use of this binary between the supposed progressive West and traditional non-West. Opinion makers who mobilise such binarised representations and claim to stand up for minoritised women in these debates are unlikely to be feminists themselves. This is not to suggest that patriarchal practices should not be criticised. Far from it. But this must happen against all patriarchal practices (Phillips, 2010). And they must take the broader context of global power inequalities into account. Questions of cultural difference need to be contextualised against the backdrop of cultural hierarchies that mark the lives of different groups of women. I would use a feminist yardstick to address difficult questions of cultural difference (Phillips, 2010), but it must be a feminism that is intersectional and, simultaneously, is anti-imperialist and one that is alive to the unequal power relations between different parts of the globe.

Unfortunately, these days discourses about cultural difference tend to exhibit an assimilationist tendency. This is a reversal of the gains previously made through political activism and campaigns. For instance, as long ago as 23 May 1966, the then Home Secretary of Britain argued against the notion of assimilation and in favour of integration. He said that integration should be viewed not "as a flattening process of assimilation but as equal opportunity accompanied by cultural diversity, in an atmosphere of mutual trust" (Jenkins, 1996). But today when politicians use the term integration, they mean assimilation. Integration, at its best, is designed to incorporate incoming groups into the economic, social, and political life on the basis of equality of opportunity as well as outcome. So, for instance, class equality is as important as cultural equality. But a discourse of integration as a mask for assimilation seeks to flatten cultural difference. The right to cultural difference has become a critical arena of contestation today.

This reappraisal of different conceptions of citizenship can be seen to foreground themes that are simultaneously relevant to diaspora studies, literary studies, and law. Finally, I conclude with a brief commentary on the way in which law diaspora and literary studies may be interconnected through the concept of governance and governmentality.

To think of law in the broader sense foregrounds Michel Foucault's concept of law as governance and governmentality (Golder, 2013). It is linked with the notion of disciplinary power with its focus on techniques of surveillance, and 'docile bodies'. This concept is intertwined with his view of power as both coercive and productive. Although Foucault may be seen to counterpose law to regulation, Hunt and Wickham (1994) argue that discipline and law supplement each other and form distinctive and pervasive forms of regulation at the very heart of modern government. Law, they suggest, is never unitary – rather it is a complex of practices, discourses, and institutions. The prison, for instance, may be constructed within a juridical framework but it operates with disciplinary techniques. In diaspora studies, practices and institutions are important. Diaspora narratives are the ground on which realities of encounters with law and disciplinary power are played out. Citizenship law, immigration law, and statutes of international governance are all relevant to the life chances of migrants. There is thus a clear link between diaspora, literary studies, and law.

If legal discourses are a dynamic product of the articulation of complex social, historical, and political forces embedded within rationalities and technologies of power, then questions of identity and difference have a critical bearing on legal narratives. How are those who have committed an offence constructed or represented in terms of their identities? How is identity to be theorised? There is an on-going debate about these concerns. As noted earlier, Stuart Hall has used both Derridean deconstruction, utilising the concept of *différance*, and Judith Butler's use of psychoanalysis to think through questions of identity.[4] I believe these insights are incisive and bring together diaspora, literary, and legal studies. In conclusion, it is important to note that the concept of intersectionality discussed throughout the text is crucial to all three areas and informs the multiple configurations of power.

---

[4] Stuart Hall and Paul Du Gay, *Questions of Cultural Identity* (London: SAGE Publications, 1996).

Chapter 9

Insurgent Knowledges, Politics of Resistance: A Conversation between Avtar Brah, Brenna Bhandar, and Rafeef Ziadah

BB/RZ: Through several decades of meticulously grounded research, you have devised a methodological approach that reworks Althusser's theory of interpellation, among other Marxian theories, to account not only for the effects of capitalist social relations but also the psychic and symbolic relations of race, migration, class, and gender. Stuart Hall states that your method, arising at a distinct historical, theoretical, and political conjuncture, could be termed 'the diasporic'. So the first question we want to ask is, could you tell us about this distinct conjuncture in terms of the historical moment, and the theoretical influences and the political landscape during which you developed the diasporic as a method?

AB: The concept of diaspora, or even the term 'diaspora', assumed currency during, I think, the mid-to-late eighties and nineties in Britain. Looking back, one of the major political moments that comes to mind was the 1989 crumbling of the Berlin Wall and the demise of the Soviet Union as a Communist bloc. So that had a very significant global impact. In Britain at the time, of course, we had Thatcherism. That ideology and practice had a very significant impact on people of colour. In the field of research and knowledge production within academia and outside academia too, there were a lot of intellectual contestations around postmodernity and modernity, poststructuralism and structuralism. So, there was a lot of both intellectual and political ferment going on. Looking specifically at the term 'diaspora', I think I'll confine myself to Britain in the post-war period. Until the 1980s, really, the term used to describe people of colour was 'immigrant'.

It wasn't a straightforward descriptor; rather, it was a mode of marginalising and pathologising the communities. In fact, even British-born young people were called second-generation or third-generation immigrants. That still happens. It irritates me when I hear that. At the same time, the terms 'ethnic relations', or 'ethnic group' were also in currency. That was thought to be a slightly more polite way of referring to people of colour, although of course the term is not necessarily just applicable to people of colour, but any ethnic group. But in Britain that was how it was used. Again, that particular term, although slightly more polite, still tended to pathologise minority ethnic groups. There was a tendency to talk about people of colour as a problem; the discourses centred around problems.

That intellectual and political climate was the backdrop against which people were beginning to think about ways to interrogate that language. How shall we talk about people whose historical trajectories touch on many continents and many countries? In what way can we talk and think about those groups without pathologising them? And the term 'diaspora' emerged in that critical ferment. In part, it was designed to critique nationalisms and get away from an undue focus on the nation state. Again, we have to remember that this was a time when globalisation was a major feature of the economy and society. The concept of diaspora was intended to enable us to think beyond the nation state and foreground communities that had links globally, so to speak. So the term emerges in that kind of a political conjuncture. Paul Gilroy's book *The Black Atlantic* (1993) uses the term 'diaspora', and Stuart Hall (1996b [1989]) used the concept as well.

Then, the term 'ethnicity' came on the horizon; Stuart Hall (1996b [1989]) coined the term 'new ethnicities', which is linked to 'diaspora' in the sense that new ethnicities were focused on generational shifts, on hybridisation, on politics of representation. Hall's focus was on the use of poststructuralist thought in relation to analysing ethnicity. He sought to develop conceptions of ethnicity that did not essentialise, pathologise, or marginalise communities. It is a non-essentialist concept which emphasises the place of history, language, and culture. So that's the kind of context in which the term 'diaspora' emerges. For many of us, it was a more positive way of conceptualising communities, and a way to deracialise them, because they were always thought of in a racialised mode at the time. So that's the context in which the term emerges.

BB/RZ: Do you want to tell us a bit more about Thatcherism and how that impacted people of colour in this country?

AB: Thatcherism, as you know, was linked to Powellism in the previous decade. Enoch Powell famously, or infamously, talked about young people, Black people, Asians, saying that they could be born in Britain but could never be *of* Britain. He talked about young 'piccanninies' and used all kinds of racialised language, and gave a speech focusing on 'the rivers of blood' that might flow in Britain, which expressed his predictions of violence that might ensue due to immigration. Margaret Thatcher built on and continued the same kind of discourse. She didn't always use the same language, but it was a very similar discourse. In a 1978 TV interview, she talked about the British people being scared that Britain might be 'swamped by people of a different culture'. That kind of language was creating many problems, giving respectability to racism. There was a lot of racial violence on the streets, which we tend to forget now, but there were many racial attacks; people had been murdered. I remember in Southall, for instance, Gurdip Chaggar was murdered in 1976 by young white people.[1] So there was a lot of racist violence.

But economically, as well, we were seeing not the emergence of neoliberalism (because it is much older than that), but neoliberalism becoming much more rampant, particularly in Thatcher's policies. There were attacks, which are happening again now, on the trade unions. You will remember that 1984 was when the miners were on strike and Thatcher was totally committed to destroying the miners.

---

[1] Gurdip Singh Chaggar, 18 years old, was stabbed to death by racists in Southall, London, on 3 June 1976.

There were figures given in the media about the huge sums of money the government spent on campaigning against the miners and their union, and the government did succeed in the end – that was one of the very sad moments in labour history. The attacks on the unions had a major impact on people of colour, partly because people of colour held jobs in places of work affected by Thatcherite policies. There were high levels of unemployment among people of colour.

All of this was happening everywhere. In 1979 in Southall, Blair Peach, a teacher, was killed by injuries sustained to the head, at the hands of police. This happened when the racist and fascist National Front came marching through Southall to hold an election rally against which the local people had gathered to protest. The police, in the form of the notorious Special Patrol Group, came in large numbers to ensure that the National Front rally did take place. In the process many protestors were injured, arrested, and taken to police stations all over London. Over 700 people, mainly Asians, were arrested and, I think, 345 were charged. Clarence Baker, the manager of the Black reggae band Misty in Roots, was so badly injured on the head that he spent considerable time in hospital. So there was a lot of that kind of political ferment going on, within which there was a great deal of contestation of, and challenges to, the racism people were experiencing. At the same time, in factories there were strikes. I was in Southall in the early 1980s, and I remember there was a strike of workers at the Chix bubble gum factory in Slough.[2] We used to go and support those women – it was mostly women who were on strike. Such events were happening all the time. Mainly the term 'diaspora' itself emerged during this time to challenge racialised regimes, which were connected to the very material, everyday lives of people because of unemployment and racist violence.

BB: You also draw a connection between the fall of the Berlin Wall – and the demise of the Soviet bloc, the massive impact that had on left

---

[2] The workers at the Chix factory in Slough went on the strike for eight months during 1979 and 1980 and won recognition of their union.

politics – and the contemporaneous racial violence against people of colour and antiracist resistance.

AB: Absolutely, that was a very major event of the period, globally too. We all went into depression, those of us who were involved in socialist projects. We were always critical of the Soviet Union, but nonetheless, globally there was a socialist presence, a project that we subscribed to. There was a huge amount of melancholia at the time. But also, internationally it's quite important, because the Black struggles – and I'll use the term 'Black' for the moment, including Asians – were always international struggles. The Left, particularly the Black Left, theorised racism in the context of histories of capitalism, colonialism and imperialism, whereas other contemporary discourses are likely to underplay these connections. But the Black Left always looked at the links between colonialism and postcolonialism; and imperialism and new imperialisms.

That, of course, shifted after the demise of Soviet Communism because the ways in which global power relations had been constituted changed. A new order, a new political order, was born now in which capitalism gained a much more pronounced ascendancy. Also, for a period, at least – although that has changed now – we found that the Soviet Union was no longer seen as a threat by the West. There was a period when the Iron Curtain was no longer seen as the Iron Curtain. So internationally, that meant the left project in Britain was affected by what happened, because it weakened the arguments for alternatives. That has changed now, of course, because Russia is again not in the good books of the West, but for a period it was not seen as a threat.

It was also the case that the Black women's groups that we had in those days, we, as Black women, always explored the ways in which our life trajectories had been constituted over periods of time in and through histories of imperialism. And the ways in which our presence here in Britain was connected with colonialism, in the sense that during the post-war period, Britain recruited Black people, people of colour, from its colonies to come and do the work the white workers didn't want to do, in the lowest rungs of the economy. So that was very important. Our presence here was connected with colonialism and such issues were always crucial to emphasise. We always foregrounded international struggles alongside our political struggles here in Britain.

BB/RZ: Do you feel that goes missing nowadays, that grounding?

AB: Yes, to some degree. Moreover, in those days we talked about class relations and capitalism. Sometimes you find nowadays that people talk about the disadvantaged 99 per cent and all that, and it's good that it's happening, but I find it quite frustrating that people don't always explicitly define and concretise capitalism. There are discussions about the wars in the Middle East, and so forth, but not enough emphasis on the histories of colonialism and imperialism, which resulted in the carving out of these different countries and created these different territorial lines, new countries and new nation states which are now having all kinds of problems. Indeed, there is insufficient problematisation of the links between capitalism and imperialism. I know we're jumping around here, but people talk about all these migrants coming from abroad, as if capitalism and imperialism has no effect in making these countries poor. Back then, there was considerable discussion about the ways in which certain parts of the world became impoverished.

There was a focus on the global inequalities and inequities – people talked about them. There was a discourse around them in the media. But now there is not the same degree of attention, although the new developments such as the Occupy Movement of 2011–12 have been of great importance and significance. Today there is much discussion and debate about all these so-called economic migrants coming here, but not enough attention to why it is mainly people from the global South who become economic migrants to the rich global North. I find this gaping absence really problematic.

BB/RZ: It's quite common in the academy for people to take up a self-described stance as 'being critical' without considering capitalism or class in any serious fashion. What do you make of the identification of being critical, or the idea of critique, when it no longer addresses precisely the issues you were just talking about?

AB: Well, it is a big problem, even in terms of resources. Of course, you have Thomas Piketty's *Capital in the Twenty-First Century* (2013) and books like that, which are important, but they're not critiques of capitalism as such from a socialist perspective. Similarly, I was excited when I came across Ha-Joon Chang's *23 Things They Don't Tell You about Capitalism* (2010). But then he clearly states that he's not against capitalism. Whereas in the eighties and nineties, there were resources, there were books – for instance Susan George's *How the Other Half Dies* (1976), which looks at global poverty and why people in certain parts of the world are actually dying. And they were quite easily accessible kinds of books, not heavy theory, although they contained a lot of theoretical insight and you could use them with students. There used to be quite a few video programmes; Channel 4, for example, did some very interesting programmes around multinational corporations, which looked at how multinationals go overseas and the ways in which they extract surplus value, particularly in special economic zones.

These were very accessible, excellently made programmes, which took away the mystique about how these multinationals operate globally. I remember throughout my teaching years using some of those kinds of resources with students, alongside the more strictly academic ones. I'm not teaching anymore, so you would know better than me what kinds of resources are available today, but I have a sense those kinds of resources are not that easily accessible. Am I right, or are there resources like that?

BB: There are resources like that to be used, but I think what has changed is the environment in which we are working; the landscape of higher education has changed a lot, and in some ways the space for doing that kind of teaching has shrunk.

AB: Now why is that? Is that because they find those kinds of critiques threatening? What is the reason?

BB: My view is shaped by my experience in the field that I'm in. Law is always a more conservative discipline. But there was, for a period of time, particularly in the seventies and eighties, a very left, vibrant, critical movement within legal studies here. That work was however, with a few very important exceptions, void of any serious engagement with issues of race, gender, colonialism, and empire. More recently, we have seen a renewed engagement with law and racial capitalism, but today, academics are increasingly isolated in the academy, and scholarly work is affected by a lack of engagement with the world outside. Alternately, where engagement does take place, it is often confined by the parameters set by an audit culture and a marketised system of education.

BB/RZ: Going back to the concept of diaspora, you have written that diaspora can be understood in four different ways – first, by looking at diaspora as an analytical concept, which I think you explained before; second by looking at diaspora as a genealogical concept; and third, the diasporic as focused on both 'routes' and 'roots', which we think is really compelling. Fourth, there is the fact that diaspora itself is an intersectional concept. So we just want to ask if you could tease out a few more of these different ways of thinking about those words.

AB: I think when I came to this term 'diaspora' and started using it, I was very acutely aware that we were talking about diaspora in many different ways. There are, of course, many discourses of diaspora, and James Clifford (1994) talks about this as well. There are different types of *discourses* of diaspora, which need to be distinguished from the actual *lived experiences* of diaspora. Then there is the *concept* of diaspora, as distinct from lived experience and histories of diaspora. I wanted to think through the question: "How can we distinguish the concept from the experience of diaspora and the discourses of diaspora?" That was how I came to the notion of thinking about diaspora as a concept in terms of genealogy. I used the Foucauldian term 'genealogy' because it simultaneously foregrounds discourse and knowledge and power, which is very important when we are thinking about diasporas and how they are constituted, how they have been lived.

Thus, there is the notion of power, and notions of how knowledge and power are always connected, how different kinds of discourses construct diasporas in different kinds of ways. I decided that I was going to think of the concept of diaspora as genealogy, and as genealogy it doesn't hark back to final origins or pure essences, or present truth claims as given rather than constructed. It occurred to me that we needed to think of diaspora as a concept in terms of an investigative technology, which looks at historical, cultural, social, and political processes in and through which diasporas are constituted. I also wanted to point to the ways in which different subaltern diasporas are positioned in relation to one another other, and not simply in relation to the dominant group in society.

Then, in terms of routes and roots – yes that's very important, of course. It was Paul Gilroy (1993), who in his book used this term, 'routes and roots', because in a way there is a contestation between routes and roots, so to speak, in thinking about diasporas. There's movement, but there is also a sense of actually putting down roots in a place to which one moves. To hold these two axes together simultaneously is critical. Diasporas are historically specific formations. Each diaspora has its own history, such that you can have diasporas which emerge out of slavery. Then there are diasporas which emerge out of labour migrations. There are diasporas which emerge out of what is happening at the moment around us, refugees coming out of wars, war-torn countries, out of poverty.

So, in all those different notions of diaspora, history is critical, because not all diasporas are the same, so we have to look at the history behind each formation of the diaspora. This term 'intersectional' – actually, I didn't come to intersectionality through the work of Kimberlé Crenshaw. I was concerned as to how questions of race, gender, class, or sexuality constantly interact. This was during the process of writing *Cartographies of Diaspora* (1996). And I used the term 'intersectionality' in *Cartographies*. I came across Crenshaw's work later. In a sense, maybe I have a slightly different take on intersectionality. I'm told that some people mainly associate the concept of intersectionality with subordinate groups whereas I think that intersectionality is about power regimes and how they intersect and position different groups differently and differentially in relation to each other. One has to look at the regimes of domination if we are to understand the ways the subordinate live their lives. But, we also have to look at how the dominant groups dominate. Intersectionality for me, first and foremost, is about embodiment. How do we embody social relations? And this is as much about the social, political, and cultural as it is about the psychic. It's about subjectivity and it's also about identity. So, I address intersections throughout *Cartographies*, but I'm talking about all these different levels noted above. I consider 'difference', which is related to intersectionality very closely, again as social relation, but also as subjectivity, as identity and as experience.

The key thing is that these different axes – class, race, gender, sexuality, disability, and so on – intersect both in our physical bodies and the social body. So, intersectionality operates at the level of the social, the physical, and the psyche. I greatly respect the debates that came afterwards and have learnt a great deal from them, but my own take on intersectionality may have been slightly different from the way it at times appears to have become valorised now.

BB/RZ: What do you think its valorisation has been about?

AB: Well, intersectionality both as a concept and a political practice emerges out of discussion and debate surrounding the experience of Black American women, especially, working-class Black American women. And this work is really important. Yet, there are other discourses where talk about intersectionality has become a mantra now. In reality, intersectionality demands a lot of hard work – analytically, politically, in every way. It's not just about the rhetorical use of three or four key words, and saying 'yes, I'm doing intersectionality' – it's really looking at grounded analysis of these different axes. It requires complex analysis. It's hard work.

BB: One of the effects of its valorisation has been that it has allowed, to some extent, the continued universalisation of particular women's experiences. For instance, in a given article there may be a couple of paragraphs that acknowledge, 'that this issue is different for women of colour or different for working-class women of colour'. In this cynical sense, it can almost be used as an insurance policy to guard against the criticism that one is not integrating analysis of race or class.

RZ: Academically, that can be the case. But then there's also activist movements where it has been very much owned by people of colour. You have the Black Lives Matter movement, for example, and the insistence of the activists in BLM that this movement will be intersectional. The hard work you're speaking of is partly on the academic level, but it's required in the social movement too. When you say 'it's hard work to do', what does that mean for an activist who would be starting today? How do you think that would play out?

AB: Well, I have to go back to my roots in Southall Black Sisters.

RZ: That's what I was hoping you would do.

AB: That was hard work, when I look back on it. I was a member of the Southall Black Sisters at its inception in 1979. Then in 1982, I left London for a job in Leicester and then in Milton Keynes, so I moved away from SBS during its second phase. But I know, firstly, that it was hard work in terms of the things we've been talking about, the interconnections that we had to make between our histories – our imperial histories, colonial histories – to make sense of what was happening to us as Black women in post-war Britain, in eighties and nineties Britain. It was also hard work in terms of dealing with patriarchal issues in relation to men with whom we were working, around questions of racism, for example, or questions about socialism. That was not easy at all, you know; it was difficult to raise patriarchal issues. We would be having a political meeting about socialism or about racism. Then to raise issues of gender was seen as failing to show solidarity with brothers, so to speak.

We were planning an antiracist and anti-fascist march from Bradford to London. The march didn't happen in the end, but we were planning one. We had a meeting with men and women in Bradford to discuss what we would do. We brought up the question of gender, and that didn't go down very well with a number of the men – not all of them, but with some of them. There were many reasons why the march didn't happen, but some of the men tended to blame us for bringing up questions of patriarchal relations as the reason for why the march did not take place. So there was the struggle with men on the political left. There was, of course, struggle within our own communities, where, as in Britain as a whole, living out the difficulty of patriarchal relations was an everyday experience for women.

We had to develop strategies to make sure people would listen to us and not just dismiss us as these difficult young women with these newfound ideas. Some of the things we did were simultaneously fun and serious. For example, we once staged a feminist version of *Ramlila*, a play based on the Hindu epic of *Ramayana*. Some people might think, 'Why would you do that?' But here we were in Southall, a predominantly Asian locality at the time, and we wanted to engage the audience with the help of political theatre. In the event, mostly women came to see the play. Our aim was to critique Sita's position as a woman, and we used the figure of a 'jester', who provided a humorous though pointed commentary on the proceedings. Here was a feminist perspective presented through an idiom that was culturally familiar to those present. We did that. It was quite a successful event. The women could identify, because they knew what it would be like if you lived the life of an 'obedient wife'. And, we were coming up with different ideas about possible alternatives.

I think you have to be able to work with people in such a way that you can facilitate the emergence of a shared common project. You have to address the contradictory 'common sense' that we all live with, that Gramsci (1971) speaks of. Unless you do that, then you're not going to make much headway with constructing new political agendas. To do that, you have to begin with where people are at, but not stay there, and not get sucked into taking up a narrow political position. But rather, try to jointly develop new discourses and practices for the creation of new political horizons, a new common sense. Those were rather difficult things to do in relation to our communities, but also in relation to ourselves. We were Asian women, we were women of African descent.

There was once a political meeting called – not by us, but by another antiracist group in Southall – in a hall belonging to a temple. Just as a venue, not for religious reasons. I know that some SBS members didn't want to go there because it was in a hall on the premises of a temple, a religious place, when we were secular. So, there were difficult debates and issues like that. There isn't a hard and fast rule for how you would go about doing such work at the ground level, if you are an activist. It's quite hard work. It takes its toll on you psychologically.

BB/RZ: We were also wondering how your own life experiences influence your theoretical and conceptual work around diaspora?

AB: I was born in India, but I was about five or six years old when I went to Africa. So I grew up in Uganda. I was in Uganda until I did my A levels. Then I went to America to study; I was in California, where I did my undergraduate degree, then Wisconsin, where I did my Master's. This was about the time when Idi Amin was coming to power. I was in Britain, on my way back to Uganda, when the Idi Amin edict was issued[3] – and even though I was a Ugandan citizen, I couldn't go back. So I was stateless for about five years in Britain, until I became a citizen. (In those days, after five years you applied for naturalisation.) Hence, I've lived in all these different countries, and diaspora is very much part and parcel of my life experience. The things we've been talking about – SBS, other politics around racism, around class and so on – all those are very much part and parcel of my life.

My analysis has always been informed by my political activism and vice versa. I think the two have gone together. So the concept of 'diaspora space', for example, emerged out of thinking through different life experiences and how to theorise about them, how to analyse them.

---

[3] On 4 August 1972, President of Uganda Idi Amin issued a decree ordering the expulsion of the 50,000 Asians who were British passport holders, forcing many to migrate to the UK, other Commonwealth nations, and the United States.

BB/RZ: We wanted to follow up with the question of belonging and your work on belonging. The Indigenous Australian scholar Aileen Moreton-Robinson (2015) draws our attention to the fact that the conjoined twin of belonging is exclusion, which may sound obvious, but she points out how that often gets lost in the discourse on belonging. Lauren Berlant (2016: 395) formulated this nicely: 'Just because we are in the room together does not mean that we belong to the room or each other: belonging is a specific genre of affect, history, and political mediation that cannot be presumed and is, indeed, a relation whose evidence and terms are always being contested.'[4] We were wondering if you could tell us a little bit about your understanding of the discourse of belonging and how that has been useful to your thinking on migration and diaspora?

AB: I think, in fact, that what these two scholars say is very important. I do find the notion of belonging compelling, because without a sense of belonging, however contested and fractured it might be, you are vulnerable as an outsider – not just physically, but psychologically and psychically, as well. We are vulnerable if we don't feel any sense of belonging – to our siblings, our families, our friends, our political allies, our 'imagined communities' as well as others that form our lifeworld. The point that Moreton-Robinson and Berlant are making is that the flip side of belonging is exclusion. Belonging only makes sense because there is exclusion. Histories of racism, class hierarchy, and heteronormativity, for instance, tell us which groups, under what conditions, have belonged or been excluded.

Apart from being predicated against the socio-economic, political, and cultural landscape, belonging is also very much part of the affective domain. These different aspects need to be held together. But we always need to be aware – it's like when Stuart Hall talks about

---

[4] Berlant continues: "Belonging is a proposition, a theory, a forensic fact, and a name for a king of attachment. The crowded but disjointed propinquity of the social calls for a proxemics, the study of sociality as a proximity quite distinct from the possessive attachment languages of belonging."

the concept of 'identity', and he says that it's a term without which he cannot do, but at the same time it's a term that he's continually interrogating. I think 'belonging' is such a term. You can't do without it, but you have to always question how it is being evoked, always remain aware how it is being used and how a sense of belonging, or a sense of alienation, is being played out. Those two may go together. If you don't feel a sense of belonging, you may become alienated. What kinds of social, political, and cultural conditions favour alienation and anomie as opposed to a sense of belonging, a sense of well-being?

I would think of it that way, to be aware of those social issues alongside the sense that it gives you a feeling of being a part of something. A sense of affirmation.

BB/RZ: I think you mentioned somewhere that a feeling of being at home is one way of describing what belonging is. Because for those of us who have moved around a lot or have come from families who were also immigrant families, migrant families, refugee families, it's quite difficult to grasp what 'belonging' actually means. For many of us, the feeling of not belonging is what becomes familiar and even a primary psychic default position. What does belonging actually look like, and what does it mean?

AB: It is a sense of feeling at home, isn't it?

BB: Yes, I think that's why I recalled that. Because I thought, okay, that's an interesting way to think about what it means to belong – feeling at home somewhere

RZ: From a Palestinian perspective, for example, when home is a colonised space you are not allowed to return to – the struggle is to hold on to return, but also your rights and new belonging where you have ended up.

AB: There's always a tension. I remember thinking about this when I first came here. At first, you feel you're in a new place; you don't feel at home at all. But then there comes a time when you do begin to feel at home, but you may not necessarily be seen by the dominant group as belonging. That is why affect and the psyche are implicated in all of that. It's also having that psychic strength to be able to say, 'I now feel at home, and I'm going to contest you who say I'm not at home.' To have that strength is very important. Political activism gives that collective strength, and our loved ones give us the personal strength. So, it is a contest all the time. Because even now, I've been here 20-odd years, more than that, but there are people who still think I'm an outsider. But I feel quite at home down here in London, and I challenge the processes that construct me as an outsider. But you're absolutely right – it's always contested, disputed, and how you feel does not necessarily reflect how others see you.

BB/RZ: In *Cartographies of Diaspora*, you explore how the new Europe has been constituted juridically, legally, politically, economically, and culturally, through race, class, and gender. You make an intervention into the discourse of new racisms by showing how the racisms that emerged in Britain in the context of debate over the EU are informed by the New Right. This related back to our earlier discussion about how terms like 'nation' and 'people' were used by Thatcher against trade unions and the working class and so-called welfare scroungers.

Alongside the austerity policies and politics that have saturated the UK and also the EU in the last decade, what differences do you perceive between the eighties and nineties, and this current moment? You mentioned Powellism and Thatcher and the language of the swarm, which came back, of course, in Cameron's comments on refugees. We were wondering if you could maybe talk a little bit about some of the similarities or differences you see between that earlier moment and what's happening today?

AB: Well, I suppose the linguistic content can sometimes be very similar. Often, immigrant groups are represented as dirty, as inherently different, as 'Other'. There's a recursivity about ways in which certain groups are described and 'Othered'. But what changes is the broader social context, and I think that has changed hugely, if you look back at the eighties. In economic terms the situation for some groups, such as the precariat class in the gig economy, has worsened. But, also, the global scene has changed so much with all the wars, ever since the war in Iraq and the Gulf in 1990. We've had several other wars since. The rise of the Islamic State as well, and the ways in which the securitisation discourses and practices have come to the fore since 9/11, for instance. All of these have actually changed the world enormously. So, the racism of which we speak has never been one racism. We talk about Islamophobia or anti-Muslim racism, which is a very specific racism. Similarly, we talk about racism that is directed at asylum seekers and refugees; that is another one. And, of course, anti-Semitism, as well as the racism that is directed at the so-called economic migrants, or against people of colour; these are all distinct forms of racism.

Even the refugees are not accepted to any great degree in Britain. Turkey and Pakistan have taken millions of refugees, and here in Britain we have taken comparatively few. Indeed, we know that most of the refugees are in the Third World countries, or what we now call the global South. The global scene, in terms of these wars and what they have done to people's lives, is just horrendous. I often think, here we sit, and talk about lofty ideals while we forget how people live in dire conditions in wartime zones.

Rather than resolving issues politically, countries, particularly countries in the West, are likely to be more and more involved in situations in which military intervention is regarded as justified.

BB: I wanted to ask you, following up on the Brexit referendum, and these different forms of racism that you're identifying, what is your diagnosis of the re-emergence of the discourse around the Commonwealth?

AB: Some people who are in favour of leaving the EU argue for the importance of the Commonwealth. They seem to assume for some reason that in the post-Brexit period, Britain will suddenly allow people from Africa and the Caribbean and India and Pakistan to enter the UK, that the doors will be open wide. The Brexit campaign has made them believe, incorrectly in my view, that there is competition between the East Europeans and people from the Commonwealth. That somehow if we didn't have people from Eastern

Europe, then we would get more people from the Commonwealth. That won't happen.

BB: It seems as though people who have been denied recognition as people who truly belong in the nation are trying to reinvigorate this discourse of empire, as if to say we have a place here that precedes that of the Eastern European migrants.

AB: You are absolutely right about that – that's true. In 2015, when Greece was in a very dire economic situation, I became very anti-EU. But on the other hand, the EU has the Social Charter,[5] whereas some in Britain don't even want to retain the Human Rights Act. I felt that because of the Social Charter, we probably needed to stay in the EU and argue for a better, more democratic EU than we have now. But the Brexit group managed to convince quite a few people that the interest of the Commonwealth would be better served if we leave. It doesn't make sense from a rational point of view but we are dealing here with the workings of ideology.

BB: Can we switch tack for a moment? We wanted you to address the shift in political identification with respect to the use of term 'Black'.

AB: There has been a splintering of the sense in which we used the term 'Black' from the 1970s onwards. Even back then, in the mid-1970s, some people didn't agree with us; they used to say, 'Asians are not Black – they don't look Black.' But at the same time, there are some women today who also want to use the term 'Black' in the sense that we used it. When we constructed the term 'Black' to refer to a political colour rather than a shade of skin, it was in the context where we were working together against shared experiences of racism. There were immigration laws, for example, against which we,

---

[5] The European Social Charter is a Council of Europe treaty that guarantees fundamental social and economic rights as a counterpart to the European Convention on Human Rights, which refers to civil and political rights. It guaranteed a broad range of everyday human rights related to employment, housing, health, education, social protection, and welfare. See 'The European Social Charter', Council of Europe official website, coe.int.

as Black communities, mobilised across the board. So, the term had a political purchase.

But nowadays, even the term 'Asian' has itself become fractured. When you use the term 'Asian', people don't necessarily identify with that. People talk about being Muslims, or Hindus, or Sikhs, so the religious identifications have become much more pronounced. The point is that unity has to be achieved through struggle and solidarity; it cannot be imposed. Because if a term doesn't have a critical purchase, then it is probably more relevant to use a term that actually does have political resonance with a new generation of people today.

I've started using the American term, 'women of colour' or 'people of colour'. Which is also problematic, because they used to use the term 'coloured' here in Britain, which was a racialised term. But people of colour has been constructed by 'non-white' groups in solidarity. And that is important.

RZ: It's interesting because religious affiliation has become much more common. This has taken place, like you're saying, in many situations, where it is your religious affiliation, even more specifically, your sect, that people are using. What do you think of that change that has happened?

AB: That's a very difficult one, isn't it? It's because it's so caught up with global politics as well. We can't talk about religion – we can talk about spiritualism. I've nothing against spiritualism – people can pursue their religious affiliation if they're spiritually oriented. But religion is no longer seen as separate from the geopolitical order at the moment.

BB: I think nowadays, rather than identifying people of colour by ethnicity, we are marginalised and racialised through –

AB: Being called Muslim.

RZ: Yes. There are certain types of racisms that have developed that are related to religion, and there are the tensions that come with building alliances along those lines. How do we nurture and build an antiracist movement around these issues?

AB: I think in terms of racism, it is quite clear. One needs to fight against Islamophobia, or any other anti-religious racism that there is. That is easier to deal with, in a way, because one takes a stand against any racism that goes around. But when I and my political allies organised in the old days, we were organising as secular groups. In a sense it was easier. But nowadays, people organise around religion; I don't know what you do in universities now, because there are so many religious groups that are organising separately. So that the term 'Asian' doesn't hold much sway – that's what I meant earlier – because in the main, students don't come together as Asians in universities. Rather, they come together as Sikhs or Hindus or Muslims or Arabs or other groups, Shias and Sunnis, and so on. I think I would still say we need to come together on broader platforms, on common political concerns. I personally wouldn't organise around religion myself, unless I was oppressed on religious grounds. The key issue is one of oppression and exploitation. We know that the reality is that people *do* organise around religion. And given that there is an international onslaught on certain religious groups, it is understandable why they come together in the way they do. It is difficult to be sanctimonious. We must take politically thought-through positions. Because I don't think we can have blueprints for all situations.

BB/RZ: Do you think there is any political currency left in thinking about secularism as a basis for feminist politics, or maybe a reconstructed secularism?

AB: Yes, I think there is need for a reconstructed secularism. Because some secularists are as fanatical as the religious groups can be, at times. But a reconstructed secularism, I think, is important. I'm always told by my Muslim friends, 'You don't realise what it means to be Muslim today, because of all this onslaught all the time.' My response is that there is that experiential dimension there which needs to be addressed, but it's such a tightrope – a very tight rope indeed. You have to look at everything as it happens and say, 'which way do I go?' I personally think that we need secular politics, but we have to be able to take on board the reality of, for instance, Islamophobia and anti-Muslim racism.

BB/RZ: We wanted to follow up with the concept of critical multiculturalism. Given the fragmentation of politics, that the issue of religion and religious identification has entered into the political landscape in a way that is much greater than in the eighties or nineties, does the concept of a critical multiculturalism still have relevance today?

AB: Yes. Well, one of the things that I think, given what you've just said, is that when people criticise multiculturalism, they often fail to make a distinction between multiculturalism as cultural diversity and multiculturalism as social policy. People were often critical of the latter, because in the eighties and nineties there were policies in local authorities which were informed by multiculturalism. I think some of those policies were problematic, but not all of those policies were wrong. After all, multiculturalism emerged out of struggle; it wasn't something that was just given to us by the state. It was a struggle to say, in education – the discourse of multiculturalism was most widely prevalent in education, that's where it was most strongly felt – that we didn't want an education system which pays no attention to the histories of colonialism and imperialism, which pays no attention to cultural diversity, to the ways in which people from the former colonies were concentrated in certain geographical locations where there were high rates of unemployment and poor housing and poor social services. That we wanted a different kind of education system, or different kind of policy that actually took into account the specific needs of different groups of people.

I think at that level it was a struggle, and it was relevant to argue for multicultural education. But then there was a debate between antiracists and multiculturalists. That was because once multiculturalism started being practised in schools and elsewhere, it became obvious that sometimes the question of racism or class was not taken very seriously. Thus, multiculturalism came to be caricatured as being about 'samosas, saris and steel drums', or something like that.

So we started talking about antiracism in education as opposed to multicultural education. That debate went on a for a decade or so. It has now gone away, because people started attacking multiculturalism. Multiculturalism is problematic if it does not address an antiracist critique. But what do we have instead? Monoculturalism? No! We may not call it multiculturalism; people are using different terms, currently. Instead of 'multiculturalism', they're trying to use the term 'interculturalism'. Basically, they're struggling with the same thing, which is, how do you address the hegemony of white British culture, even when we know that there is nothing called 'white British culture', in the singular because British culture is heterogeneous.

But nonetheless, when people talk about the 'British way of life', or 'British values', which is a current discourse, they assume there is something British which is inherently different from the rest of the world, something uniquely special, when often they're talking about very universal values, really. So, if we don't have some kind of a politics and a discourse around cultural diversity, how do we contest the discourse of 'British way of life'? In other words, you're right that 'multiculturalism' as a term now is a problem, because it has been so discredited. But how do we deal with cultural diversity? I'm not sure what kind of term we can use, other than just 'cultural diversity'. Or 'interculturalism' – to me that sounds quite similar to 'multiculturalism' anyway. Perhaps 'antiracist interculturalism'? And then there is that whole discourse about 'integration'. That term is a big problem, which is connected with 'multiculturalism'. 'Integration' in current discourses often means assimilation. That's what they mean. I don't want assimilation. I think we fought against assimilation.

So how do we construct a new term? I'm looking at you, as well. Can you think of something that can replace it, but without giving in to the assimilationist impulse?

RZ: Like you were saying, many of these things have to come out of practice. These formulations tend to come about through the struggle for something specific.

AB: It's true, it's very true.

BB: In a way, this is related to our emphasis on practice. In thinking about intersectionality, for instance, as an approach that can only have meaning in working it through both intellectually and politically. This notion is quite distinct from the idea of grasping certain identifications in a mode of strategic essentialism, which reflects a more tactical approach.

RZ: Just to change course slightly – we very recently saw a film that you had directed as part of a project on the *Darkmatter* journal website.[6] And it was stunningly beautiful.

AB: I'm glad you liked it.

RZ: It was remarkable, both as a historical record but also the method that you used. How did you decide to do that, methodologically?

AB: Well, I was working at the Department of Extramural Studies at Birkbeck College. A large part of the courses we developed were in relation to the needs of the communities we were working with. We wanted to undertake a project in West London because I got some external funding to develop educational opportunities for people who had been out of work. We identified a range of needs and organised courses relevant to those needs. One of the things we thought we would do would be to work with older adults and look at the ways in which we could collate their life histories. Because we were interested in oral histories. We said that people are dying, literally, and our oral histories in this country are not being recorded.

We thought we would do a video project to document the lives of older people and their backgrounds, and how they had experienced life in Britain. But we also wanted to skill them; it's very easy to make a film about people and interview them, but we wanted a participatory project in which older adults would learn the skills of making a film, and that's what we did. We involved a video trainer, who actually taught older adults skills to make a video film. This was followed by the older adults making a film by themselves. A colleague and the

---

6 Avtar Brah, *Aaj Kaal* [Yesterday, Today, Tomorrow], video [20 mins], available at *Darkmatter* official website, darkmatter101.org.

trainer were present, but they were there to facilitate, not to direct. So
that was all the work of the older adults, really.

RZ: And did you feel the method changed the end product?

AB: I think it did, yes. In some scenes, you find, for example, that they
sit very formally. And in other shots they become quite spontaneous,
especially at the end, where they start dancing. That's where they
really came into their own. But sometimes they were more formal,
especially at the beginning, when each of them appears individually.
Because traditionally, even when you had your photographs taken,
you sat like that, that formal pose. I think it changed with time as the
project progressed and, gradually, formality disappeared among the
participants, and they loved it. They hadn't had any opportunities
like that to talk about themselves on film. What was very interesting
was how they were very conscious about religious diversity among
themselves. There were Sikhs, Muslims, Hindus among them. But
they wanted to foreground unity. We had nothing to do with that;
that is what they decided. They talked about the partition of India,
and they talked about how people tried to be unified, and how
people used to live together in diasporas such as East Africa. So they
were also trying to construct some kind of a solidarity among themselves, working across these differences.

BB/RZ: Has cultural production been central in your activism and
research?

AB: That was the only film we did, really. So in terms of cultural production, I haven't really been involved in making videos or films,
apart from this case. But culture itself, as a concept and as a practice,
has been very central in my work. Even when I was doing my PhD,
I was thinking about how to conceptualise culture in non-essentialist forms. That has always been a problem – well, not a problem, a
challenge. It has been a challenge.

BB/RZ: Going back to the question of the university: Can you tell us
more specifically about your own experiences in the academy?
How have you experienced the change in higher education from
when you first started teaching to the period when you retired? It's

been a time of remarkable transformation in the higher education sector.

AB: University life was challenging. I didn't actually have my permanent job until 1985. In the early years after I finished my PhD, I couldn't find a permanent job. I had a lot of temporary jobs, which come with their own problems But, politically it was a huge struggle, around knowledge production partly and these different ways of theorising. I was working around issues of 'race' and ethnicity when I first started. In those days, you had discourses of 'race relations' and 'ethnic relations' associated with people like John Rex, Michael Banton – these were the big professors at the time. They had been radical in their own ways, in introducing the study of 'race' in sociology. But it was quite hard for us to develop a different critical and radical academic practice, especially feminist practice. I think everyone who was involved in this subject at the time would probably tell you that.

It was difficult whoever you were, but if you were a person of colour then it was more of a struggle. I took some pretty unpopular positions. I didn't get much support from my immediate professors in my early years. I turned to the work of scholars such as Stuart Hall for inspiration. And later, when I got to know him at the Open University, he was very supportive. In the early years, I was employed mainly on research projects. I wasn't teaching. Then, of course, in the latter half, I had to leave academia because I could not get an academic job, so I worked with the Greater London Council. That was a quite positive experience, I must say. I was in the Women's Support Unit and I had a quite a senior position there, and we took up all kinds of issues we discussed earlier, such as intersectionality. We didn't use that term, but we were trying to involve different categories of women, and funding women's projects through an intersectional lens.

That was a positive experience because we were doing new things. We were able to fund women's projects, and through that we were involving the women's groups themselves in telling us what they needed and what they wanted. So, I enjoyed that period of my working life. Then I got this job at Birkbeck College. At the time, we weren't part of Birkbeck. It was an extramural studies department within the University of London. I found this work quite creative, actually, because for the first time I was working with a group of women that I got on very well with. There was Jane Hoy, Mary Kennedy, and Nell Keddie. We had a lot of autonomy in developing courses, and we could liaise with communities, find out what they wanted, and then we could offer educational experiences. These were courses at the certificate and diploma levels. Later on, once we merged with Birkbeck College, we developed a Master's programme as well. But initially it was the certificate- and diploma-level courses.

We developed childcare courses, we had courses around anti-Semitism, and we had courses about Palestine. We organised all kinds of courses that we felt were important to communities – Caribbean studies, Irish studies, and Asian studies, under the rubric of 'community studies', as a generic term. So that was really very good, very creative and generative. Then John Solomos (a sociologist) and I developed the Master's programme in race and ethnicity in the politics department. That was one of the first Master's programmes on the subject.

BB: When was that?

AB: That would have been around 1988, I think. So that too was a creative part of my experience, I must say. And it also meant we could include our own imprint. Jane Hoy and Mary Kennedy developed a lesbian studies programme as part of women's studies output in the extramural studies department, which, again, might have been one of the first ones in Britain at the time. On the whole, I found academia quite difficult as a person of colour, although as I said, there were moments and stages where it was quite life-affirming as well. But it's changed so much since I've left, I think; in the last four or five years, things have changed so much. Some of the courses we were developing then might not have the same purchase today. Things have changed a great deal. The neoliberal university is now a serious problem.

Interviewer Biographies

Brenna Bandhar is Associate Professor at Allard law Faculty, UBC. Her work broadly examines the relationship between modern law and colonialism, and more specifically, the field of property law, relations of ownership, and their engagement with race and racism. She is the author of *Colonial Lives of Property: Law, Land and Racial Regimes of Ownership* (Duke University Press, 2018); co-editor (with Jon Goldberg-Hillier) of *Plastic Materialities: Politics, Legality and Metamorphosis in the Work of Catherine Malabou* (Duke University Press, 2015), and more recently, co-editor (with Rafeef Ziadah) of *Revolutionary Feminisms: Conversations on Collective Action and Radical Thought* (Verso Press, 2020). She is a member of the Radical Philosophy editorial collective.

Rafeef Ziadah is an academic, poet, and activist. She teaches Politics of the Middle East in the Politics and International Studies Department at SOAS, University of London. Her research interests are broadly concerned with the political economy of war and humanitarianism, racism, and the security state, with a particular focus on the Middle East. She has worked as researcher and campaigns organiser with a number of grassroots Palestinian, refugee rights, and anti-poverty campaigns. She is co-editor with Brenna Bhandar of *Revolutionary Feminisms: Conversations on Collective Action and Radical Thought* (Verso Press, 2020).

Chapter 10

Epilogue: Imagining Decolonial Futures: Politics of Alterity and Alliance

In the middle of the Covid-19 pandemic, on 25 May 2020, George Floyd, a 46-year-old Black American man, was killed in Minneapolis, Minnesota, during an arrest for allegedly using a counterfeit note. One of the arresting police officers knelt on Floyd's neck for more than eight minutes, while Floyd was handcuffed and lying face down, begging for his life, repeating the words, "I can't breathe". Two other officers further restrained Floyd while a third prevented bystanders from intervening. The video images of Floyd pinned to the ground went viral, and the viewers around the world were stunned by the horrific scenes of the killing. The incident triggered protests in the USA against police brutality, racism, and lack of police accountability. Protesters used posters and slogans with phrases such as 'Justice for George.' 'I can't breathe,' and 'Black Lives Matter'. Unrest that had begun in local protests spread nationwide in the USA, and simultaneously the horror of the incident led to protests in solidarity held globally in over 60 countries, supporting the Black Lives Matter campaign. Peaceful protests turned into major disturbances in some cases, and there were instances of curfews imposed. The mass unrest led to the activation of the National Guard in more than 30 states in the USA, including Washington, DC. Numerous statues and monuments associated with persons or processes and events connected with slavery and racism were removed or destroyed. This is far from the first killing of a civilian by law enforcement officers in the USA but its brutality touched a nerve across the world. Antiracist demonstrations were held in London and across the UK in support of the Black Lives Matter movement. Some far-right activists also congregated, claiming they were there to protect the statues. The killing of George Floyd and the worldwide response to it in the middle of the global pandemic emergency illuminated the articulation of racism, gender, class, debility, and sexuality at the heart of a major crisis we all face today. The theme of such articulations underpins the discussions in the book.

The 2012 vigilante killing of unarmed Florida teenager Trayvon Martin, and the murder of Michael Brown, an 18-year-old Black young man in Ferguson, Missouri on 9 August 2014 by a police officer, are widely regarded as igniting the flame of sustained protest and political organising that led to the formation of the Black Lives Matter Movement for justice and social transformation. As Barbara Ransby argues, the emergence of this movement is grounded in the US-based Black inter-sectional feminist tradition, which insists on the intimate connection between racial and economic justice. It emphasises the importance of "forging a praxis that centers class, gender, sexuality and empire along-side race to reflect a truly intersectional analysis" (Ransby, 2018: 160). This perspective has a legacy embedded in the radical spirit of the 1977 Combahee River Collective, who, as we saw earlier, were a Boston-based group of Black lesbian socialist feminists. They argue that

> We realise that the liberation of all oppressed peoples necessitates the destruc-tion of the political-economic system of capitalism and imperialism as well as patriarchy. We are socialists because we believe that work must be organised for the collective benefit of those who do the work and create the products, and not for the profit of bosses. Material resources must be equally distributed among those who create these resources. We are not convinced, however, that a socialist revolution that is not also a feminist and anti-racist revolution will guarantee our liberation.
>
> (cited in Ransby, 2018: 160–61)

The Combahee River Collective Statement exercised quite considerable influence within socialist feminist circles in Britain. I was for a long time a member of the Editorial Collective of the socialist feminist journal *Feminist Review*, and together with other women in the Collective drew much inspiration from the insights contained in the Combahee

River Collective Statement. *Feminist Review* has been at the forefront of attempts to address intersectional feminist politics, including having to face up to and dealing with tensions and conflicts that such a project can potentially generate. Such conflicts can make deep impact because they entail social cleavages as well as emotional investments which may touch us at the core of our being. Intersections of, say, 'race' and gender can have the effect of mobilising both positive and negative affect depending on the nature of the interaction and how in a given context we come to embody and experience racialised gender difference or racialising assemblages as Weheliye (2014) puts it. Intersectional feminist politics in Britain, as discussed in the book, have also been at the heart of British Black feminism, which over the decades has been at the centre of politics of solidarity among women with different cultural backgrounds and skin tone, especially those with African and Asian heritage. These politics of anti-chromatism have a global import and resonance.

Such coalition politics have figured questions of 'difference' at its centre. It is not my intention to rehearse here how questions of difference mark this book, though they do that deeply. What is interesting for me is the way in which the concept of intersectionality, a key heuristic in my analysis in the previous pages, inherently encodes critical modalities of 'difference' within itself. It foregrounds a fundamental way of thinking about the relations of power that underpin the problematic and problem of sameness and difference. Whether we examine questions of gender (how the concept is differently and differentially constructed, understood, analysed or lived, for instance); class (how, for example, material genealogies of inequality as well as experiential 'materialities' of everyday life are theorised, struggled over, and class inequality overcome); or, 'race' (how violence of racialised regimes is produced, circulated, codified, and experienced both historically and currently); intersectionality instantiates regimes of hierarchical difference marked by unequal power relations. Yet, at the same time, it holds the potential for nurturing politics of alliance and coalition. How 'difference' is addressed, understood, and dealt with in the social, cultural, and political realm is a barometer of the moral state of our existence. It raises critical ethical questions about our responsibilities to other humans and non-humans, and, how we collectively develop principles and values of social justice.

Questions of 'difference' are central to thinking through how alterity is figured. In a 1992 essay, Donna Haraway raises the question as to how humanity might have a figure outside the narratives of humanism. What language would such a 'posthumanist' figure speak? She looks to intercultural feminist theory as harbinger of hope:

> I want to set aside the Enlightenment figures of coherent and masterful subjectivity, the bearers of rights, holders of property in the self, legitimate sons with access to language and the power to represent, subjects endowed with inner coherence and rational clarity, the masters of theory, founders of states, and fathers of families, bombs and scientific theory.... and end by asking how recent intercultural feminist theory constructs possible postcolonial, nongeneric, and irredeemably specific figures of critical subjectivity, consciousness, and humanity – not in the sacred image of the same, but in the self-critical practice of 'difference', of the I and we that is/are never identical to itself, and so has hope of connection to others.
>
> (Haraway, 1992: 87)

In an essay published in 1999, 'The Scent Of Memory: Strangers, Our Own and Others', I attempted to think through questions of 'Otherness' and connectivity by addressing the figure of Jean, a working-class, white woman who committed suicide in 1988, and whom I only 'met' within the pages of her son's autobiographical account. My interest in her was partly spurred on by the fact that she lived in a multi-ethnic part of West London where I had researched and later worked while completing my postgraduate studies. This was a locality I loved but that Jean hated, although she lived amicably with her neighbours. Could my interest in Jean represent my desire as colonialism's Other to seek to fathom how forms of English whiteness are 'lived': as resentful whiteness or self-affirming connectivity? How did Jean experienced Asians? – as a threat in the manner of politicians such as Margaret Thatcher and Enoch

Powell or was it likely that her everyday contact with Asian children through her job as a 'dinner lady' in a primary school created bonds of connection and affection? These questions raise complex issues about the relationship between the social and the psychic in the production of racialised, gendered subjectivity and identity. I analyse this problematic in part through Althusser's concept of interpellation which takes on board conscious agency alongside a theorisation of unconscious processes. The challenge is how to undertake, individually and collectively, "nonlogocentric political practices – theoretical paradigms, political activism, as well as modes of relating to another person – which galvanise identification, empathy and affinity, and not only 'solidarity'?" (Brah, 2000: 279). In this regard it may be worth mentioning my discussion of otherness and belonging through the Urdu concepts of 'ajnabi', 'ghair', and 'apne'. These terms may be described as follows:

An 'ajnabi' is a stranger: a newcomer whom one does not yet know but who holds the promise of friendship, love, intimacy. The 'ajnabi' may have different ways of doing things but is not alien. They could become 'apne'; that is, 'one of our own'. The idea of 'ghair' is much more difficult to translate, for its point of difference is intimacy; it walks the tightrope between insider and outsider. The difference of the 'ghair' cannot be fully captured by the dichotomy of Self and Other; nor is it an essentialist category. Yet it is a form of irreducible, opaque, difference. Although these terms may often be used in contradistinction to each other, they do not represent opposites.

(Brah, 2000: 285)

In other words, a stranger can be a an 'ajnabi' but not necessarily a 'ghair', and potentially can become 'apne', one's own. The distinction is politically important. The world has many feminists. As part of my imagined community, they are 'ajnabi' (strangers) but not 'ghair'.

It is important to bear in mind that, when we foreground a particular axis of intersectional difference such as class we are not simply referencing a person's income, job, accent, or how class culture is lived. It is much more than that. Indeed, as Annette Kuhn discussing questions of class, argues, "... it is something under your skin, in your reflexes, in your psyche, at the very core of your being" (Kuhn, 1995: 288). The fact that these modalities of difference operate at the very core of your being makes them psychically highly charged by affect. The difference of an 'ajnabi' holds the promise of touching you to the core with intimacy, whereas the difference of a 'ghair' is about radical difference.

Using a somewhat different approach to analysing the problematic of alterity and difference, Sanjay Sharma mobilises Deleuze and Guattari's theoretical frame to address "multicultural encounters" in engaging a "pedagogy of cultural difference". Here questions of alterity are theorised from the vantage point of a "non-appropriative relationship to otherness" (Sharma, 2006: 4). In other words, it is an attempt to think through an alternative mode of subjectivity, a form of ethical agency, which resists the negation of otherness, and, instead, advances the Deleuzian idea of multiplicity, and affirmative, immanent difference. It emphasises Levinas's (1979) conceptualisation of dialogic encounters and the uniqueness of the other. Sharma argues that, in contrast to discussions of identity politics of difference, these theories emphasise that the 'other' possesses its own positivity and alterity. I agree with this form of analysing otherness in terms of the other's uniqueness. In Chapter 2 Gail Lewis also argued along similar lines. She addresses the figure of Black woman "not as abject figure of absolute alterity, but as separate from, equal to and essential to the self" (Lewis, 2017: 15). My own theorisation of difference also foregrounds the fact that the 'other' is separate from yet essential to self (Brah, 1996). It brings together the *intersection* of four axes of differentiation: difference understood as experience, difference analysed as social relation, difference theorised as subjectivity, and difference examined in terms of identity.

A lens on alterity, difference, and alliance brings into view how we approach the problematic of the 'human'. Needless to say, this is a hugely complex subject and reams have been written on it. My aim here is rather a modest one, and that is to consider how we might potentially contribute, both individually and collectively, to global efforts designed to create an ethical world where equality and difference can coexist through mutuality and care. Such practices are essential not only in relating to and connecting with other humans, crucial though that is, but equally to nonhumans, as well as the planet. I draw inspiration and resources of hope from the egalitarian visions of feminists and others with similar commitments. Sylvia Wynter, for instance, has been centrally engaged in unsettling Western conceptions of what it means to be 'human' (cf. Wynter, 2003). Her work traverses many different intellectual terrains ranging from natural sciences, the humanities, the social sciences, and the arts. Hers is a project that interrogates and challenges politics of domination and nurtures instead visions of interconnectedness and relationality. As Wynter argues:

We therefore now need to initiate the exploration of the new reconceptualised form of knowledge that would be called for by Fanon's redefinition of being human as that of skins (phylogeny/ ontogeny) *and* masks (sociogeny). Therefore *bios* and *mythoi*. And notice! One major implication here: *humanness* is no longer a *noun*. *Being human is a praxis.*

(Wynter, 2015: 23, original emphasis)

This is a far-reaching formulation of the multiplicity of our being human by conceptualising it as verb, as process, as praxis. Responding favourably to Judith Butler's formulation of the performative enactment of gender, Wynter argues that it can be equally applicable to other axes of differentiation such as class and race such that the performative enactment of all roles becomes praxis rather than nouns: "So here you have the idea that with being human everything is praxis" (Wynter, 2015: 33–34). Wynter's theorisation of the human, it is generally accepted, has the effect of "undoing and unsettling – *not replacing or occupying* – Western conceptions of what it means to be human" (McKittrick, 2015: 2, original emphasis).

Along the same lines, Angela Y. Davis (2015)'s collection of essays, interviews, and speeches draws out the connections between struggles and contestations against state violence and oppression. Inter alia, Davis points to the importance of Black feminism, the concept and practice of intersectionality, and prison abolitionism for contemporary progressive politics. She foregrounds the legacies of global liberation struggles against colonialism, imperialism, and capitalism, and underlines the centrality of projects such as the South African Apartheid Movement and Black Lives Matter in furthering radical political change. Her ongoing focus on a range of political struggles illuminates contemporary examples of political strife and confrontation the world over which demand urgent attention. Faced with a global catalogue of outrageous injustices, Davis has consistently, over decades, urged us to imagine, help initiate, and carry out political movements for human emancipation. She has long stood against the militarisation of policing, the workings of the prison-industrial complex and she has popularised the battle against mass incarceration, especially in the United States. As a socialist activist, she has theorised and put into practice visions of class equality that intersects with factors such as gender, race, and sexuality. Her rallying cry 'Freedom is a constant struggle', is so apt for our current predicaments.

Wynter regards 'emancipatory' politics of the social movements of the sixties as admirable but she does not idealise them. Rather, she stresses the need for constructing new political visions fit for the early twenty-first century. She also reminds us that the sixties movements were fuelled by the earlier anticolonial movements but their praxis had their own specificity and particularity. Walter Mignolo characterises Wynter's body of work and praxis as decolonial and sees her as not only challenging knowledge regimes embedded in imperial coloniality but as 'delinking' oneself from them and practising 'epistemic disobedience'. In other words "Wynter's decolonial project calls into question the concept of the Human and its epistemological underpinnings" (Mignolo, 2015: 107). In the process she valorises the epistemologies and perspectives of those who are constructed as nonhuman or less-than-human. Although Western conceptions of the human posit a notion of equality through espousing 'universality' and 'common humanity', in practice the social realm is deeply marred by prevailing patterns of inequality. The discourses of universal emancipatory politics have often proved to be illusory. The arrival of Columbus in the Americas in 1492, and Europe's other 'voyages of discovery' or which might more appropriately be described as voyages of reconnaissance and colonisation, were accompanied by the emergence of the idea of 'race', which resulted in the development of racialised formations of gendered and sexualised economies of exploitation and domination. Wynter's work represents a beacon of hope in dismantling the imperial concept of 'humanity' and constructing decolonial futures of human connectivity.

Another theme that has been central to discussions about politics of otherness and alliance has been that of mobilising the concept of cosmopolitanism, which references a world governed by overarching principles of rights and justice. It upholds an ethic of interconnectivity that celebrates cultural diversity, multiplicity, fluidity, and hybridity. With its shared value of humanness based on connection, it provides a critique of ethnocentric nationalism as well as more particularistic notions of 'multiculturalism'. Issues of cultural multiplicity remain central though they are to be distinguished from certain state policies and popular manifestations of 'multiculturalism'. I shall return to this point. Gerard Delanty (2009) distinguishes between four dimensions of cosmopolitanism: as a political philosophy embedded within normative principles associated with world citizenship and global governance; as a signifier of liberal multiculturalism with its focus on plurality and an embracing of difference; as a transnational formation that highlights the cosmopolitan underpinnings of transnational processes and global culture; and cosmopolitanism as a methodological approach. He also draws attention to the ways in which there has been a confluence between postmodernism and cosmopolitanism, especially in postcolonial theory where sustained efforts have been made to disarticulate cosmopolitanism from Western epistemic hegemonies, though Delanty cautions against viewing cosmopolitanism as a product of postmodernism. It is a commonplace to say that cosmopolitanism values the prospect of engaging in dialogue and debate across differences and thereby inscribes a sensibility of living together. This aspect has proved attractive to those who favour visions of 'world citizenship' though the notion of 'world citizenship' itself remains somewhat dis-embedded.

Instead, the idea of 'cosmopolitan citizenship' may be more appropriate in that the concept is not merely about a legal status but also points to public participation in civil society. Moreover,

It is in reconciling the rights of the individual with the need to protect minorities that the cosmopolitan moment is most evident. In this context cosmopolitan citizenship is understood in terms of a cultural shift in collective identities to include the recognition of others.

(Delanty, 2009: 57)

Citizenship commonly refers to legal membership of a state though the term 'cultural citizenship' is also invoked as a mode of belonging to a cultural group. In terms of legal status, there are few recognised global state institutions of governance other than organisations such as the United Nations, which, in the main, is a platform for discussion and debate, although some of its activities will at times assume a role similar to that of state functions as when legitimising sanctions against particular regimes or when it intervenes in ongoing wars. It is true, of course, that the United Nations, the 1948 Declaration of Human Rights, and the legal category of Crimes Against Humanity do reference an international normative order, but this is an order based on sovereign nation states.

As we have seen, cosmopolitanism endorses transnational interconnections and relations between social networks and movements, takes issue with putative 'identity politics' and seeks to initiate new conversations surrounding questions of identity, belonging, and citizenship. These new ways of theorising non-essentialist forms of what may, in my view, be conceptualised as 'identificatory assemblages' would be designed to displace rather than completely replace 'identity centric' discourses and practices. Clearly, incidents such as the murders discussed above that led to the emergence of Black Lives Matter movement raise urgent questions about the necessity for devising strategies suited to living amicably with one another on the basis of shared agendas. Cosmopolitanism poses such problematics acutely. It is important to recognise that while cosmopolitan optics are inherently about processes that go beyond the nation state, they do not necessarily entail an elimination of the nation state. Issues of the local and locality remain crucial to imagining 'home and belonging.' Identification with the nation state can, indeed often does, co-exist with global affiliations, sentiments, and associations. This is partly, though by no means entirely, due to global movements of migrants, diasporics, and other members of transnational communities. In other words, there is little that is contradictory in claiming local and personal identifications while emphasising humanity as a whole.

One of the criticisms that is likely to be levelled at cosmopolitanism as a strategy is that it is only available to the elite who have the resources to travel, be exposed to other cultures, become bi- or multilingual, and develop global visions of the common good. The stereotype of the cosmopolitan is that of someone who is financially well off, a privileged frequent traveller with a lavish lifestyle: "... wealthy jet setters, corporate managers, intergovernmental bureaucrats, artists, tax dodgers, academics and intellectuals" (Vertovec and Cohen, 2002: 6). Though this might have been historically the case, it does not completely match reality today when travel is not confined to the elite nor, indeed, is exposure to other cultures and lifestyles in our globalised world. A stance of openness or cosmopolitan disposition/outlook is also not a characteristic only of the elite. There can be subaltern forms of cosmopolitanism as well. But, the social conditions underlining subaltern, middle-class, or elite cosmopolitanism are far from being the same. Rather they are different and distinctive formations. Moreover, it is important to appreciate that the rhetoric of cosmopolitanism can mask deep global inequalities. Yet, as discussed above, there is much that is affirmative about cosmopolitan imaginaries. Ethnic and cultural diversity may be common today in places of work, in schools, neighbourhoods, clubs, and arenas where people socialise, and this may be described as 'everyday cosmopolitanism.' Cosmopolitanism is likely to be counterposed to particularity, but, as must be clear in this discussion, I am suggesting that the two are interconnected. The cosmopolitan ideal can coexist with and accompany specific attachments and commitments. Simultaneous membership of different communities involving multiple and plural loyalties and identifications is a common condition of sociality today. The origins of the word cosmopolitanism are decidedly Western, but this does not imply that cosmopolitan visions did not find fertile ground in non-Western social formations. Over the last decade, a number of scholars have mapped different manifestations of Muslim cosmopolitanism that poses a challenge to Western liberal-centric constructions of the idea. Indeed, as Sami Zubaida (2002) notes, the coming together of many peoples and cultures was an integral feature of Arab and Muslim empires from the Abbasid court of the eighth and ninth century, which had a cosmopolitan milieu that mixed Arab religion with Persian culture, to the Muslim period in Spain that valorised cosmopolitan cultural interaction as did the Ottoman Empire with its cosmopolitan cities of Istanbul, Cairo, and Alexandria. Similarly, Haines (2015) reminds us of the inclusive cosmopolitan community, the ummah, of believers and non-believers, of Muslims and non-Muslims, that is thought to have flourished in Medina during the time of Prophet Mohammed. Hindu religious leaders such as Swami Viveknananda regarded Hinduism as the pinnacle of universal spirituality. As Vander Veers (2002) argues, a popular cosmopolitan consciousness that was grounded in the notion of a universal spirituality came to the fore in the nineteenth century. This was distinct from the secular versions associated with European Enlightenment. He demonstrates how Nietzsche, who was an abiding critic of Christian morality in the German-speaking world, nonetheless evinces a degree of admiration for the Vedanta philosophy. Also discrete from European cosmopolitanism was the Chinese historical and contemporary discourses and practices that work against the hegemony of seeing the other as the image of the self (Kwok Bun, 2002). The point is that although there are different cosmopolitanisms in the world – ranging from the 'discrepant cosmopolitanism' of Clifford (1998), 'oppositional cosmopolitanism' of Schein (1998) to the 'vernacular cosmopolitanism' of Hall (2002) – they share a common commitment to the ideal of ethics of interconnectivity.

Feminist Interculturality, Decolonial Insurgent Cosmopolitanism, and Social Justice

I began this chapter with a discussion of the inspirational politics of the Combahee River Collective and their mobilisation of an intersectional frame long before the term intersectionality came into existence. I now suggest that the main thrust of their political message remains singularly relevant in facing up to our current predicaments. There is certainly an urgent need for seeking radical transformation of the socio-economic, political, and cultural relations associated with formations of capitalism, coloniality, imperialism, racism, ableism, heteronormativity, and patriarchal social arrangements. The Combahee River Collective's quest for economic justice that can do away with poverty, immiseration, and want in the world is hugely commendable, apposite, and essential for dealing with social conditions underpinning the present conjuncture. As Ransby (2018) emphasises above, it is necessary to hold on to a 'truly intersectional analysis', though, of course, undertaking such an analysis is a complex task that would entail disentangling relational workings of the different axes at various levels: the level of the economic, the political, the cultural, the social, the personal, and the psychic. Questions of how these processes are embodied and experienced would be central. Intersectional embodiment means that we are placed in relation to multiple others, within and across intersecting modalities of power. A cosmopolitan imagination helps illuminate local and global connections and a cosmopolitan sensibility enhances the capacity for care and obligation to others. It foregrounds the importance of simultaneously upholding the principle of diversity as well as that of shared public culture. Hence, it emphasises feminist politics of interculturality. In discussing the notion of 'cosmopolitan feminism' Nira Yuval Davis reminds us that feminists have always tended to foreground the politics of 'global sisterhood' (Yuval-Davis, 2011). Questions of human rights, she points out, were likely to be addressed through recognition and entitlement of people, not as citizens of particular states or as a result of belonging to a given cultural or religious community, but rather as being part of the human race. The discourse of women's rights as human rights has proved to be particularly empowering in regard, for instance, to struggles against violence against women. Yuval-Davis describes transversal politics as dialogical politics in which the participants see themselves as advocates of specific collectivities and categories, instead of being their representatives. Shared values and empathetic connection, mutual respect and mutual trust, are central to transversal politics.

Interestingly, Delanty speaks of "cosmopolitan multiculturalism beyond liberal multiculturalism" (Delanty, 2009: 133), arguing that the creation of multicultural populations cannot be understood within the purview of national policies alone but rather necessitates the mobilisations of globally oriented perspectives. Accordingly, a cosmopolitan interculturalism calls for dialogues that go beyond the local and the national. A key issue facing intercultural societies is whether we can be both equal and different at the same time. The answer, of course, is in the affirmative. Equality is the underlying rationale for egalitarian politics. Difference, as argued throughout the book, is complex to theorise and practice but absolutely essential in developing an imagination that does not reduce everything to the economy of the 'Same'. Indeed, difference accompanied by equality is precisely what contributes to the realisation of common visions of social justice.

It is generally accepted that 'liberal multiculturalism' is not fully equipped to deal with systematic and structural forms of exclusion because it is not designed to radically change mainstream social arrangements. Hence, interculturalism – my preferred nomenclature, not least because, as seen before, interculturalism is a non-essentialist concept – must be understood as going beyond 'tolerance' to embrace politics of social equality in the interest of bringing about radical change. The main obstacles to this type of change taking place are those posed by such factors as structural racism, class divisions, and other forms of intersectional cleavages that underline deeply ingrained practices of everyday life. The concept of 'cosmopolitan multiculturalism' is certainly attractive because it is not merely about the plurality of cultures but more about "the recognition of difference and the search for an alternative political order" (Delanty, 2009: 150). In a related though somewhat different vein, Boaventura de Sousa Santos (2007) advocates what he calls 'insurgent cosmopolitanism' or a 'counter-hegemonic globalisation from below', consisting of transnationally organised resistance against inequities and inequalities, discrimination, exploitation and oppression through linkages among "organizations and movements united in concrete struggles against exclusion, subordinate inclusion, the destruction of livelihoods and ecological destruction, political oppression, cultural suppression etc" (de Sousa Santos, 2007: 9). Insurgent cosmopolitanism defines the responses, struggles, and politics of resistance by oppressed groups aiming to unite through translocal/local linkages "on both class and non-class basis, the victims of exploitation as well as the victims of social exclusion, of sexual, ethnic, racist and religious discrimination" (de Sousa Santos, 2007: 10). While the discourse of 'multiculturalism' is generally associated with the global North, 'insurgent cosmopolitanism' is more closely, though by no means exclusively, associated with knowledge regimes from the global South. It is important to note that the concept of 'insurgent cosmopolitanism' is not a general theory of emancipation that collapses differences or ignores local identities but rather it is fully live to principles of equality and difference. I am certainly partial to the aims of this project. The continued viability of such a project cannot, however, be taken for granted and it needs to be continually fought for and subjected to questioning and revision as necessary, depending upon the circumstances. Importantly, in a later publication, de Santos (2014) underscores the importance of intercultural translation understood as consisting of

searching for isomorphic concerns and underlying assumptions among cultures, identifying differences and similarities, and developing, whenever appropriate, new hybrid forms of cultural understanding and intercommunication that may be useful in favouring interactions and strengthening alliances among social movements fighting, in different cultural contexts, against capitalism, colonialism and patriarchy and for social justice, human dignity or human decency.

(de Sousa Santos, 2014: 212)

This is a wide-ranging, politically astute agenda.

Culture, as is now widely accepted, is not an integrated whole but rather an amalgam of intersecting signifying practices. Intercultural translation draws attention to the critical issue of how best to create non-hierarchical communication and achieve shared meanings across culturally diverse social worlds. This process entails the play of power though ideally one would aim for equal power relations designed to facilitate genuine reciprocity. Importantly, sharing meanings involves also sharing passions, feelings, and emotions. Projects for radical transformation therefore involve the heart as much as the head. Indeed, they must engage our whole being. This view is particularly embedded in feminist politics. There are those who believe that politics is more of an intellectual endeavour, that emotionality can 'get in the way', be a hindrance, digression, and deflection from the path. But I endorse a politics of emancipation that engages the mind as well as sentiment. Cultural translation is central to social emancipation – I use the idea of culture here in its broadest sense of referring to signifying practices or meaning-making operations. These processes of translation are inherently part of the life of contact zones where subjects, subjectivities, and identities come face to face with realities of intercultural communication. I use the term contact zone following Mary Louise Pratt as "social spaces where disparate cultures meet, clash and grapple with each other, often in highly asymmetrical relations of domination and subordination – like colonialism, slavery or their aftermaths as they are lived out across the globe today" (Pratt, 1992: 4). Clearly, such contact zones are not neutral spaces. They offer possibility of both confrontation and mediation/negotiation. The challenge is to remain open to learning from other people's knowledge and experience and try and create a life-affirming relationship that is collaborative and is simultaneously advantageous to all parties. It is a project that mobilises and acts resolutely against all forms of oppressions and exploitation. And, with equal determination, it seeks to strengthen projects of mutual support and empowerment that challenge and work against effects of capitalism, neocoloniality, heteronormativity, racism, and patriarchal social relations. In other words, it mobilises, propagates, and activates decolonial politics.

Bibliography

Abbas, T. (2020). 'Islamophobia as Racialized Biopolitics in the United Kingdom'. *Philosophy and Social Criticism*, 46(5), pp. 497–511.

Agamben, G. (1998). *Homo Sacer: Sovereign Paper and Bare Life*, trans. Daniel Heller-Roazen. Stanford: Stanford University Press.

Ahmed, L. (1992). *Women and Gender in Islam: Historic Roots of Modern Debate*. New Haven: Yale University Press.

Ahmed, S. (2004). *The Cultural Politics of Emotion*. Edinburgh: Edinburgh University Press.

Ahmed, S. (2012). *On Being Included: Racism and Diversity in Institutional Life*. Durham and London: Duke University Press.

Ahmed, S. (2014). *Willful Subjects*. Durham: Duke University Press.

Ahmed, S. (2019). *What's the Use?: On the Uses of Use*. Durham and London: Duke University Press.

Althusser, L. (1971). *Lenin and Philosophy and Other Essays*. London: New Left Books.

Amos, V., Lewis, G., Mama, A., and Parmar, P. (eds) (1984). Many Voices, One Chant: Black Feminist Perspectives [Special Issue]. *Feminist Review*, 17(1), pp. 3–19.

Anderson, B. (1983). *Imagined Communities: Reflections on the Origins and Spread of Nationalism*. London and New York: Verso.

Anderson, B. (2013). *Us and Them? The Dangerous Politics of Immigration Control*. Oxford: Oxford University Press.

Anthias, F. (2002). 'Beyond Feminism and Multiculturalism: Locating Difference and the Politics of Location'. *Women's Studies International Forum*, 25(3), pp. 275–286.

Anthias, F. (2012). 'Hierarchies of Social Location, Class and Intersectionality: Towards a Translocational Frame'. *International Sociology*, 28(1), pp. 121–38.

Anthias, F. (2020). *Translocational Belongings: Intersectional Dilemmas and Social Inequalities*. London and New York: Routledge.

Anthias, F. and Yuval-Davis, N. (1992). *Racialized Boundaries: Race, Nation, Gender, Colour and Class and the Anti-racist Struggle.* New York: Routledge.

Anwar, M. (1998). *Between Cultures: Continuity and Change in the Lives of Young Asians.* London: Routledge.

Anzaldua, G. (1987). *Borderlands/La Frontera: The New Mestiza.* San Francisco: Spinsters/Aunt Lute Books.

Appiah, K. A. (2007). *Cosmopolitanism: Ethics in a World of Strangers.* London: Penguin Books.

Asad, T. (1973). *Anthropology & the Colonial Encounter.* London: Ithaca Press.

Asad, T. (2003). *Formations of the Secular: Christianity, Islam, Modernity.* Stanford: Stanford University Press.

Asad, T. (2018). *Secular Translations: Nation-State, Modern Self, and Calculative Reasons.* New York and Chichester, West Sussex: Columbia University Press.

Back, L. and Brah, A. (2012). 'Activism, Imagination and Writing: Avtar Brah Reflects on Her Life and Work with Les Beck.' *Feminist Review*, 100(1), 39–51. doi:10.1057/fr.2011.66.

Back, L. and Sinha, S. (2018) *Migrant City.* London: Routledge.

Baddiel, D. (2021). *Jews Don't Count.* London: TLS.

Baksh-Soodeen, R. and Harcourt, W. (2015). *The Oxford Handbook of Transnational Feminist Movements.* New York: Oxford University Press.

Balibar, E. (2002). *Politics and the Other Scene.* London: Verso Books.

Balibar, E. (2004). *We, the People of Europe? Reflections on Transnational Citizenship.* Princeton and Oxford: Princeton University Press.

Barth, F. (ed.) (1969, reissued 1998). *Ethnic Groups and Boundaries: The Social Organization of Cultural Difference.* Illinois: Waveland Press.

Bauböck, R. and Faist, T. (2010). *Diaspora and Transnationalism: Concepts, Theories and Methods.* Amsterdam: Amsterdam University Press.

Bauman, Z. (1993). *Postmodern Ethics.* Oxford: Blackwell Publishing.

Beckett, A. (2019). 'Age of Perpetual Crisis. How the 2010s Disrupted Everything but Resolved Nothing'. *The Guardian*, 17 December 2019. Retrieved from: www.theguardian.com/society/2019/dec/17/decade-of-perpetual-crisis-2010s-disrupted-everything-but-resolved-nothing

Belsey, C. (2002). *Poststructuralism: A Very Short Introduction*. Oxford: Oxford University Press.

Benhabib, S. (2004). *The Rights of Others: Aliens, Residents, and Citizens*. Cambridge: Cambridge University Press.

Benhabib, S. (2008). *Another Cosmopolitanism*. Oxford: Oxford University Press.

Berlant, L. (2016). 'The Commons: Infrastructures for Troubling Times'. *Environment and Planning D: Society and Space*, 34(3), pp. 393–419.

Betts, A. 'Smuggling Doesn't Cause Migration. We Are Ignoring the Real Problem'. *The Observer*, 26 April, p. 18.

Bhabha, H. K. (1994/2004). *The Location of Culture*. London: Routledge.

Bhabha, H. K. (2013). 'Living Side by Side: On Culture and Security'. Keynote Presentation at CoHaB International Conference on Diasporic Constructions of Home and Belonging. Munster University, Germany, 23 September.

Bhambra, G. K. (2007). *Rethinking Modernity: Postcolonialism and the Sociological Imagination*. Houndmills: Palgrave Macmillan.

Bhambra, G. K. (2014). 'Postcolonial and Decolonial Dialogues', *Postcolonial Studies*, 17(2), pp. 115–121.

Bhambra, G. K. and Narayan, J. (eds) (2016). *European Cosmopolitanism: Colonial Histories and Postcolonial Societies*. International Library of Sociology series. London: Routledge.

Bhambra, G. K. (2017). 'Brexit, Trump, and "Methodological Whiteness": On the Misrecognition of Race and Class'. *The British Journal of Sociology*, 68, pp. 214–232.

Bhambra, G. K. and Holmwood, J. (2021). *Colonialism and Modern Social Theory*. Cambridge: Polity.

Bhandar, B. (2018). *Colonial Lives of Property: Law, Land and Racial Regimes of Ownership*. Durham and London: Duke University Press.

Bhandar, B. and Ziadah, R. (2020). *Revolutionary Feminisms: Conversations on Collective Activism and Radical Thought*. London and New York: Verso.

Bharucha, N. E., Rajeswaran, S., and Stierstorfer, K. (2018). *Beyond Borders and Boundaries: Diasporic Images and Representations in Literature and Cinema*. Mumbai: University of Mumbai, CoHab IDC.

Bhattacharyya, G. (2018). *Rethinking Racial Capitalism: Questions of Reproduction and Survival*. London and New York: Rowman and Littlefield International.

Bienkov, A. (2020). 'Boris Johnson's Long Record of Sexist, Homophobic and Racist Comments'. *Business Insider*, 9 June 2020. Retrieved from: www. businessinsider.com/boris-johnson-record-sexist-homophobic-and-racist-comments-bumboys-piccaninnies-2019-6

Black Feminists Blogspots. (2010). *About*. Retrieved from: http://blackfeminists. blogspot.ca/p/about.html

Brah, A. (1993). 'Re-framing Europe: En-gendered Racisms, Ethnicities and Nationalisms in Contemporary Western Europe'. *Feminist Review*, 45(1), pp. 9–29.

Brah, A. (1993). ' "Race" and "Culture" in the Gendering of Labour Markets: South Asian Young Muslim Women and the Labour Market'. *New Community*, 19(3), pp. 441–458.

Brah, A. (1996). *Cartographies of Diaspora, Contesting Identities*. London and New York: Routledge.

Brah, A. (2000). 'The Scent of Memory: Strangers, Our Own, and Others'. In A. Brah and A. Coombes (eds) *Hybridity and Its Discontents: Politics, Science, Culture*. London: Routledge.

Brah, A. (2002). 'Global Mobilities, Local Predicaments: Globalization and the Critical Imagination'. *Feminist Review*, 70(1), pp. 30–45.

Brah, A. (2013). 'Diasporic Constructions of Home and Belonging'. A paper given on a panel for the Diaspora Studies in the 21st Century Conference, University of Muenster, Germany. Retrieved from: www.youtube.com/watch?v=DZcıınSJbNjM

Brah, A. and Coombes, A. (2000). *Hybridity and Its Discontents: Politics, Science, Culture*. London: Routledge.

Brah, A. and Phoenix, A. (2004). ' "Ain't I A Woman"? Revisiting Intersectionality'. *Journal of International Women's Studies*, 5(3), pp. 75–86.

Brah, A., Hickman, M., and Mac an Ghaill, M. (1999a). *Global Futures: Migration, Environment, and Globalization*. New York: St Martin's Press.

Brah, A., Hickman, M., and Mac an Ghaill, M. (1999b). *Thinking Identities: Ethnicity, Racism and Culture*. New York: St Martin's Press.

Brah, A., Szeman, I., and Gedalof, I. (2015). 'Introduction: Feminism and the Politics of Austerity'. *Feminist Review*, 109(1), pp. 1–7. doi: 10.1057/fr.2014.59.

Braidotti, R. (1994). *Nomadic Subjects: Embodiment and Sexual Difference in Contemporary Feminist Theory*. New York: Columbia University Press.

Braidotti, R. (2006). *Transpositions: On Nomadic Ethics*. Cambridge: Polity Press.

Braziel, E. J. (2008). *Diaspora: An Introduction*. Oxford: Blackwell.

Braziel, E. J. and Anita Mannur, A. (2003). *Theorizing Diaspora*. Oxford: Blackwell.

Bryan, B., Dadzie, S., and Scafe, S. (1985). *Heart of the Race: Black Women's Lives in Britain*. London: Virago.

Butler, J. (1990). *Gender Trouble: Feminism and the Subversion of Identity*. New York and London: Routledge.

Butler, J. (1993). *Bodies That Matter: On the Discursive Limits of "Sex"*. New York and London: Routledge.

Butler, J. (2015). *Notes Toward a Performative Theory of Assembly*. London: Harvard University Press.

Campaign Against Racism and Fascism/Southall Rights. (1981). *Southall: Birth of a Black Community*. London: Institute of Race Relations and Southall Rights.

Carpi, D. and Stierstorfer, K. (eds) (2017). *Diaspora, Law and Literature*. Berlin and Boston: DeGruyter.

Centre for Contemporary Cultural Studies, University of Birmingham. (1982). *The Empire Strikes Back: Race and Racism in the 70s' Britain*. London: Routledge.

Chaffey, D. (2021). *Global Social Media Research Summary 2021*. 23 July 2021. Retrieved from: www.smartinsights.com/social-media-marketing/social-media-strategy/new-global-social-media-research/

Cho, S., Crenshaw, K. W., and McCall, L. (2013). 'Toward a Field of Intersectionality Studies: Theory, Applications, Praxis'. *Signs*, 38, pp. 941–965. doi:10.1086/669608.

Clifford, J. (1994). 'Diasporas'. *Cultural Anthology*, 9(3), pp. 302–338.

Clifford, J. (1997). *Routes: Travel and Translation in the Late Twentieth Century*. Cambridge, MA: Harvard University Press.

Clifford, J. (1998). 'Mixed Feelings'. In P. Cheah and B. Robbins (eds) *Cosmopolitics: Thinking and Feeling Beyond the Nation*. Minneapolis: University of Minnesota Press.

Cohen, R. (1997). *Global Diasporas: An Introduction*. London: Routledge.

Cohen, R. and Fischer, C. (2019). *Routledge Handbook of Diaspora Studies*. London and New York: Routledge. https://doi.org/10.4324/9781315209050.

Collins, P. H. (2019). *Intersectionality as Critical Theory*. Durham: Duke University Press.

Collins, P. H. and Bilge, S. (2016). *Intersectionality*. Cambridge: Polity Press.

Combahee River Collective. (1977). 'Combahee River Collective Statement.' Retrieved from: http://circuitous.org/scraps/combahee.html [Accessed 13 November 2016].

Cooper, V. and Whyte, D. (eds) (2017). *The Violence of Austerity*. London: Pluto Press.

Crenshaw, K. W. (1989). 'Demarginalizing the Intersection of Race and Sex: A Black Feminist Critique of Antidiscrimination Doctrine, Feminist Theory and Antiracist Politics.' *University of Chicago Legal Forum*, 1989(1), pp. 139-167.

Crenshaw, K. W. (1991). 'Mapping the Margins: Intersectionality, Identity Politics, and Violence Against Women of Colour'. *Stanford Law Review*, 43(6), pp. 1241-1299.

Cresswell, T. (2006). *On the Move: Mobility in the Modern Western World*. New York and London: Routledge.

Davis, A. Y. (1990/1974). *Angela Davis: An Autobiography*. London: The Women's Press.

Davis, A. Y. (2015). *Freedom is a Constant Struggle: Ferguson, Palestine, and the Foundations of a Movement*. London: Haymarket Books.

Davis, K. (2011). 'Intersectionality as Buzzword: A Sociology of Science Perspective on What Makes a Theory Successful.' In H. Lutz, M. T. Herrera Vivar, and L. Supik (eds) *Framing Intersectionality: Debates on a Multi-faceted Concept in Gender Studies*. London: Ashgate.

de Sousa Santos, B. (2007). *Another Knowledge Is Possible: Beyond Northern Epistemologies*. London and New York: Verso.

de Sousa Santos, B. (ed.) (2010). *Voices of the World*. London and New York: Verso.

de Sousa Santos, B. (2014). *Epistemologies of the South: Justice Against Epistemicide*. Boulder and London: Paradigm Publishers.

Delanty, G. (2000). *Citizenship in a Global Age: Society, Culture, Politics*. Buckingham: Open University Press.

Delanty, G. (2009). *The Cosmopolitan Imagination: The Renewal of Critical Social Theory*. Cambridge: Cambridge University Press.

Deleuze, G. and Guattari, F. (1986). *Nomadology: The War Machine*. New York: Semiotext.

Dhaliwal, S. and Yuval-Davis, N. (2014). *Women Against Fundamentalism: Stories of Dissent and Solidarity*. London: Lawrence and Wishart.

Dufoix, S. (2008). *Diaspora.* Berkeley: University of California Press.

Eddo-Lodge, R. (2017). *Why I'm No Longer Talking to White People about Race.* London: Bloomsbury Circus.

El-Enany, N. (2020). *(B)Ordering Britain: Law, Race, and Empire.* Manchester: Manchester University Press.

El-Tayeb, F. (2011). *European Others: Queering Ethnicity in Postnational Europe.* Minneapolis: University of Minnesota Press.

European Commission. Directorate-General for Employment, Social Affairs and Equal Opportunities. (2007). *Tackling Multiple Discrimination: Practices, Policies and Laws, Volume 118.* Luxembourg: Office for Official Publications of the European Communities. Retrieved from: http://ec.europa.eu/social/main.jsp? catId=738&pubId=51

Fanon, F. (1967). *The Wretched of the Earth.* London: Penguin.

Farahani, F. (2017). *Gender, Sexuality, and Diaspora.* London: Routledge.

Farris, S. (2017). *In the Name of Women's Rights: The Rise of Femonationalism.* Durham: Duke University Press.

Fine. S. (2019). 'All at Sea: Europe's Crisis of Solidarity on Migration.' *European Council of Foreign Relations.* 14 October 2019. Retrieved from: https://ecfr.eu/ publication/all_at_sea_europes_crisis_of_solidarity_on_migration/

Frankenberg, R. (1993). *White Women, Race Matters: The Social Construction of Whiteness.* Minneapolis: University of Minnesota Press.

Frohmader, C. and Meekosha, H. (2012). 'Recognition, Respect and Rights: Disabled Women in a Globalized World.' In D. Goodley, B. Hughes, and L. Davis (eds) *Disability and Social Theory: New Developments and Directions.* New York: Palgrave Macmillan.

Gedalof, I. (1999). *Against Purity: Rethinking Identity with Indian and Western Feminisms.* London: Routledge.

Gedalof, I. (2018). *Narratives of Difference in an Age of Austerity.* London: Palgrave Macmillan.

Gentleman, A. (2019). *The Windrush Betrayal: Exposing the Hostile Environment.* London: Guardian Faber.

George, S. (1976). *How the Other Half Dies.* Harmondsworth: Penguin.

Gill, A. K. and Brah, A. (2014). 'Interrogating Cultural Narratives About "Honour"-Based Violence'. *European Journal of Women's Studies*, 21(1), pp. 72–86. doi: 10.1177/1350506813510424.

Gilroy, P. (1993). *The Black Atlantic: Modernity and Double Consciousness*. Cambridge, MA: Harvard University Press.

Gilroy, P. (1997). 'Diaspora and the Detours of Identity'. In K. Woodward (ed.) *Identity and Difference*. London: SAGE Publications.

Gilroy, P. (2006). *Postcolonial Melancholia*. Cambridge: Cambridge University Press.

Golder, B. (2013). *Re-Reading Foucault: On Law, Power and Rights*. New York: Routledge.

Goodfellow, M. (2019). *The Hostile Environment: How Immigrants Became Scapegoats*. London and New York: Verso Officials.

Goodman, R. T. (ed.) (2019). *The Bloomsbury Handbook of 21st-Century Feminist Theory*. London and New York: Bloomsbury Academic.

Gopal, P. (2019). *Insurgent Empire: Anticolonial Resistance and British Dissent*. London and New York: Verso.

Gopinath, G. (2005). *Impossible Desires: Queer Diasporas and South Asian Public Cultures*. Durham: Duke University Press.

Gopinath, G. (2018). *Unruly Visions: The Aesthetic Practices of Queer Diaspora*. Durham: Duke University Press.

Gordon, A. F. (2008). *Ghostly Matters: Haunting and the Sociological Imagination*. London and Minneapolis: University of Minnesota Press.

Gordon, A. F. (2017). *The Hawthorne Archive: Letters from the Utopian Margins*. New York: Fordham University Press.

Gramsci, A. (1971). *Selection from the Prison Notebooks of Antonio Gramsci*. Q. Hoare and G. Nowell-Smith (eds). New York: International Publishers, pp. 77–80, 82–83.

Grewal, S. et al. (1988). *Charting the Journey: Writings by Black and Third World Women*. London: Sheba Feminist Press.

Guardian Editorial (2017). *Refugee Policy Is Wrong and Short Sighted*. The Guardian, 9 July.

Gunaratnam, Y. (2013). *Death and the Migrant: Bodies, Borders and Care*. London: Bloomsbury.

Gunaratnam, Y. (2014). 'Black British Feminisms: Many Chants'. *Feminist Review*, pp. 1–10.

Gupta, R. (2003). *From Heartbreakers to Jailbreakers: Southhall Black Sisters*. London: Zed Press.

Guy-Sheftall, B. (1995). 'A Black Feminist Statement'. *Words of Fire: An Anthology of African American Feminist Thought*. New York: The Free Press.

Ha-Joon, C. (2010). *23 Things They Don't Tell You About Capitalism*. London: Penguin Books.

Haines, C. (2015). 'Being Muslim, Being Cosmopolitan: Transgressing the Liberal Global'. *Journal of International and Global Studies*, 7(1), pp. 32–49.

Hall, C. (1992). *White, Male and Middle Class: Explorations in Feminism and History*. London: Verso.

Hall, S. (1980). 'Race, Articulation and Societies Structured in Dominance in United Nations Education, Scientific and Cultural Organization'. *Sociological Theories: Race and Colonialism*. Paris: UNESCO.

Hall. S. (1990). 'Cultural Identity and Diaspora'. In J. Rutherford (ed.) *Identity, Community, Culture*. London: Lawrence and Wishart.

Hall, S. (1996a). 'Gramsci's Relevance for the Study of Race and Ethnicity'. In D. Morley and K. Chen (eds) *Stuart Hall: Critical Dialogues in Cultural Studies*. London: Routledge.

Hall, S. (1996b [1989]). 'New Ethnicities'. In D. Morley and K. Chen (eds) *Stuart Hall: Critical Dialogues in Cultural Studies*. London: Routledge.

Hall, S. (1996c). 'Who Needs Identity?' In S. Hall and P. Du Gay (eds) *Questions of Cultural Identity*. Thousand Oaks: SAGE Publications.

Hall, S. (1996d). 'When Was 'the Postcolonial'? Thinking at the Limit'. In L. Curtis and I. Chambers (eds) *The Postcolonial Question: Common Skies, Divided Horizons*. London: Routledge.

Hall, S. (1997). 'Cultural Identity and Diaspora'. In K. Woodward (ed.) *Identity and Difference*. London: SAGE Publications.

Hall, S. (2002). 'Political Belonging in a World of Multiple Identities'. In S. Vertovec and R. Cohen (eds) *Conceiving Cosmopolitanism: Theory, Context and Practice*. Oxford: Oxford University Press.

Hall, S. (2011). 'The Neoliberal Revolution'. *Cultural Studies*, 25(6), pp. 705–728. http://dx.doi.org/10.1080/09502386.2011.619886.

Hall, S. (2012). 'Avtar Brah's Cartographies: Moment, Method, Meaning'. *Feminist Review*, 100(1), pp. 27–38.

Hall, S. and Du Gay, P. (1996). *Questions of Cultural Identity*. London and Thousand Oaks: SAGE Publications.

Hall, S. and Jefferson, T. (1975). *Resistance Through Rituals: Youth Subcultures in Post-War Britain*. London: Hutchinson.

Hall, S., Critcher, C., Jefferson, T. and Clarke, J. (1978). *Policing the Crisis: Mugging, the State, and Law and Order*. London: Macmillan.

Hall, S., Massey, D., and Rustin, M. (2013). 'After Neoliberalism: Analysing the Present (Framing Statement)'. In S. Hall, D. Massey, and M. Rustin (eds) *After Neoliberalism? The Kilburn Manifesto*. London: Lawrence and Wishart. Retrieved from: www.lwbooks.co.uk/journals/soundings/pdfs/manifestoframing statement.pdf

Hamid, M. (2007). *The Reluctant Fundamentalist*. Toronto: Bond Street Books.

Haraway, D. (1988). 'Situated Knowledges: The Science Question in Feminism and the Privilege of Partial Perspective'. *Feminist Studies*, 14(3), pp. 575–599.

Haraway, D. (1992). 'Ecce Homo, ain't (ar'n't) I a Woman, and Inappropriate/d Others: The Human in a Post-Humanist Landscape'. In J. Butler and J. W. Scott (eds) *Feminists Theorize the Political*. New York: Routledge.

Hark, S. and Villa, P. I. (2020). *The Future of Difference: Beyond the Toxic Entanglement of Racism, Sexism and Feminism*. London, New York: Verso.

Hartman, S. V. (2019). *Wayward Lives, Beautiful Experiments: Intimate Histories of Social Upheaval* (First edition). New York: W.W. Norton and Company, Inc.

Harvey, D. (1989). *The Condition of the Postmodernity: An Inquiry into the Origins of Cultural Change*. Oxford: Blackwell.

Harvey, D. (2003). *The New Imperialism*. Oxford: Oxford University Press.

Harvey, D. (2009). *Cosmopolitanism and the Geographies of Freedom*. New York: Columbia University Press.

Hastings, D. and Wilson, T. M. (1999). *Borders: Frontiers of Identity, Nation and State*. Oxford and New York: Berg.

Hattenstone, S. (2020). 'The Virus Piggybacked on Racism: Why Did Covid-19 Hit BAME Families So Hard? *The Guardian*, 8 August. Retrieved from: www.theguardian.com/world/2020/aug/08/the-virus-piggybacked-on-racism-why-did-covid-19-hit-bame-families-so-hard

Hemmings, C. (2011) *Why Stories Matter: The Political Grammar of Feminist Theory*. Durham: Duke University Press.

Henry, A. (2001). 'Stuart Hall and Cultural Studies: Theory Letting You Off the Hook?' In L. Stone and K. Weiler (eds) *Feminist Engagements: Revisioning Educational and Cultural Theory*. New York: Routledge.

Hesse, B. (2000). *Un/settled Multiculturalisms: Diasporas, Entanglements, Transcriptions*. London: Zed Books.

Hunt, A. and Wickham, G. (1994). *Foucault and Law: Towards a Sociology of Law as Governance*. London: Pluto Press.

International Organization for Migration. (2020). *UN World Migration Report 2020*. Geneva: IOM.

Ipsos MORI. (2018). *A Review of Survey Research on Muslims in Britain*. London.

Isin, E. F. (2008). 'Theorizing Acts of Citizenship.' In E. F. Isin and G. M. Nielsen (eds) *Acts of Citizenship*. London: Palgrave Macmillan.

Isin, E. F. and Wood, P. K. (1990). *Citizenship and Identity*. London: SAGE Publications.

Isin, E. F. and Nielsen, G. M. (2008). *Acts of Citizenship*. London: Zed Books.

Jenkins, R. (1966). Speech given on 23 May 1966. British Hansard.

Jenkins, R. (1997). *Rethinking Ethnicity: Arguments and Explorations*. London: SAGE Publications.

Jones, H. (2021). *Violent Ignorance: Confronting Racism and Migration Control*. London: Zed Books.

Jones, H. et al. (2017). *Go Home? The Politics of Immigration Controversies*. Manchester: Manchester University Press.

Jones, S. and Jackson, J. (2015). 'UN Criticizes Sun over "Cockroaches" Slur on Migrants.' *The Guardian*, 25 April, pp. 6.

Jonsson, T. (2016). 'The Narrative Reproduction of White Feminist Racism.' *Feminist Review*, 113, pp. 50–67.

Kaplan, C. K. (1996). *Questions of Travel.* Durham: Duke University Press.

Kaufmann, E. (2019). *White Shift: Populism, Immigration and the Future of White Majorities.* London: Penguin Books.

Kenny, K. (2013). *Diaspora: A Very Short Introduction.* Oxford: Oxford University Press.

Khan, M. (2019). *It's Not About the Burqa: Muslim Women on Faith, Feminism, Sexuality and Race.* London: Picador.

Kivisto, P. and Faist, T. (2007). *Citizenship: Discourse, Theory and Transnational Prospects.* Oxford: Blackwell.

Knap, G. A. (2005). 'Race, Class and Gender: Reclaiming Baggage in Fast Travelling Theories'. *European Journal of Women's Studies,* 1 August 2005. https://doi.org/ 10.1177/1350506805054267.

Knott, K. (2010). 'Space and Movement'. In K. Knott and S. McLoughlin (eds) *Diasporas: Concepts, Intersections, Identities.* London: Zed Press.

Knott, K. and McLoughlin. S. (2010). *Diasporas: Concepts, Intersections, Identities.* London: Zed Press.

Kuhn, A. (1995). *Family Secrets: Acts of Memory and Imagination.* London: Verso.

Kwok-Bun, C. (2002). 'Both Sides, Now: Culture Contact, Hybridization, and Cosmopolitanism'. In S. Vertovec and R. Cohen (eds) *Conceiving Cosmopolitanism: Theory, Context and Practice.* Oxford: Oxford University Press.

Kymlicka, W. (1989). *Liberalism, Community and Culture.* Oxford: Oxford University Press.

Levinas, E. (1979). *Totality and Infinity: An Essay on Exteriority.* Boston: Nijhoff Publishers.

Lewis, R. (1996). *Gendering Orientalism: Race, Femininity and Representation.* London and New York: Routledge.

Lewis, R. (2004). *Rethinking Orientalism: Women, Travel and the Ottoman Harem.* New Brunswick, NJ: Rutgers University Press.

Lewis, R. (2015). *Muslim Fashion: Contemporary Style Culture.* Durham: Duke University Press.

Lewis, G. (2013). 'Unsafe Travel: Experiencing Intersectionality and Feminist Displacements'. *Signs,* 38(4), pp. 869–892.

Lewis, G. (2017). 'Questions of Presence'. *Feminist Review*, 117(1), pp. 1–19. doi: 10.1057/s41305-017-0088-1.

Lewis, G. (2020). 'Once More with My Sistren: Black Feminism and the Challenge of Object Use'. *Feminist Review*, 126(1), pp. 1–18. doi: 10.1177/0141778920944372.

Lister, R. (1998a). *Citizenship: Feminist Perspectives*. New York: NYU Press.

Lister, R. (1998b). 'Citizenship and Difference: Toward a Differentiated Universalism'. *European Journal of Social Theory*, 1(1), pp. 71–90. doi: 10.1177/136843198001001006.

Livingstone, J. and Puar, J. K. (2011). *Interspecies, Social Text*, 29(106), pp. 3–14.

Lorde, A. (2017). *Your Silence Will Not Protect You*. Madrid: Silver Press.

Lott, T. (1996). *The Scent of Dried Roses: Our Family and the End of English Suburbia*. London: Viking.

Lugones, M. (2010). 'Toward a Decolonial Feminism'. *Hypatia*, 25(4), pp. 742–759.

Lustgarten, A. (2015). 'Our Tears Won't Solve This Refugee Scandal. Only Justice Will'. *The Guardian*, 18 April, p. 30.

Lutz, H., Vivar, M. T. H., and Supik, L. (2011). *Framing Intersectionality: Debates on a Multi-faceted Concept in Gender Studies*. London: Ashgate.

Lykke, N. (2011). 'Intersectional Analysis: Black Box or Useful Critical Feminist Thinking Technology?' In H. Lutz, M. T. H. Vivar, and L. Supik (eds) *Framing Intersectionality: Debates on a Multi-faceted Concept in Gender Studies*. London: Ashgate.

Mani, L. (2009). *Sacred Secular: Contemplative Cultural Critique*. London and New Delhi: Routledge.

McCall, L. (2005). 'The Complexity of Intersectionality'. *Signs*, 33(1), pp. 1771–1800.

McKittrick, K. (2015). *Sylvia Wynter: On Being Human as Praxis*. Durham: Duke University Press.

Meekosha, H. (2006). 'What the Hell Are You? An Intercategorical Analysis of Race, Ethnicity, Gender and Disability in the Australian Body Politic'. *Scandinavian Journal of Disability Research*, 8(1), pp. 161–176.

Meghji, A. (2021). *Decolonizing Sociology. An Introduction*. Cambridge: Polity.

Mignolo, W. D. (2007). 'Delinking the Rhetoric of Modernity, the Logic of Coloniality, and the Grammar of Decoloniality'. *Cultural Studies*, 21(2–3), pp. 449–514.

Mignolo, W. D. (2011). *The Darker Side of Western Modernity: Global Futures, Decolonial Options*. Durham: Duke University Press.

Mignolo, W. D. (2015). 'Sylvia Wynter: What Does It Mean to be Human?' In K. McKittrick (ed.) *Sylvia Winter: On Being Human as Praxis*. Durham and London: Duke University Press.

Mignolo, W. D. and Walsh, C. E. (2018). *On Decoloniality: Concepts, Analytics, Praxis*. Durham and London: Duke University Press.

Mirza, H. S. (1997). *Black British Feminism: A Reader*. London: Routledge.

Modood, T. (2010). *Still Not Easy Being British: Struggles for a Multicultural Citizenship*. London: Trentham Books.

Mohanty, C. T. (1992). 'Feminist Encounters: Locating the Politics of Experience.' In M. Barrett and A. Philips (eds) *Destabilizing Theory: Contemporary Feminist Debates*. Cambridge: Polity Press.

Mohanty, C. T. (2003). *Feminism Without Borders: Decolonizing Theory, Practicing Solidarity*. Durham: Duke University Press.

Mondon, A. and Winter, A. (2020). *Reactionary Democracy: How Racism and the Populist Far Right Became Mainstream*. London and New York: Verso.

Moosavi, L. (2012). 'Muslims Are Well-Integrated in Britain – But No One Seems to Believe It.' *The Guardian*, 3 July.

Moraga, C. and Anzaldúa, G. (eds) (1981). *This Bridge Called My Back: Writings by Radical Women of Colour*. London: Persephone Press.

Morley, D. and Chen, K. H. (2010). *Critical Dialogues in Cultural Studies*. New York: Routledge.

Morrison, T. (1987). *Beloved*. New York: Vintage.

Moreton-Robinson, A. (2015). *The White Possessive: Property, Power and Indigenous Sovereignty*. Minneapolis: University of Minnesota Press.

Mulinary, D. and Neergard, A. (2014). 'We Are Sweden Democrats because We Care for Others: Exploring Racism in the Swedish Extreme Right.' *The European Journal of Women's Studies*, 21(1), pp. 43–56.

Nail, T. (2015). *The Figure of the Migrant*. Stanford: Stanford University Press.

Nash, J. C. (2008). 'Re-thinking Intersectionality.' *Feminist Review*, 89(1), pp. 1–15.

Nash, J. C. (2019). *Black Feminism Reimagined: After Intersectionality.* Durham: Duke University Press.

Nayak, A. (2003). *Race, Place, and Globalization: Youth Cultures in a Changing World.* Oxford: Berg.

Nazir, P. (1986). 'Marxism and the National Question: Class and Ideology in the Making of Pakistan'. *Journal of Contemporary Asia,* 16(4), pp. 491–507.

Nazir, P. (1991). *Local Development in the Global Economy.* New York and London: Routledge.

Nazir, P. (2007). 'Political Islam and the Media'. *Policy Perspectives,* 4(2), pp. 21–39. Retrieved from: www.jstor.org/stable/42909172

Nazir, P. (2010). 'War on Terror in Pakistan and Afghanistan: Discursive and Political Contestations'. *Critical Studies on Terrorism,* 3(1), pp. 63–81. doi: 10.1080/17539151003594236.

Ngũgĩ wa Thiong'o. (1986). *Decolonising the Mind: The Politics of Language in African Literature.* Harlow, Essex: Pearson Education Ltd.

Observer. (2015). Editorial. *The Observer,* 19 April 2015, p. 36.

Offe, C. (1984). *Contradictions of the Welfare State,* trans. John Keane. Cambridge, MA: MIT Press.

Olusoga, D. (2019). 'How Did We Get Here? The Decade That Left Us Reeling'. *The Observer,* 22 December. Retrieved from: www.theguardian.com/world/2019/dec/22/2010s-decade-that-left-us-reeling

Parekh, B. (2006). *Rethinking Multiculturalism: Cultural Diversity and Political Theory.* Houndmills, Basingstoke: Palgrave Macmillan.

Patel, S. (2010). *Migritude.* New York: Kaya Press.

Penfield, C. (2014). 'Towards a Theory of Transversal Politics: Deleuze and Foucault's Block of Becoming'. *Foucault Studies,* 17, pp. 134–172.

Penney, J. (2014). *After Queer Theory: The Limits of Sexual Politics.* London: Pluto Press.

Phillips, A. (2010). *Gender and Culture.* Cambridge: Polity Press.

Phoenix, A. and Pattynama, P. (2006) 'Intersectionality'. *European Journal of Women's Studies,* 13(3), pp. 187–192. doi: 10.1177/1350506806065751.

Piketty, T. (2013). *Capital in the Twenty-First Century*. Cambridge, MA: Harvard University Press.

Pratt, M. B. (1984). 'Identity: Skin/Blood/Heart'. In E. Bulkin, B. Smith, and B. M. Pratt (eds) *Yours in Struggle: Three Feminist Perspectives on Racism and Anti-Semitism*. New York: Long Hall.

Pratt, M. L. (1992). *Imperial Eyes: Travel Writing and Transculturation*. London and New York: Routledge.

Puar, J. K. (2007). *Terrorist Assemblages: Homonationalism in Queer Times*. Durham and London: Duke University Press.

Puar, J. K. (2012a). 'Coda: The Cost of Getting Better: Suicide, Sensation, Switchpoints'. *GLQ: A Journal of Lesbian and Gay Studies*, 18(1), 149–158.

Puar, J. K. (2012b). 'I Would Rather Be a Cyborg than a Goddess: Becoming Intersectional in Assemblage Theory'. *Philosphia: A Journal of Feminist Philosophy*, 2(1), pp. 49–66.

Puar, J. K. (2017). *The Right to Maim: Debility, Capacity, Disability*. Durham and London: Duke University Press.

Purkayastha, B. (2010). 'Interrogating Intersectionality: Contemporary Globalisation and Racialised Gendering in the Lives of Highly Educated South Asian Americans and their Children'. *Journal of Intercultural Studies*, 31(1), pp. 29–47.

Puwar, N. (2004). *Space Invaders: Race, Gender and Bodies out of Place*. Oxford and New York: Berg.

Puwar, N. (2012). 'Mediations on Making Aaj Kaal'. *Feminist Review*, 100(1), pp. 124–141.

Puwar, N. (2019). 'Puzzlement of a Dejá Vu: Illuminaries of the Global South'. *The Sociological Review*, pp. 1–17. doi: 10.117710038026119890254.

Quijano, A. (2007). 'Coloniality and Modernity/Rationality'. *Cultural Studies*, 21(2), pp. 168–178. doi: 10.1080/09502380601164353

Rankin, J. (2019). 'EU Declares Migration Crisis Over as It Hits Out at "Fake News"'. *The Guardian*, 6 March. Retrieved from: www.theguardian.com/world/2019/mar/06/eu-declares-migration-crisis-over-hits-out-fake-news-european-commission

Ransby, B. (2018). *Making All Black Lives Matter: Reimagining Freedom in the 21st Century*. Oakland: University of California Press.

Rattansi, A. (2011). *Multiculturalism: A Very Short Introduction*. Oxford: Oxford University Press.

Rawwida, B. and Harcourt, W. (2015). *Oxford Handbook of Transnational Feminist Movements: Knowledge, Power and Social Change*. Oxford: Oxford University Press.

Rice-Oakley, M. (2015) 'It Is Not Our Caring That Is the Real Killer'. *The Guardian*, 20 April, p. 5.

Rich, A. (1984). 'Notes Towards a Politics of Location'. In *Blood, Bread and Poetry: Selected Prose 1979–1985*. New York: W. W. Norton & Company.

Rich, A. (2018). *Essential Essays: Culture, Politics and the Art of Poetry*. New York: W. W. Norton & Company.

Richman, P. (1999). 'A Diaspora Ramayana in Southall, Greater London'. *Journal of the American Academy of Religion*, 67(1), pp. 33–57.

Robbins. B. (1998). 'Introduction Part I: Actually Existing Cosmopolitanism'. In P. Cheah and B. Robbins (eds) *Cosmopolitics: Thinking and Feeling Beyond the Nation*. Minneapolis: University of Minnesota Press.

Rogaly, B. (2020). *Stories from a Migrant City: Living and Working Together in the Shadow of Brexit*. Manchester: Manchester University Press.

Roman, L. G. (1993). 'White Is a Color! White Defensiveness, Postmodernism, and Antiracist Pedagogy'. In C. McCarthy and W. Crichlow (eds) *Race, Identity, and Representation in Education*. New York and London: Routledge.

Roseneil, S. (2013). *Beyond Citizenship? Feminism and the Transformation of Belonging*. London: Palgrave Macmillan.

Roseneil, S., Crowhurst, I., Hellesund, T., and Santos A. C. (2011). 'Intimate Citizenship and Gendered Well-Being: The Claims and Interventions of Women's Movement in Europe. In A. Woodward et al. (eds) *Social Movements: Gendering Well-Being*. Aldershot: Ashgate.

Rumford, C. (2006). 'Theorizing Borders'. *European Journal of Social Theory*, 9(2), pp. 155–169.

Rumford, C. (2014). *Cosmopolitan Borders*. Basingstoke: Palgrave Macmillan.

Rutherford, A. (2020). *How to Argue with a Racist: History, Science, Race and Reality*. London: Weidenfeld & Nicolson.

Safran, W. (1991). 'Diasporas in Modern Societies: Myths of Homeland and Return'. *Diaspora: A Journal of Transnational Studies*, 1(1), pp. 83–99. doi: 10.1353/dsp.1991.0004.

Said, E. (1978). *Orientalism.* New York: Pantheon Books.

Said, E. (1983). *The World, the Text and the Critic.* Cambridge, MA: Harvard University Press.

Said, E. (1994). *Culture and Imperialism.* London: Vintage.

Sanghera, S. (2021). *Empireland: How Imperialism Has Shaped Britain.* London: Viking Penguin Random House.

Sayyid, B. (1997). *A Fundamental Fear: Eurocentrism and the Emergence of Islamism.* London: Zed Books.

Schein, L. (1998). 'Forged Transnationality and Oppositional Cosmopolitanism'. In M. P. Smith and L. E. Guarnizo (eds) *Transnationalism from Below: Comparative Urban and Community Research.* New Brunswick, NJ: Transaction Publishers.

Scott, J. W. (1992). 'Experience'. In J. Butler and J. W. Scott (eds) *Feminists Theorize the Political.* New York: Routledge.

Sharma, S. (2006). *Multicultural Encounters.* Basingstoke: Palgrave Macmillan.

Sheller, M. and Urry, J. (2006). *The New Mobilities Paradigm. Environment and Planning A: Economy and Space.* London: SAGE Publications.

Sian, K. P. (2013). *Unsettling Sikh and Muslim Conflict: Mistaken Identities, Forced Conversations and Postcolonial Formations.* Lanham: Lexington Books.

Sian, K. P. (ed.) (2014). *Conversations in Postcolonial Thought.* London: Palgrave Macmillan.

Singh, J. (2018). *Unthinking Mastery: Dehumanism and Decolonial Entanglements.* Durham and London: Duke University Press.

Skeggs, B. (2004). *Class, Self, Culture.* London: Routledge.

Smith, L. T. (1999). *Decolonising Methodologies: Research and Indigenous Peoples.* London: Zed Press.

Solomos, J. (2003). *Race and Racism in Britain.* London: Palgrave Macmillan.

Southall Black Sisters. (1990). *Against the Grain: A Celebration of Survival and Struggle.* London: SBS.

Stevis-Gridneff, M. (2019). 'Europe Keeps Asylum Seekers at a Distance, This Time in Rwanda'. *The New York Times,* 8 September 2019. Retrieved from: www.nytimes.com/2019/09/08/world/europe/migrants-africa-rwanda.html

Stierstorfer, K. and Wilson, J. (eds) (2018). *The Routledge Diaspora Studies Reader*. London and New York: Routledge.

Sudbury, J. (1998). *Other Kinds of Dreams: Black Women's Organisations and the Politics of Transformation*. London: Routledge.

Swaby, N. A. (2014). 'Disparate in Voice, Sympathetic in Direction: Gendered Political Blackness and the Politics of Solidarity'. *Feminist Review*, 108, pp. 11–25.

Taylor, C. (1994). *Multiculturalism: Examining the Politics of Recognition*. Princeton: Princeton University Press.

Thatcher, M. (1978). 'TV Interview for Granada World in Action', interviewed by Gordon Burns for *Granada TV*, 27 January 1978. Retrieved from: www.margaretthatcher.org/document/103485

Trade Union Congress. (2016). 'Still Just a Bit of Banter: Sexual Harassment in the Workplace'. London: Trade Union Congress. Retrieved from: www.tuc.org.uk/sites/default/file/sexualharrassment.report2016.pdf

Travis, A. (2007). 'Officials Launch Drive to Seek Out Illegal Immigrants at Work'. *The Guardian*, 15 May. Retrieved from: www.theguardian.com/uk/2007/may/16/immigration.immigrationandpublicservices

Travis, A. (2013). 'Immigration Bill: Theresa May Defends Plans to Create 'Hostile Environment'. *The Guardian*, 10 October. Retrieved from www.theguardian.com/politics/2013/oct/10/immigration-bill-theresa-may-hostile-environment

Tudor, A. (2017). 'Dimensions of Transnationalism'. *Feminist Review*, 117(1), pp. 20–40. doi: 10.1057/s41305-017-0092-5.

Tuitt, P. (2004). *Race, Law, Resistance*. London: The Glass House Press.

UN DESA. (2020). *International; Migration 2020 Highlights*. New York: United Nations.

UNHCR. (2020) *UNHCR Refugee Data Finder*. Retrieved from: www.unhcr.org/refugee-statistics/

United Nations. (2016). *Number of International Migrants Reached 244 Million in 2015*. 12 January 2016. Retrieved from: www.un.org/sustainabledevelopment/blog/2016/01/244-million-international-migrants-living-abroad-worldwide-new-un-statistics-reveal/

Valluvan, S. (2019). *Race and Nation in Twenty-First-Century Britain*. Manchester: Manchester University Press.

Van Der Veer, P. (2002). 'Colonial Cosmopolitanism'. In S. Vertovec and R. Cohen (eds) *Conceiving Cosmopolitanism: Theory, Context and Practice*. Oxford: Oxford University Press.

Verges, F. (2021). *A Decolonial Feminism*. Translated by Ashley J . Boherer with the author. London: Pluto Press.

Vertovec, S. and Cohen, R. (eds) (2002). *Conceiving Cosmopolitanism: Theory, Context and Practice*. Oxford: Oxford University Press.

Virdee, S. (2014). *Racism, Class and the Racialised Outsider*. Houndmills, Basingstoke: Palgrave Macmillan.

Visas and Immigration. (2015). 'Ancestry Visa'. GOV.UK. Retrieved from: www.gov.uk/ancestry-visa/overview

Walia, H. (2013). *Undoing Border Imperialism*. Oakland and Edinburgh: AK Press.

Weedon, C. (1987). *Feminist Practice and Poststructuralist Theory*. Oxford: Blackwell.

Weheliye, A. G. (2014). *Habeas Viscus: Racializing Assemblages, Biopolitics, and Black Feminist Theories of the Human*. Durham and London: Duke University Press.

Whitley, L. M. (2015). 'More Than a Line: Borders as Embodied Site'. PhD Thesis. Goldsmiths College, University of London.

Wilson, A. (1978). *Finding A Voice: Asian Women in Britain*. London: Virago.

Wilson, J. M. (2012). 'The Contemporary Terrorist Novel and Religious Fundamentalism: Richard Flanagan, Mohsin Hamid, Orhan Pamuk'. In C. Pesso-Miquel and K. Stierstorfer (eds) *Burning Books: Negotiations between Fundamentalism and Literature*, vol. 10, AMS Studies in Cultural History. New York: AMS Press Inc.

Woodward, K. (ed) (1997). *Identity and Difference*. London: SAGE Publications. in association with the Open University.

Wynter, S. (2003). 'Unsettling the Coloniality of Being/Power/Truth/Freedom: Towards the Human, After Man, Its Overrepresentation – An Argument'. *CR: The New Centennial Review*, 3(3), pp. 257–337. doi: 10.1353/ncr.2004.0015.

Wynter, S. and McKittrick, K. (2015). 'Unparalleled Catastrophe for Our Species? Or, to Give Humanness a Different Future: Conversations'. In K. McKittrick (ed.) *Sylvia Winter: On Being Human as Praxis*. Durham and London: Duke University Press.

Young, I. M. (1990). *Justice and the Politics of Difference*. Princeton: Princeton University Press.

Younge, G. (2015). 'No One Makes This Journey Just to Pick up Benefits'. *The Guardian*, 27 April, p. 27.

Yuval-Davis, N. (1997). *Gender and Nation*. London: SAGE Publications.

Yuval-Davis, N. (2006). 'Intersectionality and Feminist Politics'. *European Journal of Women's Studies*, 13(3), pp. 193–209.

Yuval-Davis, N. (2011). *The Politics of Belonging: Intersectional Contestations*. London: SAGE Publications.

Yuval-Davis, N. and Anthias, F. (eds) (1989). *Women-Nation-State*. Houndsmills, Basingstoke: The Macmillan Press.

Yuval-Davis, N., Wemyss, G., and Cassidy, K. (2019). *Bordering*. Cambridge: Polity Press.

Zack, N. (2005). *Inclusive Feminism: A Third Wave Theory of Women's Commonality*. Lanham: Rowman & Littlefield.

Zubaida, S. (2002). 'Middle Eastern Experiences of Cosmopolitanism'. In S. Vertovec and R. Cohen (eds) *Conceiving Cosmopolitanism: Theory, Context, and Practice*. Oxford: Oxford University Press.

Filmography

Aaj Kaal. (1990). [Video]. Extra-Mural Studies, Birkbeck College, University of London, 20 minutes. See www.darkmatter101.org/site/2012/04/03/aaj-kaal-yesterday-today-tomorrow-video/

Against the Grain: A Celebration of Survival and Struggle. (1979–1989). [Film]. Southall Black Sisters. SBS, 21 Avenue Road, Southall, Middlesex, UB1 3BL.

Index